Your

FIRST

Book of

Personal Computing

by Joe Kraynak

FOZ
6/09
$/100

alpha
books

A Division of Macmillan Computer Publishing
A Prentice Hall Macmillan Company
201 West 103rd Street, Indianapolis, Indiana 46290 USA

And to my children, Nicholas and Alexandra Kraynak, who prove every day that anything is possible.

International Standard Book Number: 1-56761-503-1
Library of Congress Catalog Card Number: 94-71518

97 96 95   8 7 6 5 4 3 2 1

Interpretation of the printing code: the rightmost number of the first series of numbers is the year of the book's printing; the rightmost number of the second series of numbers is the number of the book's printing. For example, a printing code of 94-1 shows that the first printing of the book occurred in 1995.

Printed in the United States of America

PUBLISHER
Marie Butler-Knight

MANAGING EDITOR
Elizabeth Keaffaber

PRODUCT DEVELOPMENT MANAGER
Faithe Wempen

ACQUISITIONS MANAGER
Barry Pruett

SENIOR DEVELOPMENT EDITOR
Seta Frantz

PRODUCTION EDITOR
Kelly Oliver

MANUSCRIPT EDITOR
Audra Gable

EDITORIAL ASSISTANT
Martha O'Sullivan

EDITORIAL INTERN
Lara Young

ILLUSTRATORS
Katherine Hanley, Jeff Yesh

BOOK DESIGNER
Barbara Kordesh

INDEXER
Rebecca Mayfield

PRODUCTION TEAM
Gary Adair, Dan Caparo, Brad Chinn, Kim Cofer, David Dean, Cynthia Drouin, Jennifer Eberhardt, Erika Millen, Beth Rago, Bobbi Satterfield, Karen Walsh, Robert Wolf

SPECIAL THANKS TO CHRIS DENNY FOR ENSURING THE TECHNICAL ACCURACY OF THIS BOOK.

CONTENTS

PART 2 USING AN OPERATING SYSTEM 57

PART 3   APPLICATIONS: DOING SOME REAL WORK   105

INTRODUCTION

It's the 90's, and personal computers (PCs) are everywhere. You see them at work, in home offices and dens, in schools, and even on commercials and sitcoms. To make it in the modern world, you have to be PC literate. You must know how to turn on a PC and use it to do something productive. But what exactly do you need to know? And where do you start?

You start with *Your First Book of Personal Computing*. This book is based on the assumption that you don't have to know how a computer works in order to use one. *Your First Book* focuses on practical, hands-on tasks, including:

- How to boot (start) your computer (and restart it when all else fails).

- How to enter DOS (which rhymes with "boss") commands and use DOS to run your applications.

- How to start and use Microsoft Windows.

- How to use an Apple Macintosh computer.

- What kind of programs you can run on your computer and what you can do with them.

- How to use a modem to connect to another computer or an online service.

- How to play computer compact discs on a CD-ROM drive.

- How to buy a computer that's not overly obsolete and properly maintain it.

- How to get out (and stay out) of trouble.

In short, *Your First Book of Personal Computing* is your guide to computers and to the software that you use to do your work.

HOW TO USE THIS BOOK

Although this book is as simple to read as the back of a cereal box, we have included a few unique elements that you won't find on most cereal boxes.

First, each chapter starts with a picture (on the left hand page) that shows what you'll learn in the chapter, and lists the page numbers where you'll find that information. At the end of most chapters are three special sections: "More You Can Do," "Exercises," and "Chapter Digest." "More You Can Do" provides ideas and suggestions on how you can use the information you learned to go beyond what you've learned. "Exercises" leads you through practical hands-on tasks designed to give you practice with what you've learned. And "Chapter Digest" provides a quick review of the chapter, scanning the important points and providing shortcuts for the tasks explained in the chapter.

In addition, each chapter contains numbered steps and plenty of colorful screen shots, leading you step-by-step through the common tasks of computing. You'll learn exactly what you need to do and what to expect as you perform each task.

ACKNOWLEDGMENTS

Although all books are team projects, this book required a special team—one consisting of both novices and experts. The novices offered their insights into what beginners need to know; the experts supplied the necessary information. Thanks to the following people for helping to nurture this book from its inception to its current form:

Liz Keaffaber and Kelly Oliver for coordinating my work.

Faithe Wempen, Seta Frantz, Audra Gable, and Lara Young for keeping my language clear and direct.

Marie Butler-Knight and Barry Pruett for giving me the opportunity, resources, and guidance I needed to perfect the book.

Chris Denny for patiently answering my technical questions and reviewing my material for accuracy.

TRADEMARKS

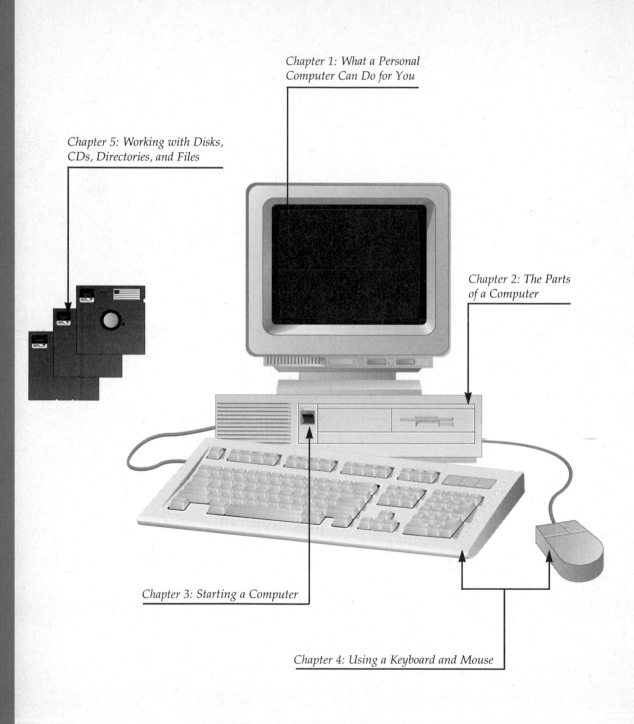

Chapter 1: What a Personal
Computer Can Do for You

Chapter 5: Working with Disks,
CDs, Directories, and Files

Chapter 2: The Parts
of a Computer

Chapter 3: Starting a Computer

Chapter 4: Using a Keyboard and Mouse

PART 1

COMPUTER BASICS

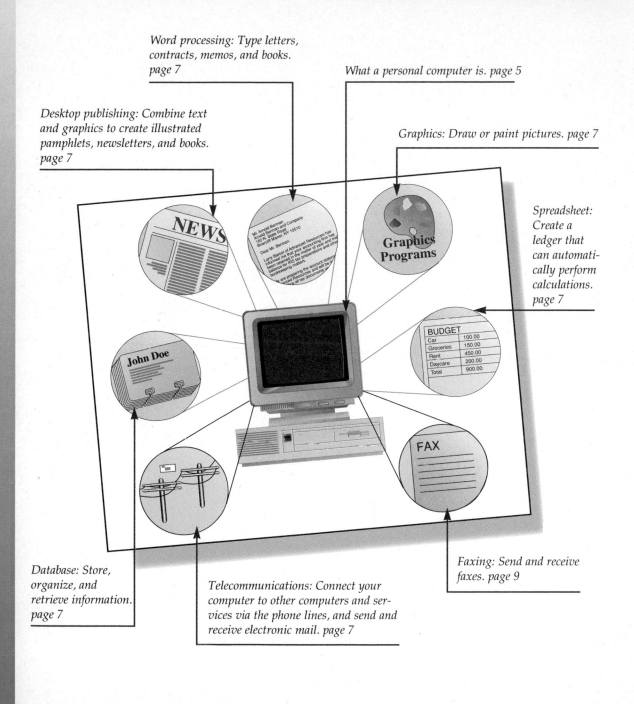

Word processing: Type letters, contracts, memos, and books. page 7

What a personal computer is. page 5

Desktop publishing: Combine text and graphics to create illustrated pamphlets, newsletters, and books. page 7

Graphics: Draw or paint pictures. page 7

Spreadsheet: Create a ledger that can automatically perform calculations. page 7

Faxing: Send and receive faxes. page 9

Database: Store, organize, and retrieve information. page 7

Telecommunications: Connect your computer to other computers and services via the phone lines, and send and receive electronic mail. page 7

WHAT A PERSONAL COMPUTER CAN DO FOR YOU

P ersonal computers are useful tools for writing letters and memos, balancing checkbooks and budgets, keeping track of accounts receivable and mailing lists, plotting stock market trends, sending mail electronically, and even playing games. If you can perform a task using a pencil, some paper, and a calculator, chances are that you can perform the same task more efficiently and accurately using a computer.

The Definition of a Personal Computer

What You Can Do with a Computer

Types of Computer Programs

What Makes a Computer Such a Useful Tool

WHAT IS A PERSONAL COMPUTER?

A personal computer is a general purpose machine that a qualified person can program to perform specific tasks. The programs are instructions that usually come on one or more disks. Each program enables the computer to perform a single task, such as total sales figures, draw graphs, or create greeting cards.

The term "personal" describes the computer's ability to act on its own. In other words, it doesn't rely on a central (mainframe) computer. In the old days, computers were too expensive for businesses to plop one on every employee's desk. So businesses would set up a powerful central computer and connect weaker, inexpensive computers to it. In other words, the central computer did all the heavy work.

As computers became less expensive, businesses found that they could plop a powerful computer on every employee's desk. These individual, liberated computers are called personal computers. A typical IBM Personal Computer is shown here.

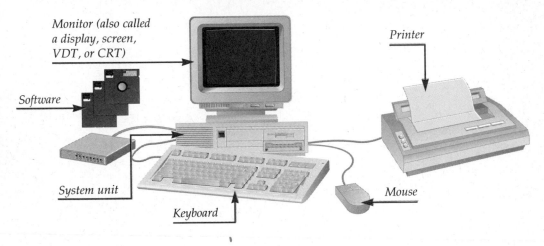

Monitor (also called a display, screen, VDT, or CRT)

Printer

Software

System unit

Keyboard

Mouse

COMPUTER PROGRAMS: WHAT THEY ARE AND WHAT THEY DO

Tip: Some people use the term personal computer (or PC) specifically to describe the IBM Personal Computer. However, in this book, we use "personal computer" to refer to other types of personal computers as well, including PC-compatibles, Apple II, Macintosh, and Amiga. This book focuses on the two most popular types of personal computers—the Macintosh and the IBM PC.

A personal computer is fairly useless without a set of instructions that tell it how to do something. A computer needs two types of instructions: operating system instructions, which get the computer up and running; and applications—programs that enable the computer to perform a specific task, such as balance a budget or draw a graph.

Fortunately, you don't have to write your own programs. You can purchase programs specifically designed to perform one or more tasks. The following table lists a few of the tasks you may now be performing manually and the computer alternatives. In Chapters 8–16, you will learn more about each type of program.

Task	Manual Method	Computer Alternative
Writing letters	Typewriter	Word processor
Balancing a budget	Calculator	Spreadsheet or finance program
Storing names and addresses	Rolodex	Database
Generating purchase orders	Calculator, typewriter	Accounting program
Drawing pictures	Pen, paints, paper	Graphics program
Sending mail	Pen, envelope, stamp	Modem and telecommunications program or online service
Balancing a checkbook	Paper, calculator	Personal finance program
Keeping a schedule	Calendar	Personal information manager (PIM)
Learning a subject	Books, tapes	Educational program
Creating newsletters	Typewriter, scissors and glue	Desktop publishing program
Repairing and recovering from computer problems	Not applicable	Utility program
Having fun	Board games	Computer games

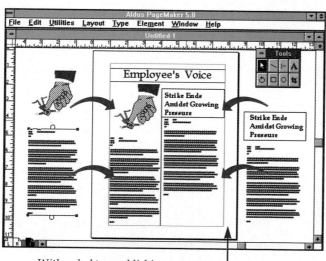

With a desktop publishing program, you cut and paste on the screen.

HOW DOES A COMPUTER DO WHAT IT DOES?

As you can see, the computer can perform a wide variety of tasks, depending on your requirements and on the programs you have. Despite this variation, all computers perform six basic functions: they store, retrieve, edit, display, print, and transfer information. These functions are explained in the following list:

- **Store** A computer can store a lot of data in a very small space by storing it on magnetic disks rather than on paper. These disks are similar to cassette tapes. A single disk can hold several chapters of a book. A small box of disks can hold an entire filing cabinet of work. A hard disk (typically inside the system unit), can store hundreds of times more data than a floppy disk.

- **Retrieve** Once you've stored information on a disk, you can use the computer to read the information off the disk. That way you can continue to work with it.

- **Display** Whenever you create a document or retrieve a previously created document, the computer displays it on your monitor's screen. The display enables you to watch what you're doing with your document.

The screen displays an electronic version of a résumé created in Microsoft Word for Windows.

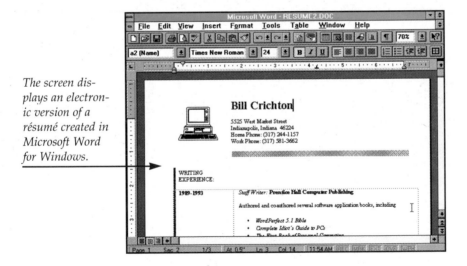

- **Edit** After you retrieve a document, you can change it by adding, deleting, or rearranging information. When the data is exactly as you want it, you can save the revised version to a disk.

- **Print** Although a computer stores each document electronically on disk, it can transform the document into a printed version.

PART 1

- **Send and Receive** If you have a modem (a device that enables your computer to transfer data over the phone lines), or if your computer is connected to other computers through network cables, you can use your computer to communicate with other people's computers. You can send and receive electronic mail and retrieve documents and programs from an online information service. You can even play a computer game with a friend or relative who lives in another state or country!

MORE THINGS A PERSONAL COMPUTER CAN DO

This chapter briefly introduced some of the tasks that a computer can perform. The following list reveals a few more advanced capabilities:

- With a fax modem (a special type of modem that can make your computer act like a fax machine) and the proper application, a personal computer can send faxes to and receive faxes from other fax machines.

- With a CD-ROM drive and an encyclopedia on compact disc, a computer can retrieve articles from the encyclopedia very quickly and can play short movie clips in addition to displaying text. With a sound card and speakers, a computer can also play sounds.

An encyclopedia on CD lets you read, watch, and listen.

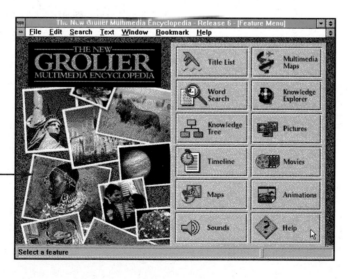

- With a specialized database, such as a movie guide, a personal computer can give you quick access to a vast pool of information.

EXERCISE

Practice your knowledge of software by matching the software type in the first column with its function in the second column.

Database   Balance a checkbook, track a budget, amortize loans

Desktop publishing   Balance accounts, track schedules, estimate job costs, create graphs

Graphics   Connect to another computer, transfer files over the phone lines

Online service   Draw pictures, make slide shows, create animations

Personal finance   Make appointments, keep an address book, make to-do lists

Personal information manager   Make greeting cards, create flyers, lay out books

Spreadsheet   Manage files, fix damaged disks, recover damaged files, tune your computer

Utility   Store information, sort records, generate reports

Word processing   Talk with other users, get news, transfer files

Telecommunications   Type letters, write books, publish newsletters

CHAPTER DIGEST

A Computer Is a Tool That...

- Can be programmed to perform a variety of tasks.

- Records your work, so you need not recreate your work to change it.

- Performs repetitive tasks tirelessly and with great precision.

- Allows you to customize and design your work to meet your exact needs.

Two Computer Components

- Hardware is the equipment (system unit, printer, keyboard, mouse).

- Software programs are the instructions that tell the computer what to do.

Two Types of Software

- Operating system software

- Applications

Creating a Document

Enter data→Save→Edit→Format→Print

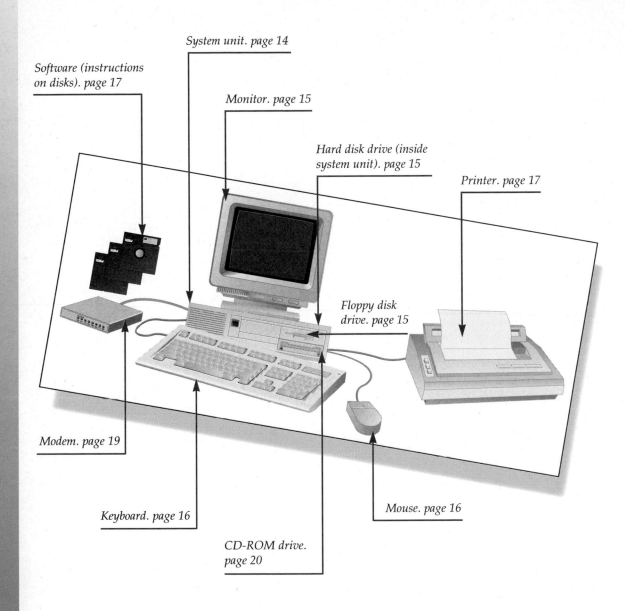

Software (instructions on disks). page 17

System unit. page 14

Monitor. page 15

Hard disk drive (inside system unit). page 15

Printer. page 17

Floppy disk drive. page 15

Modem. page 19

Keyboard. page 16

Mouse. page 16

CD-ROM drive. page 20

THE PARTS OF A COMPUTER

I f you had to assemble your own computer from scratch, you would have a long shopping list. First, you would need the hardware. *Hardware* is the machinery that makes up your comput er. You also need *software*, the instructions that tell your computer what to do and how to do it. In this chapter, you will learn about the various parts of a computer and about the types of software a computer needs.

HARDWARE: THE PARTS THAT MAKE UP A COMPUTER

Although most people refer to a computer as a single entity, a computer is actually a collection of parts, each contributing to the operation of the computer. In the following sections, you will learn each part's function. At the end of this chapter, you will learn how all the parts work together.

> **Tip:** To understand the relationship between hardware and software, think of the computer as a person—you, for example. The hardware is your body and brain. The software is everything you learned from school and from your various experiences.

LOOKING INSIDE THE SYSTEM UNIT

The *system unit* is the central (and most expensive) part of a computer. All data and program instructions flow through the system unit on their way to the other parts of the computer. Most IBM PCs and compatibles have a system unit that is separate from the rest of the computer. Some Macintosh computers combine the system unit and monitor.

The system unit is the central part of any computer.

The system unit contains the following elements that enable your computer to carry out the most complex of computer operations:

Random access memory (RAM)   RAM (which rhymes with "clam") consists of several components called chips that store information and program instructions electronically. The information remains in RAM only as long as the power to the computer is on. If you open a document in RAM and then turn off the computer or experience a power outage, RAM "forgets" your document. What you saved on disk is safe, but any changes you made to the document are lost. That's why it is so important to store information magnetically on disk.

Read only memory (ROM)   ROM (which rhymes with "mom") permanently stores the instructions that your computer uses to start up and communicate with the other parts of the computer (including the keyboard). You probably won't deal much with ROM.

Central processing unit   The central processing unit (CPU, pronounced "sea-pea-you") is the brain of the computer. The CPU carries out the program instructions and handles the information you enter.

Input and output ports   On the back of the system unit are several receptacles called ports. You connect your keyboard, mouse, monitor, printer, modem, and other devices to the system unit using these ports.

Floppy disk drives   A floppy disk drive appears as a slot on the front of the computer (your computer may have more than one). It enables you to feed program instructions and other information to your computer via floppy disks. The disk drive reads the information from the disk and stores the information in RAM where the CPU can work with it.

Hard disk drive   A hard disk drive comes complete with non-removable disks. It acts as a giant floppy disk drive and usually sits inside your computer. You'll learn more about disk drives in Chapter 5.

Power switch   If you have an older computer, the power switch is on the back or side of the system unit. On newer models, the power switch (or power button) is on the front. On some Macs, the keyboard has a power key.

> *Tip: The system unit is the central part of the computer. Devices you attach to the system unit are called* peripherals. *They include the monitor, printer, keyboard, mouse, modem, and joystick. Some manufacturers consider only nonessential devices peripherals, and don't consider the keyboard and monitor peripherals.*

VIEWING YOUR WORK ON A MONITOR

A *monitor* is like a fancy TV screen that lets you see what's happening as you work. Whenever you run a program, the program displays a screen, menu, or prompt (a brief message) that allows you to enter a command or type text. Whatever you type appears on-screen, allowing you to see exactly which keys you are pressing. The monitor goes by many names; you may hear it referred to as a screen, a CRT (Cathode Ray Tube), or a VDT (Video Display Terminal).

The monitor shows you what's going on.

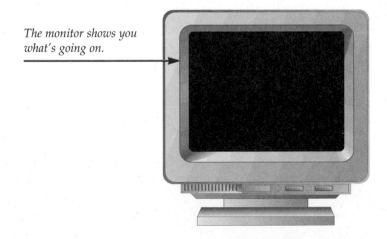

Typing with a Keyboard

A *keyboard* is the main device you use for entering information and commands into the computer. A computer keyboard is like a typewriter keyboard with several extra keys. You use the extra keys mainly to enter commands and move around on-screen. You will learn more about using a keyboard in Chapter 4.

Pointing with a Mouse

The *mouse* owes its name to its physical appearance; it has a small, oval body and a tail. The mouse tail is the cable that connects the mouse to your computer. The mouse is designed to make moving around on-screen more natural—a little like using a pencil. You slide the mouse on the mouse pad or table in the direction you want to move. The mouse pointer (on-screen) moves in the direction the mouse moves. (You will learn more about using a mouse in Chapter 4.)

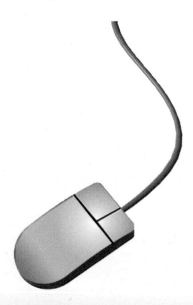

MAKING PAPER DOCUMENTS WITH A PRINTER

When you finish creating and perfecting your work, you will surely want to share it with someone. The most common way to share your work is to *print* the computer information onto paper. Chapter 20 lists the various types of printers.

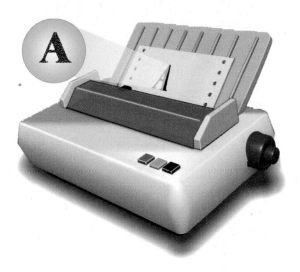

SOFTWARE: COMPUTER INSTRUCTIONS ON DISKS

Before your computer can do anything useful, it needs an education—some instructions that tell it what to do. In the computer world, these instructions are called *software* or *programs*.

Although you can write your own programs, most users buy software developed by professional programmers. This type of software comes on disks. If you have a hard disk drive, you will normally install the software on the hard drive. Most software comes with an installation program that copies the software from the disks you bought to the hard disk. It also performs any other operations required to make the software usable.

As you learned in the last chapter, your computer uses two types of software: *operating system software* and *application software*. The following sections explain each type of software.

OPERATING SYSTEM SOFTWARE

The *operating system* software tells the computer how to get and store information on disks, how to display information on-screen, and how to use the computer's RAM and CPU. In addition, it sets the rules by which all other programs (applications) have to play. The operating system is usually installed on your computer (on its hard disk) when you purchase it, so that the computer is ready to work.

There are two commonly used operating systems for IBM PCs and compatibles: MS-DOS (pronounced emm-ess-dawss) and OS/2 (oh-ess two). The most popular operating system for Macintosh computers is called "System."

The *version number* of the operating system is usually included in its name. For example, popular versions of operating systems include MS-DOS 6.0, OS/2 2.1, and System 7. Version numbers tell you how recent the software is—the higher the number, the more recent the version.

In Chapter 6, you will learn how to use the most popular PC operating system: MS-DOS. In Chapter 7, you will learn how to work with Microsoft Windows, an environment that runs on top of DOS and is designed to make a PC easier to use. Chapter 8 provides details for working with System 7 on a Macintosh.

APPLICATION SOFTWARE

With an operating system, a computer has the basics, but it cannot apply itself to any practical task, such as helping you write letters or figuring out whether refinancing your home would save you money.

What a computer needs in order to perform such tasks is *application software*. This software consists of a set of specialized instructions your computer uses to apply itself to a useful task. This is the software you buy to do your work: write letters, balance your checkbook, or play Tetris. In Chapters 9–16, you will learn about the various types of applications and their uses.

HOW THE COMPONENTS WORK TOGETHER

As you enter information (sometimes called data) or commands into a computer, electrical impulses are generated. The CPU translates and temporarily stores these impulses in RAM. The CPU then sends the information to your monitor so you can see what you're doing.

For example, to create a document, you must first enter a command to run the application you want to use. The disk drive reads the application's instructions off the disk and stores them in RAM where the CPU can access them. The CPU displays the application on your screen, providing you with a work area and additional commands.

As you type, the keyboard sends data to the computer, which stores the data in RAM and echoes the data to the monitor (so you can see it). When you finish a document, you should save it permanently to a floppy disk or to your hard drive. Whenever you want to work on the document again, you load the document from the disk into the application program you used to create it.

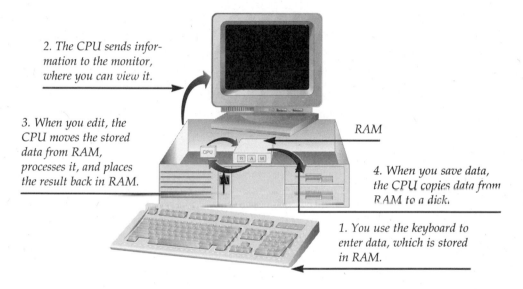

2. The CPU sends information to the monitor, where you can view it.

3. When you edit, the CPU moves the stored data from RAM, processes it, and places the result back in RAM.

RAM

4. When you save data, the CPU copies data from RAM to a disk.

1. You use the keyboard to enter data, which is stored in RAM.

MORE COMPUTER PARTS

In addition to the standard parts that make up a computer, you can add other equipment, depending on your needs. The following list shows some of the more popular peripheral devices you can add to a computer:

- **Modem**   Through the use of modems, two computers can share information over the phone lines. For example, one person in Chicago can transfer information from an IBM computer to a Macintosh computer in Los Angeles.

- **Joystick**   A joystick looks like a stick shift lever on a car, and gives you greater control when you use your computer to play arcade games.

- **Sound board**   By adding a sound board (and a pair of speakers), you give the PC sound capabilities that equal those of a standard TV. You can connect a microphone to the sound board to record voices and other sounds, and connect a musical instrument to record music. (You must have the appropriate software to record voices or music.) If you have a Mac, you don't have to worry about adding a sound board; it is built in.

- **CD-ROM drive**   CD-ROM (pronounced see-dee-rahm) stands for compact disc read-only memory. A CD-ROM drive uses the same kind of discs you play in an audio CD player. Instead of music, computer compact discs store computer files and programs. A single disc can store an entire set of encyclopedias (including text, pictures, sounds, movie clips, and animation).

EXERCISE

To test your knowledge of computer parts, write the correct names next to the following parts.

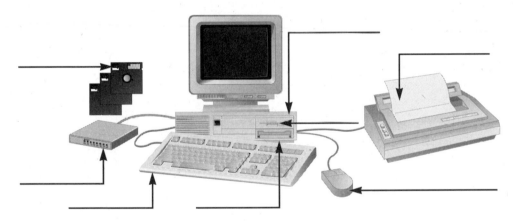

CHAPTER DIGEST

Hardware: Parts of a Computer

- *Monitor*—Displays your computer data.

- *Keyboard*—Used to enter information or commands into the computer.

- *System unit*—Acts as the "brain" of the computer, processing data and program instructions as you work.

- *Hard drive*—Stores information (data and programs) on a non-removable (fixed) disk.

- *Floppy disk drive*—Retrieves or stores information on portable diskettes.

- *Mouse*—Used to select commands, words, or pictures on the monitor.

- *Printer*—Transfers computer information onto paper.

- *Modem*—Transmits information between computers using a telephone line.

Software: Computer Instructions

- *Software*—Instructions that tell your computer how to function and how to do something useful.

- *Operating system*—Instructions that tell a computer how to perform basic tasks, such as how to save data and use computer memory.

- *Application*—Instructions that tell a computer how to perform a specific task, such as writing a letter or balancing a checkbook.

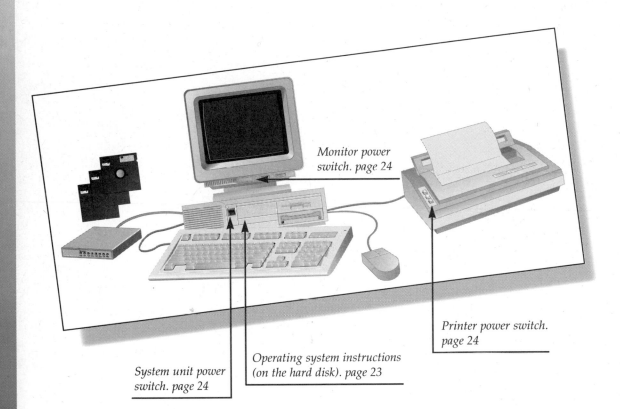

Monitor power switch. page 24

Printer power switch. page 24

Operating system instructions (on the hard disk). page 23

System unit power switch. page 24

3

STARTING A COMPUTER

I n order for a computer to do anything useful, you have to turn it on. In this chapter, you will learn how to turn on a PC and a Macintosh. You will also learn what to expect as your computer "wakes up," and what to do if something does not happen as expected.

The following section explains how to start an IBM PC or compatible computer. If you have a Macintosh computer, skip ahead to the section called "Starting a Macintosh Computer."

STARTING A PC

Before you can use your computer, you must turn it on with the operating system (usually DOS) in place. This procedure is called *booting*. Most PCs now come with a hard disk (inside the computer) that already has DOS on it. The following steps assume you have a newer computer with a hard disk.

1 Make sure the floppy disk drives do not contain floppy disks.

2 Make sure all your computer equipment is properly connected and is plugged in.

3 If all your computer equipment is plugged into a surge protector or power strip, flip the switch on the power strip to turn it on. (Users commonly plug all their computer equipment into a surge protector to protect the electronic components from sudden jumps in power, which can damage equipment.)

4 Flip the power switch or press the power button on the monitor to turn it on. By turning on the monitor first, you can read any messages that your computer might display during startup.

5 If desired, flip the power switch on the printer to turn it on. (You may have to hunt for the switch.)

6 Flip the power switch or press the power button on the system unit to turn it on. The power switch is usually on the right side or back of the system unit.

As your computer boots, you'll see some text on-screen as the computer goes through its internal checks. The disk drive lights will go on and off, and you will hear the floppy disk drives grind. The computer is basically making sure all its parts are still in working order.

WHAT YOU'LL SEE NEXT

After a while, the system quiets down, and the display stops changing. What you see next depends on your computer's setup. Here are the four most common things you'll see:

- **Microsoft Windows** Many newer computers are set up to run Microsoft Windows automatically. When you start your computer, you'll see a screen that looks something like the one shown here.

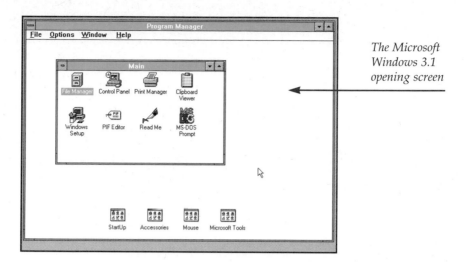

The Microsoft Windows 3.1 opening screen

- **The DOS prompt** In the old days, all computers were set up to display a DOS prompt, such as one of the following:

C:\\>

or this

A:\\>

or this

A>

- **A navigational screen** In an attempt to help new users learn how to operate a computer, some computer manufacturers (such as Packard Bell) set up their computers to run a computer navigator. The navigator may include a person's voice, animation, and a series of buttons that let you explore your computer.

- **A menu** Some computers come with a menu of all the programs that are on the computer. If you see such a menu, don't panic. Just read everything on the screen (especially the stuff at the bottom). The screen will often include messages that tell you what to do next or how to get help.

Packard Bell's Navigator helps you start using your PC.

WHAT COULD POSSIBLY GO WRONG?

If you don't see the DOS prompt, Windows, the Navigator, a menu, or some similar feature, don't panic. Several things may be going on:

- **Nothing happens.** If you hear no noise and see no flashing lights, your computer or one of its parts may not be plugged in. Turn everything off, then make sure everything is connected and is plugged into an outlet.

- **Blank screen.** If your screen is still blank, make sure your monitor is on. If it's on, the brightness knob may be turned way down. Try cranking the brightness up.

- **Non-system disk or disk error.** If you see a message telling you that there is a non-system disk in the drive, try the following solutions:

  If you left a disk in the floppy drive by mistake, remove the disk and then press any key on the keyboard.

  If that doesn't work, your computer may not have a hard disk drive. You will have to boot the computer from a floppy disk. Insert the DOS Program disk (Disk 1) into the floppy disk drive, close the drive door, and press any key to continue the boot operation.

  If your computer has a hard disk drive, DOS may not be installed on it. Check the manual that came with your computer to find out how to install DOS.

REBOOTING OR RESETTING A PC

During the day, your computer may lock up, refusing to do any more work. You try to type or move the mouse, and nothing responds.

When this happens, you will be tempted to turn the computer off and then on. Resist the temptation. Try to *warm boot* the computer first. A warm boot tells the computer to reread the operating instructions without turning the power on and off. To warm boot the computer, hold down Ctrl and Alt while pressing Del.

If your computer does not respond to a warm boot (if nothing happens), look for a Reset button on the system unit and press it. If that doesn't work, turn everything off, wait about one minute, then turn everything back on.

STARTING A MACINTOSH COMPUTER

Turning on a Macintosh is not much different from turning on a PC. With a Mac, you still have to turn on the power with the operating system instructions in place. The main difference is that the Mac has fewer switches, and the switches may be located in different places. Follow these steps to start a Macintosh computer:

1. Make sure the floppy disk drives do not contain floppy disks.

2. Make sure your Mac is plugged into an electrical outlet.

3. If your Mac is plugged into a surge protector or power strip, flip the switch on the power strip to turn it on.

4. If you have a Mac that has a separate monitor, flip the power switch or press the power button on the monitor to turn it on.

5. If you plan on using your printer, flip the power switch on the printer to turn it on.

6. Flip the power switch or press the button on the back of the Mac to turn it on.

   Or, if you have a Macintosh II, Centris, or Quadra, and a keyboard that has a power key, press the power key. (The power key is in the upper right corner of the keyboard and has a right pointing arrow on it.)

If everything goes as it should, you should first hear a "boing" or chime meaning the Mac is waking up. You will then see a smiling Mac icon (an icon is a small picture that appears on-screen), and then a "Welcome to Macintosh" message. Finally, you will see the Macintosh opening screen.

The Macintosh opening screen →

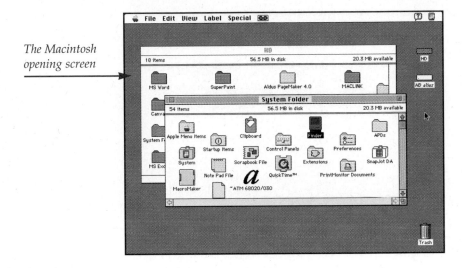

WHAT COULD POSSIBLY GO WRONG?

If you don't hear a "boing" and the Mac fails to show the opening screen, several things may be going on:

Nothing happens. If you hear no noise and see no flashing lights, your Mac or one of its parts may not be plugged in. Make sure everything is connected and is plugged into an outlet.

Blank screen. If your screen is still blank, make sure it is on. If it's on, the brightness knob may be turned way down. Try turning the brightness up.

 Flashing question mark icon. If you see a disk that has a question mark icon inside it, the Mac is telling you that it needs the operating system disk. Try the following solutions:

- If you left a disk in the floppy drive by mistake, remove the disk and press any key on the keyboard.

- If that doesn't work, your Mac may not have a hard disk drive. You will have to boot the computer from a floppy disk. Insert the System disk into the floppy disk drive, then press the Reset button (or turn the power off, wait 15 seconds, and flip the power back on).

Loud, unfamiliar tones. If you don't hear the typical "boing" or chime, your Mac may have a serious hardware problem. Look for the sad Mac icon on-screen and a number that indicates the cause of the problem.

 Sad Mac icon. If you see a Mac icon with a sad face, your Mac probably has a serious problem. For example, the system files or disk may be damaged. Write down the number that appears under the Mac icon and seek professional help.

WHAT TO DO IF YOUR MAC STOPS RESPONDING

While you're working, your Mac may lock up, or you may receive an error message indicating an unrecoverable error. When this happens, try the following steps to regain control of your Mac:

- Hold down the ⌘ key while pressing . (the period key). This frees a program that may be caught up in an unending command loop.

- If ⌘+. doesn't work, hold down the ⌘ key and the Option key while pressing the Esc key. This forces the currently active program (the one causing problems) to quit.

- If your Mac is still stuck, press the Reset button (assuming your Mac has a Reset button).

> *Tip: Sometimes, a Mac will refuse to eject a disk when you press the floppy disk eject button. When this happens, hold down the eject button while turning the Mac off and then on. This will usually make the Mac cough up the disk.*

- If your Mac doesn't have a Reset button or the Reset button doesn't free your Mac, try restarting your Mac with the power switch.

- If you are still having problems, turn the Mac off and wait a few minutes. To restart the Mac, hold down Shift while flipping the power switch on. This boots the Mac without automatically loading some programs.

Turning Off a Computer

Turning off your computer is more complicated than turning it on. The reason for this is that you have probably done other things with your computer since starting it. To turn off the computer, you have to first back out of whatever you were doing. Take the following steps to turn off your computer.

1 *Save anything you've been doing on a disk.* As you create or edit a document, your work is stored in RAM, which requires electricity to remember things. If you turn off the power without saving your work on a disk, the computer forgets your work.

2 *Quit any programs you are currently using.* When you close a program, it prompts you to save all your work to disk, and then it shuts itself down properly. If you turn off the power without quitting your programs, you might lose your work.

3 *If you are shutting down a Macintosh, open the Special menu and select Shut down.* The Mac puts away hidden files, darkens the screen, and may display a message indicating that it's okay to turn off the computer.

If Windows is running, press Alt+F4 *or open the File menu and select Exit Windows.* If you shut down a PC when Windows is running, you risk losing data and damaging files. You should exit Windows and return to the DOS prompt before turning off the computer.

4 *Turn off your computer.* Flip the power button on the power strip, or flip each switch or button on the individual computer parts.

More About Booting and Rebooting

The following list provides some more advanced tips about booting and rebooting a computer:

- When you boot a PC, it reads a set of startup commands in two files (CONFIG.SYS and AUTOEXEC.BAT). If you have trouble booting your computer, press and release the F8 key when you see the message **Starting MS-DOS**. If you have DOS version 5 or later, it enables you to step through the commands to see which one is causing problems. You can bypass all the commands by pressing and releasing the F5 key when you see the **Starting MS-DOS** message.

- Because rebooting from Microsoft Windows can cause data loss and other problems, Windows has a reboot safety net. If you press $\boxed{Ctrl}+\boxed{Alt}+\boxed{Del}$ in Windows, you see a screen that lets you quit the application that is giving you problems and return to Windows. Reboot from Windows only when nothing else works.

- Many users choose to leave their computers on all the time. There are pros and cons to this approach. Leaving the computer on all the time does save wear and tear on some of the electrical components. However, this also increases energy consumption and shortens the life of some components, such as the fan that cools the other components.

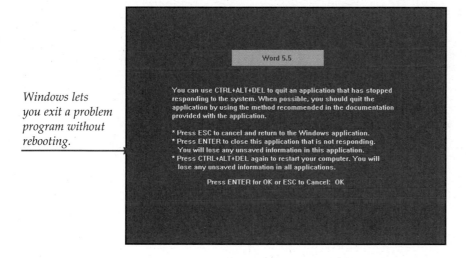

Windows lets you exit a problem program without rebooting.

EXERCISES

Although it's not a great idea to keep booting and rebooting your computer, you should be comfortable with the process. Perform the following exercises for practice.

BOOTING A PC

1 Remove any floppy disks.

2 Turn on the power strip, if you have one.

3 Turn on the monitor.

4 Turn on any other peripheral devices.

5 Turn on the system unit.

REBOOTING A PC

1 If Windows is running, press [Alt]+[F4] until you see the Exit Windows dialog box, then press Enter.

2 Wait until the DOS prompt appears.

3 Press [Ctrl]+[Alt]+[Del].

BOOTING A MAC

1 Remove any floppy disks.

2 Turn on the power strip, if you have one.

3 Turn on the monitor, if it has a separate switch.

4 Turn on any other peripheral devices.

5 Flip the power switch on the Mac or press the power key on the keyboard.

Computer Basics

CHAPTER DIGEST

Startup Terminology

- *Boot*   To start your computer with the operating system instructions in place (on a disk in one of the computer's disk drives)

- *Cold boot*   To boot a computer by turning on its power

- *Warm boot*   To reboot a computer that is already running, without turning the power off and then on

- *Reset*   To restart a computer without turning the power off and on

Turning On an IBM Personal Computer

Remove floppy disks→Turn on power strip→Turn on monitor→Turn on system unit

Turning On a Macintosh

Remove floppy disks→Turn on power strip→Turn on monitor→Flip power switch on Mac or press power button on keyboard

Reboot a PC

Press (Ctrl)+(Alt)+(Del)

Reboot a Mac

Press (⌘)+(.)
or
Press (⌘)+(Option)+(Esc)
or
Press Reset
or
Flip the power switch off→wait 15 seconds→Flip the power switch on

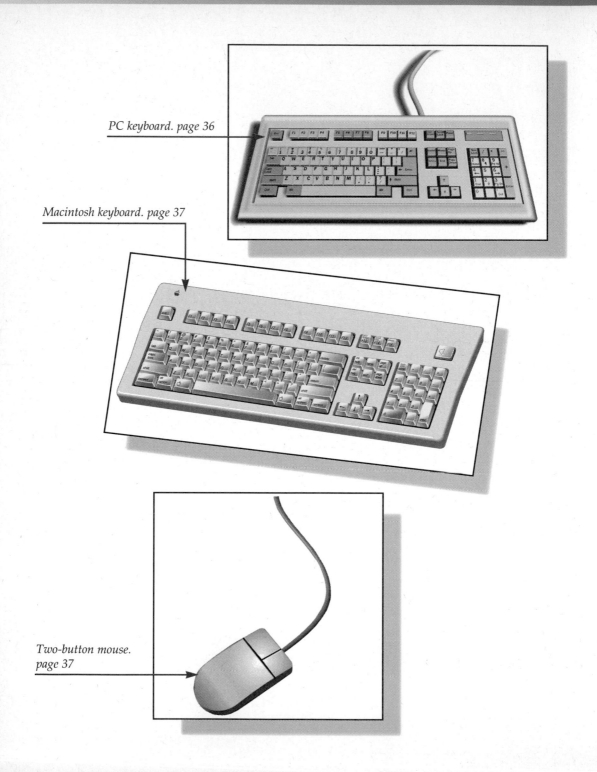

PC keyboard. page 36

Macintosh keyboard. page 37

Two-button mouse. page 37

USING A KEYBOARD AND MOUSE

4

I f you were to compare a computer to a car, the keyboard and mouse would be the computer's steering wheel. You use the keyboard and mouse to enter commands that tell the computer what to do, to type text and numbers, and to draw illustrations. In this chapter, you will learn the basics of using a keyboard and mouse to control your computer.

USING A KEYBOARD

Although no two keyboards look exactly alike, they all have a set of typewriter keys for entering letters and numbers, and keys for moving around on-screen. Following is a list of the keys you'll find on most keyboards:

- **Alphanumeric keys**   *Alphanumeric* is a fancy term for "letters and numbers." This area of the keyboard also includes a Shift key (for uppercase letters), an Enter (or Return) key, a Space bar, a Tab key, and a Backspace key.

- **Arrow keys**   Also known as *cursor-movement* keys, the arrow keys move the cursor (the blinking line or box) around on-screen.

- **Numeric keypad**   Most keyboards include a numeric keypad, whose keys act as both cursor-movement keys and number keys. This keypad includes a Num Lock key. With Num Lock turned off, you use the numeric keypad to move around on-screen. With Num Lock turned on, you use the keypad to type numbers, just as you would enter numbers on an adding machine.

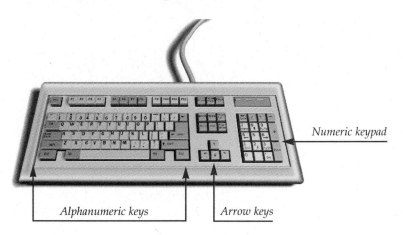

Numeric keypad

Alphanumeric keys   *Arrow keys*

SPECIAL PC KEYS

The PC keyboard has several special keys that you may not see on other types of keyboards. Most of these keys are reserved for quickly entering commands in a program. The following list describes most of the special keys:

Key	Description
F1	**Function keys** Use the function keys to enter commands and get quick help. The function of each key varies from program to program.
Ctrl Alt	**Ctrl and Alt keys** The Ctrl (Control) and Alt (Alternative) keys make the other keys on the keyboard act differently from the way they normally act. For example, if you press the F1 key by itself, the computer may display a help screen. But if you hold down the Ctrl key and press the F1 key (Ctrl+F1, in computer lingo), the computer carries out an entirely different command. You can also use the Alt key with the number keys (on the numeric keypad) to type special symbols or foreign characters.
Esc	**Esc key** You can use the Esc (Escape) key in most programs to back out of a menu or cancel a command.

SPECIAL MACINTOSH KEYS

Because a Macintosh relies more on a mouse than on the keyboard for entering commands, the Macintosh keyboard is less complex. For example, some Macintosh keyboards do not have function keys. However, the Macintosh does have the following special keys:

Key	Description
⌘	**Command (Apple or Clover) key** You hold down the Command key and press other keys (usually letters or numbers) to enter commands. A Macintosh usually lets you enter the same command using the mouse (to select a command from a menu); the Command key offers a faster alternative.
Option	**Option (Alt) key** Use the Option key with other keys to type symbols and special foreign language characters.
Ctrl	**Control key** In advanced applications, you use Control along with the Command key and other keys to quickly enter commands.
Esc	**Esc (Escape) key** You may sometimes use the Esc key to cancel an operation, but there are usually easier ways to cancel.

POINTING WITH A MOUSE

If you have a mouse and a program that *supports* (allows you to use) a mouse, a mouse pointer appears on-screen when you start the program. The appearance of the pointer varies depending on the program. Sometimes it looks like a tall rectangle. Other times, it looks like an arrow. It may even appear as a cross-hair pointer (like what you see when you look through a rifle sight).

> *Tip: If you start a program and you don't see the mouse pointer, roll the mouse around on your desk (or mouse pad) until the pointer comes into view.*

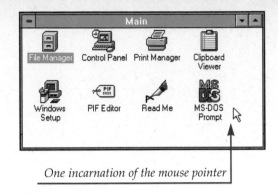

One incarnation of the mouse pointer

MOUSE POINTING TECHNIQUES

With a mouse, you don't have to remember a book full of commands, or which function key or command key to press to issue a command. You simply point to an on-screen item or menu, and then press and release the mouse button. When using the mouse, you need to know the following actions:

- **Point**   Roll the mouse on the mouse pad until the mouse pointer is over the item you want. When you point at a command or object on screen, nothing happens.

- **Click**   Once you have pointed to something, you can select it by *clicking* (pressing and releasing) the mouse button without moving the mouse. If the mouse has more than one button, you'll usually use the left mouse button. Programs reserve the right mouse button for canceling a selection or for other special actions.

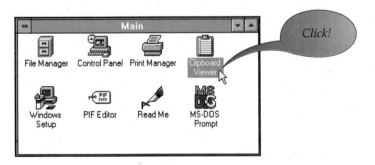

- **Double-click**   Press and release the left mouse button twice quickly without moving the mouse. You double-click to give a command, select a file, or start a program.

- **Drag**   Hold down the mouse button while moving the mouse. You drag to select characters or words, move something on-screen, or draw a line or shape.

GETTING COMFORTABLE WITH A MOUSE

Using a mouse sounds easy, right? Well, it is once you get used to it. The following tips will help you get started:

- **Hold still when clicking.** If you move the mouse when you're clicking, you might just move the mouse pointer off the item you wanted to select.

- **Click to select, double-click to enter.** If you click on something, you select it, but nothing happens. If you want something to happen, click-click (double-click).

- **Quick with the double-click.** Two clicks is not a double-click. If you click twice slowly, you will select an item twice.

> *Tip: Both a cursor and an insertion point show you where the text you type will appear. A cursor is a horizontal line that appears below characters or a flashing box. The insertion point is a vertical line that appears between characters. Although they are basically the same, in DOS programs you see the cursor, and in Macintosh and Windows programs you usually see an insertion point.*

MAKING YOUR MOUSE BEHAVE

You can change the mouse settings to make the mouse behave the way you want it to. Typically, you can change three things about your mouse's behavior: the speed at which the pointer moves across the screen, the speed at which you must click twice for a double-click, and the orientation of the mouse buttons for left- or right-hand use.

In Microsoft Windows, for example, you double-click on the Mouse icon (in the Control Panel window) to display the mouse settings. You can then enter your preferences. Refer to your Windows manual for details.

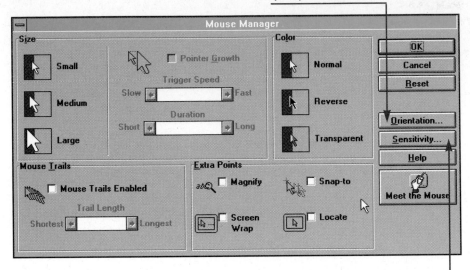

CHAPTER 4

Swap mouse buttons for left-handed use.

Increase the double-click interval and control the speed of the mouse pointer.

MORE KEYBOARD AND MOUSE TIPS

Now that you know the basics of how to use a keyboard and mouse, following is a list of some more advanced keys and features:

- Avoid the [Remap] key. If you have a fancy keyboard, it may have a [Remap] key that allows you to make one key act like another. For example, you can have the [F12] key type an asterisk. If you press the Remap key by mistake and continue typing, you may remap all your keys.

- Avoid the [Scroll Lock] key. In most applications, when you press the down arrow key, the cursor moves down. With Scroll Lock on, the cursor remains in position, and the text moves up or down.

- Press [Esc] or [Ctrl]+[Break] to stop an action.

- In some applications, you can use the right mouse button for quick access to commands. Try right-clicking in an application to see if it supports the right mouse button.

EXERCISES

To become comfortable with a keyboard and mouse, perform the following exercises for practice.

LOCATING KEYS

Draw a line from the label to the correct key.

Escape (Esc)   *Function keys*   *Num Lock light*

Caps Lock

Control (Ctrl)

Caps Lock light

Num Lock

Numeric keypad

Alternative (Alt)   *Forward slash (/)*   *Arrow keys*

MOUSE CALISTHENICS

The following steps assume you are working on a Mac, running Windows, or using an application that supports a mouse.

1 Slide the mouse across your desk until the pointer is resting on an object or a point on the desktop.

2 Press and release the left mouse button without moving the pointer.

3 Press and release the left mouse button twice without moving the pointer.

4 Hold down the left mouse button while sliding the mouse.

CHAPTER DIGEST

PC Keyboard

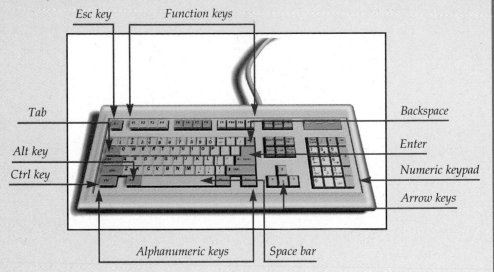

Esc key   Function keys

Tab

Alt key

Ctrl key

Backspace

Enter

Numeric keypad

Arrow keys

Alphanumeric keys   Space bar

Macintosh Keyboard

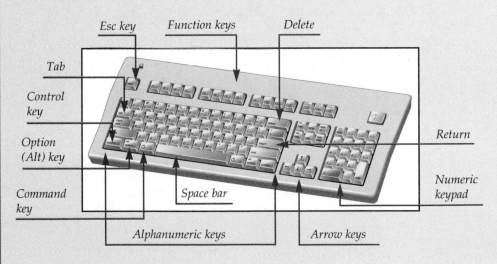

Esc key   Function keys   Delete

Tab

Control key

Option (Alt) key

Command key

Return

Numeric keypad

Space bar

Alphanumeric keys   Arrow keys

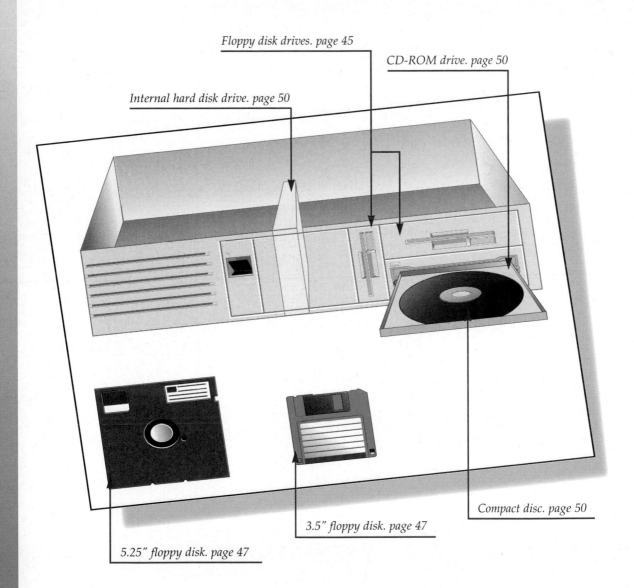

Floppy disk drives. page 45

CD-ROM drive. page 50

Internal hard disk drive. page 50

Compact disc. page 50

3.5" floppy disk. page 47

5.25" floppy disk. page 47

Working with Disks, CDs, Directories, and Files

Chapter 5

One of the most important jobs you have as a computer user is to feed information to your computer on disks. The computer uses a *disk drive* to read information and program instructions off the disks and store it in memory where the computer can use the information. In this chapter, you will learn how to work with disks and with the information on the disks.

Storing Information on Disks

Floppy Disk Drives

Hard Disk Drives

CD-ROM Drives

How to Handle Floppy Disks

Preparing Floppy Disks to Store Data

Disk Drives and Their Names

Most computers have at least two disk drives. On an PC, the disk drives are assigned letters: A, B, C, and so on. Letters A and B represent the floppy disk drives—on the front of the system unit. Letter C stands for the hard disk drive. Letter D usually corresponds to the CD-ROM drive (if your system has one). Note that your computer may have different drive letters than the ones labeled on the following figure.

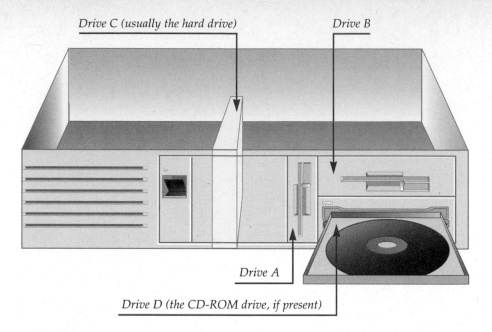

Drive C (usually the hard drive)

Drive B

Drive A

Drive D (the CD-ROM drive, if present)

A Macintosh computer handles drives a little differently. Instead of using letters, a Mac displays an icon (a small picture that represents an object) for each disk drive that contains a disk.

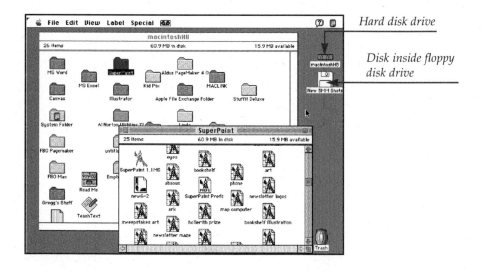

Hard disk drive

Disk inside floppy disk drive

FLOPPY DISKS

Floppy disks are the disks you insert into your computer's floppy disk drive (usually located on the front of the computer). You typically use floppy disks to install programs, back up files (duplicate files to prevent data loss), or share files with another person.

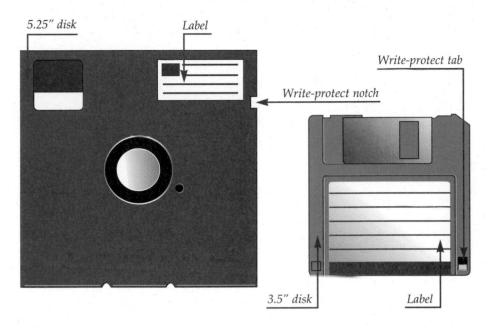

5.25" disk Label Write-protect tab Write-protect notch 3.5" disk Label

Two characteristics describe floppy disks: *size* and *capacity*. You can measure size with a ruler. The size tells you which floppy drive the disk will fit in. You can get 3.5" disks or 5.25" disks, as shown here.

Capacity refers to the amount of information the disk can hold; it's sort of like pints, quarts, and gallons. Capacity is measured in *kilobytes (K)* and *megabytes (MB)*. Each *byte* consists of 8 *bits* and is used to store a single character—A, B, C, 1, 2, 3, and so on. (For example, 01000001 is a byte that represents an uppercase A; each 1 or 0 is a bit.) A kilobyte is 1,024 bytes—1,024 characters. A megabyte is a little over a million bytes.

Tip: A hard disk drive can be divided (or partitioned) into one or more drives. On a PC, each partition has a separate drive letter—for example, drive C, D, E, and so on. The actual hard disk drive is called the physical *drive; each partition is called a* logical *drive. By dividing a physical drive, you make the drive more manageable.*

A disk's capacity depends on whether it stores information on one side of the disk (single-sided) or both sides (double-sided) and on how much information it lets you cram into a given amount of space (the disk's *density*). The following table shows the four basic types of floppy disks used in PCs and how much information each type can hold.

Disk Size	Disk Type	Disk Capacity	Approximate Number of Typed Pages
5.25"	Double-sided Double-density (DS/DD)	360K	150 pages
5.25"	Double-sided High-density (DS/HD)	1.2MB	500 pages
3.5"	Double-sided Double-density (DS/DD)	720K	300 pages
3.5"	Double-sided High-density (DS/HD)	1.44MB	600 pages

If you have purchased your computer recently, it is equipped with a *high density* disk drive, which can store more data on a disk per inch of disk space. You should purchase high density disks (of the right physical size—5.25" or 3.5") to use in that drive. Boxes of disks have their density and size clearly labeled. Even if your computer has two floppy drives, if the computer is new, both drives are probably high density (check your owner's manual to be sure). If your computer is older, you may have a *double density* disk drive. You should purchase double density disks to use in that drive.

THE CARE AND HANDLING OF FLOPPY DISKS

Floppy disks are fragile. If you damage a disk, you may destroy the data stored on that disk, or the disk may no longer store data reliably. You should follow a few simple precautions to prevent damage:

- Keep the disk in a safe place when not in use. Dust, dirt, coffee, and any other foreign matter can damage a disk.

- When labeling a disk, write on the label before sticking it on the disk, so that the pressure from your pen does not damage the disk. If a disk already has a label, write gently with a felt-tip pen.

- Keep disks away from heat sources, such as photocopy machines or the top of your monitor. Heat can warp the disk.

- Keep disks away from magnetic fields. (Telephones and computer speakers have magnets in them.) Disks store information magnetically, so a magnet can erase data from the disk.

INSERTING AND EJECTING A FLOPPY DISK FROM A DRIVE

A disk will fit into a drive any number of ways—upside-down, sideways, backwards—but it will work only if you insert it properly. To insert the disk, hold it by its label with the label facing up (or to the left, if the drive slot is vertical), and insert the disk into the drive. If the floppy drive has a lever or a door, flip the lever or close the door.

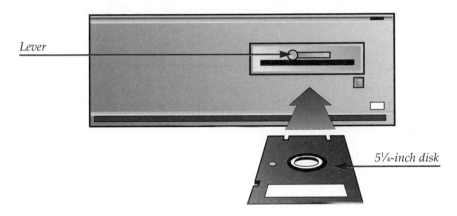

Lever

5¼-inch disk

Before removing a disk from a drive, make sure the drive light is off. If the drive light is on, the drive is reading information from the disk or writing information to the disk. Removing the disk during either of these operations may damage the disk and drive and may cause you to lose data.

Most 3.5" drives have an eject button. Press the button to eject the disk, and then gently pull the disk from the drive. Most 5.25" drives have a lever or door. Flip the lever or open the door, and then gently pull the disk from the drive. On a Macintosh, the disk will usually pop out after you exit a program, but you can also use the keyboard to eject a disk: hold down the ⌘ key and press E.

> *Tip: A quick way to eject a floppy disk from a Mac drive is to drag the disk's icon over the Trash icon and release the mouse button. Some Mac floppy drives also come with eject buttons, like those on PC drives.*

BEFORE YOU USE A FLOPPY DISK

You get a brand-new box of disks. Can you use them to store information? Maybe. If the disks came *preformatted*, you can use them right out of the box. If they are not formatted, you'll have to do it yourself, with the help of your computer. To determine whether the disks are formatted and to figure out the formatted capacity of the disks, read the box.

> *Tip: If you have trouble with preformatted floppies, reformat the disks on your computer. Sometimes the alignment of the read/write heads of one drive differ just enough from the alignment of the read/write heads on another drive to make a disk formatted in one drive unreadable in another.*

Formatting divides a disk into small storage areas and creates a *file allocation table* (FAT) on the disk. Whenever you save a file to disk, the parts of the file are saved in one or more of these storage areas. The FAT functions as a classroom seating chart does, telling your computer the location of all its storage areas.

You will learn to format a disk for use with an PC in Chapter 6. In Chapter 8, you can learn how to format (initialize) a disk with a Macintosh computer.

WORKING WITH A HARD DISK

The hard disk drive is like a big floppy disk drive complete with disk. (Typically, you don't take the disk out; it stays in the drive forever.) To get information onto the hard disk, you copy information to it from floppy disks or save the files you create directly to the hard disk. The information stays on the hard disk until you choose to erase the information. When the computer needs information, it goes directly to the hard disk, reads the information into memory, and continues working. You don't have to feed it floppies.

THE CD-ROM DRIVE: D?

If you're lucky, your computer will have a CD-ROM drive. If it's an internal CD-ROM drive, it will be near the floppy drives. If it's an external drive, it will stand alone, connected with a cable to your system unit. Either way, the CD-ROM drive is usually drive D.

Some CD-ROM drives come with a removable carriage called a caddy. You place a CD into the caddy and then insert the caddy into the drive. Some drives have a built-in caddy. You press a button to open the caddy, and then you place the CD in the caddy and push it closed.

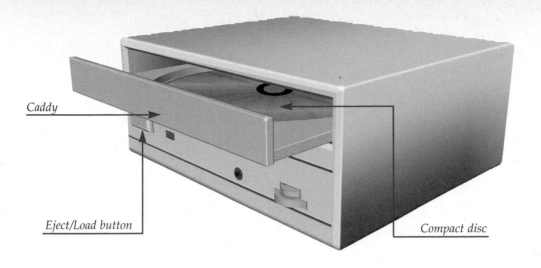

Caddy

Eject/Load button

Compact disc

DISKLESS WORK STATIONS

If your computer is part of a network, it may not have any disk drives. If that's the case, forget all this talk about floppy disks and hard disks. Your network probably has a *server* with a large disk drive that stores all the information and programs everyone in the company needs. A person called the *network administrator* manages the network and makes sure everything runs smoothly. In such a case, you will work with the drives on the server just as if those drives were your computer's internal hard drives.

UNDERSTANDING FILES

Most applications let you create files to store your work. When you create a file, you're essentially naming your work and recording it on a disk so you can "play it back" later.

FILE NAMES

On PCs, file names consist of a *base name* and an *extension*; for example, CHAPTER9.DOC consists of the base name CHAPTER9, a period, and the extension DOC. The extension helps identify the type of file (in this case **DOC**ument), and helps you group your files so you can enter commands that affect an entire group of files. The following table lists some common file extensions.

File Extension	File Type
.BAK	Backup file
.BAT	Batch file (a collection of commands)
.COM	Command (program) file
.DAT	Data file
.DBF	dBASE file
.DOC	Document or Microsoft Word file
.EXE	Executable program file
.HLP	Help file
.OVL	Overlay file
.PCX	PC Paintbrush file
.TXT	Text (ASCII) file
.WKS, .WK1, .WK2, or .WK3	Lotus 1-2-3 files
.WP or .WPF	WordPerfect file
.WS	WordStar file

A PC is particular about the file names it allows. The base name can be eight characters or less, and the extension can be three characters or less and must be preceded by a period. (This is the only place a period can appear in the file name.) The following characters are not allowed in file names:

   " . / \ [ ] : * < > | + ; , ? space

A Macintosh offers more flexibility in naming files. Macintosh file names can be up to 31 characters, although most programs will display only the first 24 characters of the file's name. You can include any character in the file name except for a colon (:), and you can use spaces. The following file name would be valid on a Macintosh:

   "Johnson You're Hired" letter

ORGANIZING FILES ON A FLOPPY DISK

Organizing files on a floppy disk is not difficult, because you normally don't store many files per disk. Even if you store as many as 30 files on a single disk, you can search through a list of files fairly quickly. However, you should follow three procedures to make the information more accessible:

- Give each file a unique name that helps you remember what's in the file. For example, JOHNSON.LTR tells you the name of the person the document concerns (Johnson) and the type of document (LTR for Letter).

- Label each disk with the date and the types of files stored on it, so you'll know what's on the disk and which disk holds the most recent revisions.

- Copy any files you don't use very often to separate disks, and erase the original files from the disks you use often. (Refer to Chapters 6–8 to learn how to copy files.)

ORGANIZING FILES ON A HARD DISK

Because hard disks can store thousands of files, you need to group related files. On a PC, you group files by using *directories* and *subdirectories*. A directory acts like a drawer in a filing cabinet, and subdirectories act as folders. Directories and subdirectories form a structure that looks like a family tree.

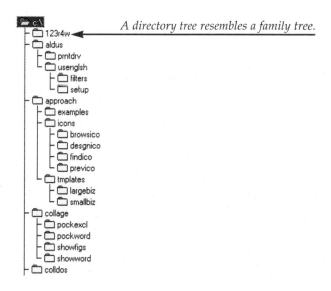

A directory tree resembles a family tree.

To tell a PC where to look for a file, you type a path. For example, you may need to tell your computer to get the CUB file that's in subdirectory LION, in the directory ZOO, on drive C. The path would look like this:

c:\zoo\lion\cub

A Macintosh computer uses *folders* (represented on-screen by icons that look like folders) to group files. Each folder can contain additional folders and/or individual files. To open a folder, you double-click on its icon.

CHAPTER 5

EXERCISES

IDENTIFYING PC DISK DRIVES FROM DOS

1 Make sure the DOS prompt is displayed (**C:\>**).

2 Type **a:** and press ⏎Enter. If no disk is in drive A, you'll hear a grinding sound and see the following message on-screen.

```
C:\>a:

General failure reading drive A
Abort, Retry, Fail?
```

3 Insert a formatted disk into drive A, and close the drive door, if it has one.

4 Press ⃞R for Retry. **A:\>** should appear on the screen.

5 Type **d:** and press ⏎Enter. If you see a message that says **Invalid drive specification,** your computer has no drive D (most new computers go only up to C, unless they have CD-ROM drives). If you do have a drive D, you might have an E, F, and G. Try changing to those drives.

IDENTIFYING PC DISK DRIVES IN WINDOWS

1 Run Windows.

2 Double-click on the ⃞Main icon.

3 Double-click on the ⃞File Manager icon.

4 Look at the disk icons at the top of the window.

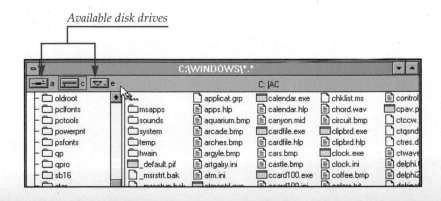

Available disk drives

CHAPTER DIGEST

Inserting a Floppy Disk

1. Insert disk.

2. Close door, if present.

3. Label facing up

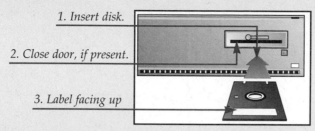

Ejecting a Floppy Disk (PC)

1. Make sure light is off.

2. Press Eject button.

3. Remove disk.

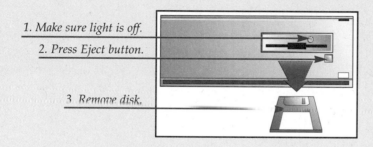

Ejecting a Floppy Disk (Macintosh)

Press ⌘+E→Remove disk

File Name Rules

DOS: Use 8 characters, a period, and three character extension. Do not use the following: " . / \ [ ] : * < > | + ; , ? **space**

Mac: Use up to 31 characters but not a colon (:).

Chapter 6: Entering DOS Commands

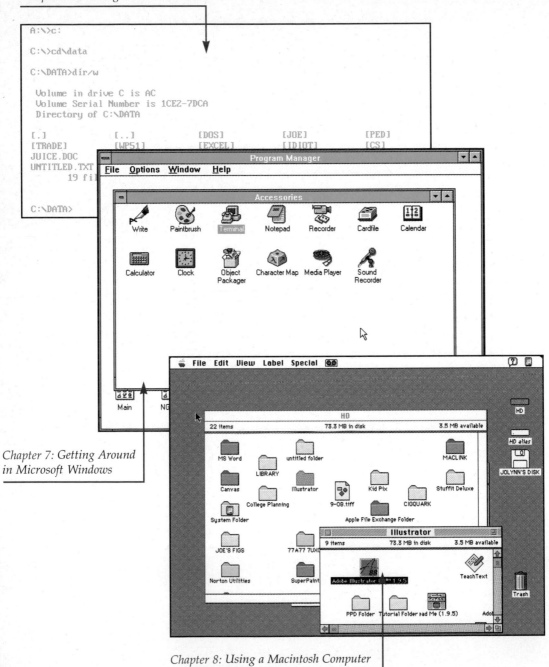

```
A:\>c:

C:\>cd\data

C:\DATA>dir/w

 Volume in drive C is AC
 Volume Serial Number is 1CE2-7DCA
 Directory of C:\DATA

[.]            [..]           [DOS]          [JOE]          [PED]
[TRADE]        [WP51]         [EXCEL]        [IDIOT]        [CS]
JUICE.DOC
UNTITLED.TXT
        19 fil

C:\DATA>
```

Chapter 7: Getting Around
in Microsoft Windows

Chapter 8: Using a Macintosh Computer

PART 2

USING AN OPERATING SYSTEM

Changing disk drives.
page 60

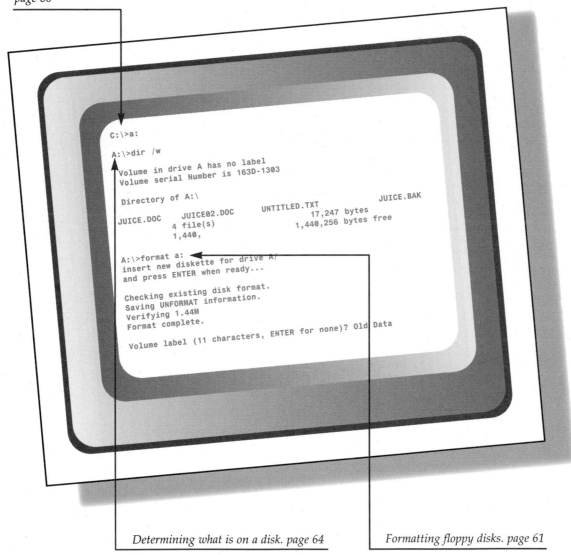

```
C:\>a:

A:\>dir /w

Volume in drive A has no label
Volume serial Number is 163D-1303

Directory of A:\
                                    UNTITLED.TXT                 JUICE.BAK
JUICE.DOC     JUICE02.DOC                    17,247 bytes
              4 file(s)              1,440,256 bytes free
              1,440,

A:\>format a:
insert new diskette for drive A/
and press ENTER when ready...

Checking existing disk format.
Saving UNFORMAT information.
Verifying 1.44M
Format complete.

Volume label (11 characters, ENTER for none)? Old Data
```

Determining what is on a disk. page 64

Formatting floppy disks. page 61

Chapter 6

ENTERING DOS COMMANDS

Entering Commands at the DOS Prompt

Activating a Disk Drive

Viewing a List of Files

Running an Application from the DOS Prompt

Formatting Floppy Disks

When you boot a PC or compatible computer (see Chapter 3), you might encounter the infamous DOS prompt (for example, C:\>), a symbol that provides little clue as to what to do next. Your job is to type some command at the prompt to run an application or perform some other useful task. But what do you type and how do you type it? This chapter will teach you the most commonly used DOS commands and the correct way to enter them.

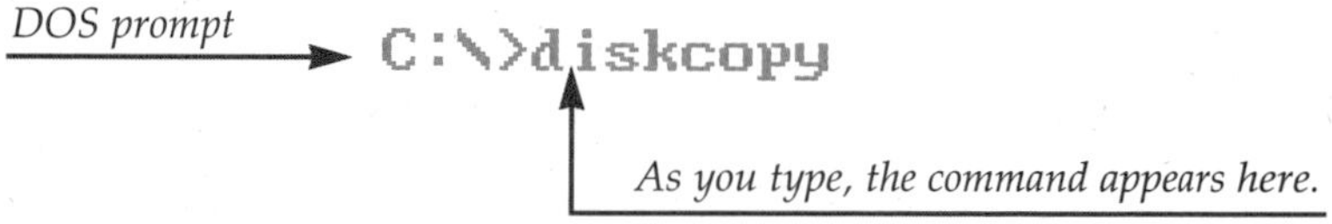

DOS prompt
C:\>diskcopy
As you type, the command appears here.

PARTS OF A DOS COMMAND

Before you start typing commands at the DOS prompt, you should know the various parts of a DOS command. For example, this typical DOS command consists of four elements:

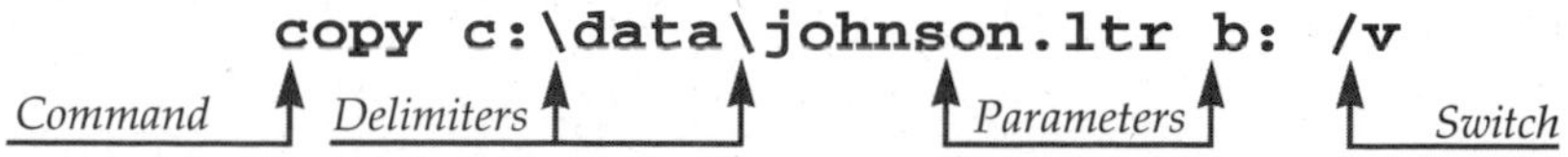

copy c:\data\johnson.ltr b: /v
Command
Delimiters
Parameters
Switch

- **Command** This is the name of the DOS command (in the example on the previous page, it's **copy**). It tells DOS which action to carry out.

- **Delimiters** Delimiters are spaces and special characters (such as /, \, and :) that break down the command line for DOS. Think of delimiters as spaces and punctuation marks.

- **Parameters** Parameters specify the objects on which you want DOS to perform the action. In the example, **c:\data\johnson.ltr** is a parameter.

- **Switches** Switches allow you to control how the command performs its action. In the command on the previous page, the **/v** switch tells DOS to verify the copy operation to make sure the copy matches the original.

CHANGING TO A DISK DRIVE

Before you can work with the files on a disk, you need to tell DOS which drive to use. To change to a disk drive, here's what you do:

1 Make sure there is a formatted disk in the drive. (A hard drive has a formatted disk inside it. Any floppy disk that has files on it is formatted.)

2 Type the letter of the drive to which you want to change followed by a colon. For example, type **a:**.

3 Press ⏎Enter. The DOS prompt changes to show the letter of the active drive, for example **A:\>**.

4 To change back to drive C, type **c:** and press ⏎Enter.

Tip: If you change to a drive that does not contain a formatted disk, an error message like this will appear:

**Not ready reading drive A
Abort, Retry, Fail?**

Insert a formatted disk in the drive, close the drive door, and press ⓇR for Retry.

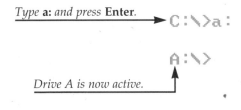

*Type **a:** and press **Enter**.*   →   C:\>a:

A:\>

Drive A is now active. ↑

FORMATTING A NEW FLOPPY DISK

Before you can store data on a disk, you must *format* the disk. Formatting divides a disk into small storage areas and creates a *file allocation table* (FAT) on the disk that acts as a map, telling your computer the location of all its storage areas.

You normally format a disk only once: when it is brand new. If you format a disk that contains data, that data is erased during the formatting process. Before you format a disk, make sure the disk is blank or that it contains data you will never again need.

Before you start formatting disks, you have to ask yourself the following questions:

- **What kind of floppy disk drives do I have?** What capacity is the disk drive? Is it high-density (1.2M or 1.44M) or double-density (360K or 720K)? The documentation that came with your computer will tell you whether you have high- or double-density drives.

- **What kind of floppy disks do I want to format?** Do you have high-density or double-density disks? Check the disks or the box in which the disks came.

This matters for two reasons. First, you *cannot* format a high-density disk in a double-density disk drive (for example, a 1.2 megabyte disk in a 360 kilobyte drive). Second, you *can* format a double-density disk in a high-density drive, but you have to use a special command switch. Keep the disk and drive densities in mind when working through the following sections.

If you are formatting a brand-new disk in a drive whose capacity matches the capacity of the disk (for example a 1.2M disk in a 1.2M disk drive), perform the following steps to format the disk:

1 Insert the blank disk you want to format into one of the floppy disk drives.

2 Type **format** followed by a space, the letter of the drive that contains the blank floppy disk, and a colon. For example, type **format b:** to format the disk in drive B.

3 Press ⏎Enter. DOS starts to format the disk. When DOS is done formatting, it displays a message asking if you want to type a volume label.

4 To label the disk, type a volume label (up to 11 characters) and press ⏎Enter. (This volume label will appear whenever you display a file list for this disk.) DOS displays a message asking if you want to format another disk.

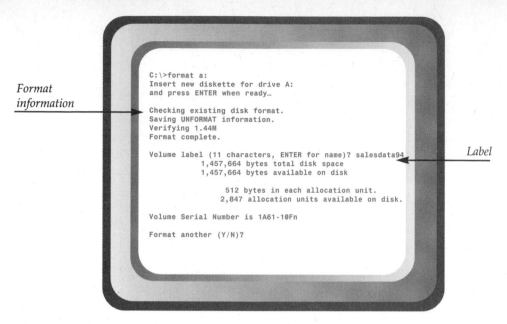

Format
information

```
C:\>format a:
Insert new diskette for drive A:
and press ENTER when ready...

Checking existing disk format.
Saving UNFORMAT information.
Verifying 1.44M
Format complete.

Volume label (11 characters, ENTER for name)? salesdata94
           1,457,664 bytes total disk space
           1,457,664 bytes available on disk

               512 bytes in each allocation unit.
           2,847 allocation units available on disk.

Volume Serial Number is 1A61-10Fn

Format another (Y/N)?
```

Label

5 Remove the formatted disk from the drive.

6 To format another disk, insert it into the floppy disk drive, and press Ⓨ. Otherwise, press Ⓝ to stop formatting.

To format a low-density disk in a high-density drive (for example, a 360K disk in a 1.2M disk drive), you need to add the /F switch to the FORMAT command. The /F switch allows you to specify the capacity of the for-matted disk, as shown in the following examples:

> *Tip: If you choose to enter a volume name, it can be up to 11 characters and can include spaces. You cannot use tabs or any of the following characters:*
>
> *?/ \ | . , ; : + =
> [ ] ( ) & ^ < > "*

- To format a 360K disk in a 1.2M drive, use the /F:360 switch. For example, type **format a: /f:360** and press ⏎Enter.

- To format a 720K disk in a 1.44M drive, use the /F:720 switch. For example, type **format b: /f:720** and press ⏎Enter.

CHANGING TO A DIRECTORY

Hard disks and CDs usually have several divisions, called directories, each of which contains a group of related files. You may need to change to a directory to view a list of files in that directory or to run an application. To change directories, perform the following steps:

1 Change to the drive that contains the directory, as explained earlier.

2 Type **cd ***dirname* (where *dirname* is the name of the directory you want to change to). For example, to change to the \DOS directory, type **cd \dos**.

```
A:\>c:

C:\>cd \dos

C:\DOS>cd \

C:\>
```

Changes to the root directory ⟶ (points to `C:\>cd \dos`)

Changes to the DOS directory ⟵ (points to `C:\DOS>cd \`)

3 Press [⏎Enter].

4 To change back to the root directory, type **cd ** and press [⏎Enter].

Directories can contain subdirectories (subdivisions of the directory). Let's say you want to work with the files in a subdirectory named C:\DATA\BOOKS. You can change to the subdirectory in either of two ways. The first way is to enter two CD commands:

1 Type **cd \data** and press [⏎Enter] to change to C:\DATA. (The backslash tells DOS to start at the root directory.)

2 Type **cd books** and press [⏎Enter] to change to C:\DATA\BOOKS. (Note that you omit the backslash here, because you don't want to start back at the root directory.)

The other way to change to a subdirectory is to use a single CD command followed by a complete list of directories that lead to the subdirectory:

1 Type **cd \data\books**.

2 Press [⏎Enter].

> *Tip: To move up one directory level in a tree, type cd .. and press [⏎Enter].*

CHAPTER 6

DISPLAYING A LIST OF FILES

Once you have changed to the drive and directory that contains the files you want to work with, you can view a list of the files on that drive and directory by doing this:

- Type **dir** and press ⏎Enter. A file list appears. If the list scrolls by too quickly to read, try one of the following options to slow down the list or display more file names at one time.

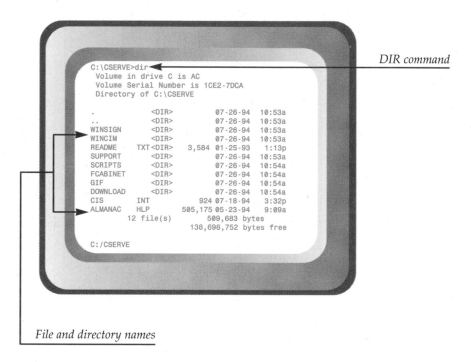

DIR command

File and directory names

- Type **dir /w** and press ⏎Enter. The /W (wide) switch tells DOS to display only the names of the files and to display the file names in several columns across the screen.

- Type **dir /p** and press ⏎Enter. (The /P stands for "page"—a screenful.)

With DIR /P, DOS displays one screenful of file names.

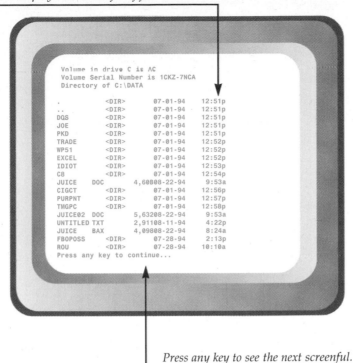

```
Volume in drive C is AC
Volume Serial Number is 1CKZ-7NCA
Directory of C:\DATA

.            <DIR>      07-01-94   12:51p
..           <DIR>      07-01-94   12:51p
DQS          <DIR>      07-01-94   12:51p
JOE          <DIR>      07-01-94   12:51p
PKD          <DIR>      07-01-94   12:51p
TRADE        <DIR>      07-01-94   12:52p
WP51         <DIR>      07-01-94   12:52p
EXCEL        <DIR>      07-01-94   12:52p
IDIOT        <DIR>      07-01-94   12:53p
C8           <DIR>      07-01-94   12:54p
JUICE    DOC       4,608 08-22-94    9:53a
CIGCT        <DIR>      07-01-94   12:56p
PURPNT       <DIR>      07-01-94   12:57p
TMGPC        <DIR>      07-01-94   12:58p
JUICE02  DOC       5,632 08-22-94    9:53a
UNTITLED TXT       2,911 08-11-94    4:22p
JUICE    BAX       4,098 08-22-94    8:24a
FBOPOSS      <DIR>      07-28-94    2:13p
ROU          <DIR>      07-28-94   10:10a
Press any key to continue...
```

Press any key to see the next screenful.

- Type **dir /a:d** and press <u>↵Enter</u>. (The /A:D stands for attribute:directories.) DOS displays the names of the subdirectories in the current directory. No file names appear.

You may not want to view all the files in a directory. You may, for example, want to view only those files that have the .EXE extension or the .COM extension. To view a group of files, you can use *wild-card characters*.

A wild-card character is any character that takes the place of another character or a group of characters. In DOS, you can use two wild-characters: a question mark (?) and an asterisk (*). The question mark stands in for any single character. The asterisk stands in for any group of characters. Here are some ways you can use wild-card entries with the DIR command:

- Type **dir *.com** and press <u>↵Enter</u> to view a list of all files with the .COM file name extension (for example, HELP.COM, EDIT.COM, and TREE.COM).

- Type **dir ???.*** and press <u>↵Enter</u> to view a list of all files that have a file name of three letters or fewer (for example, EGA.SYS, SYS.COM, and FC.EXE).

- Type **dir s???.*** and press <u>↵Enter</u> to view a list of all files whose file name starts with S and has four letters or fewer (for example, SORT.EXE and SYS.COM).

CHAPTER 6

Entering DOS Commands

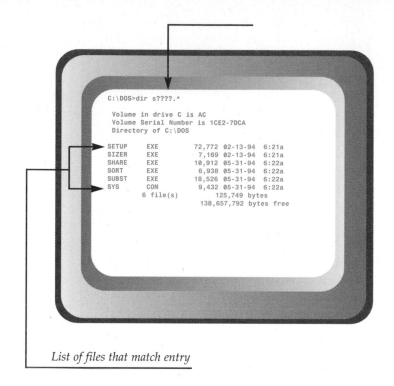

```
C:\DOS>dir s????.*

    Volume in drive C is AC
    Volume Serial Number is 1CE2-7DCA
    Directory of C:\DOS

SETUP    EXE      72,772 02-13-94  6:21a
SIZER    EXE       7,169 02-13-94  6:21a
SHARE    EXE      10,912 05-31-94  6:22a
SORT     EXE       6,938 05-31-94  6:22a
SUBST    EXE      18,526 05-31-94  6:22a
SYS      COM       9,432 05-31-94  6:22a
         6 file(s)        125,749 bytes
                      138,657,792 bytes free
```

List of files that match entry

MAKING A DIRECTORY

If your computer has a hard disk, you should save the files you create in separate directories. However, in order to save a file to a directory, that directory must exist; you must have previously created it. To make a directory, you use the MKDIR or MD (Make Directory) command followed by the name you want to give to the directory:

1 Change to the drive and directory under which you want the new directory to appear. For example, to create a directory called SAMPLE under the DOS directory, type **c:** and press ⏎Enter, and then type **cd \dos** and press ⏎Enter.

2 Type **md** and a space followed by the name you want to give the directory; for example, type **md sample**. Press ⏎Enter. You can now change to the SAMPLE directory as explained earlier.

Deleting a Directory

Having too many directories can be as confusing as having all your files lumped into one. To delete a directory, take the following steps:

1 Change to the drive and directory that is directly above the directory you want to delete. For example, to delete the SAMPLE directory under the DOS directory, type **c:** and press [⏎Enter], and then type **cd \dos** and press [⏎Enter].

2 Type **rd** and a space, followed by the name of the directory you want to delete; for example, type **rd sample**. Press [⏎Enter]. The directory is deleted.

Copying Files

You may want to copy files to share them with a colleague or to create duplicate files for editing. To copy a file, here's what you do:

1 Change to the drive and directory that contains the files you want to copy. For example, if you want to copy files from the C:\DATA\BOOKS directory, change to this directory.

2 Type **copy** *file1.ext* **d:***directory*, where *file1.ext* is the name of the file you want to copy, and *d:\directory* is the drive and directory where you want the file copied. (See the examples listed in the following table.)

3 Press [⏎Enter]. DOS copies the file.

> *Tip: You can't use just any name for a directory. A directory name can consist of up to eight characters with a three character extension (just like a file name). You can use any characters except the following:*
>
> ```
> "   .   /
> \   [   ]
> :   *   <
> >   |   +
> ;   ,   ?
> ```
>
> *And don't use the extension—it will just complicate things later.*

> *Tip: The RD command does not allow you to remove a directory that contains files or subdirectories. To remove the directory, you must first delete all its files and subdirectories. In DOS 6, you can use the DELTREE command to remove a directory and all its files, but this is a very risky operation, because you don't see what you are deleting.*

CHAPTER 6

Command	What it does
copy *.doc a:	Copies all files that have the .DOC extension from the current directory to the disk in drive A.
copy chap09.doc b:	Copies only the file named CHAP09.DOC from the current directory to the disk in drive B.
copy *.doc c:\samples	Copies all files that have the .DOC extension from the current directory to a directory named C:\SAMPLES.
copy *.* c:\samples\books	Copies all files from the current directory to C:\SAMPLES\BOOKS.
copy chap09.* c:\samples	Copies all files named CHAP09 (CHAP09.DOC, CHAP09.BAK, etc.) from the current directory to C:\SAMPLES.

DELETING FILES

If you are sure you no longer need a file, you can delete the file from a disk in order to prevent the disk from getting cluttered. However, before you delete a file, make sure you will no longer need it; you may not be able to get the file back. To delete a single file, perform the following steps:

> *Tip: Before you can copy files to a directory, you must have previously created the directory. If you try to copy a file to a directory that does not exist, DOS displays an error*

1 Change to the drive and directory that contains the file you want to delete.

2 Type **del** *filename.ext*, where *filename.ext* is the name of the file you want to delete.

3 Press `⏎Enter`. DOS deletes the file.

You can delete a group of files by using wild-card characters. For example, to delete all files that have the .BAK extension, you would change to the drive and directory where those files are stored and type **del *.bak**.

RUNNING AN APPLICATION

Although you use DOS to change to a drive and directory, view file names, and perform other disk- and file-management tasks, you usually use DOS to run an application such as a word-processing program. When you run an application, DOS moves to the side and lets the application take over. From that point on, you will see little of DOS.

To run an application from DOS, take the following steps:

1 Change to the drive and directory where the application's files are stored. For example, say you want to run WordPerfect, and the WordPerfect files are in C:\WP60. You would change to the C drive and then type **cd \wp60** and press ⏎Enter.

2 Type the command required to run the application and press ⏎Enter. For example, to run WordPerfect, you would type **wp** and press ⏎Enter. (The documentation that came with the application will tell you what to type. The following table lists commands for popular programs.) The program starts and displays a screen or menu where you can start working.

To run this program	*Type this command and press Enter*
America OnLine	aol
Carmen Sandiego	carmen
dBASE	dbase
Harvard Graphics	hg
Lotus 1-2-3	123
Microsoft Windows	win
Microsoft Word	word
Microsoft Works	works
Paradox	paradox
PC Tools	pcshell OR pctools
PFS: First Choice	first
PFS: First Publisher	fp
PRODIGY	prodigy
Professional Write	pw
Q&A	qa
Quattro Pro	q
Quicken	q
TurboTax	ttax
WordPerfect	wp
WordStar	ws

GETTING HELP FOR DOS COMMANDS

If you have DOS version 5.0 or later (6.0, 6.22), you can get on-screen help for all the available DOS commands. To get help, here's what you do:

> *Tip: DOS Help can teach you how to use the Help feature. Press the F1 key when the list of commands appears. Hold down the Alt key while pressing B to go back to the list of DOS commands.*

1 Type **help** and press Enter. A list of all the DOS commands appears.

2 Press the PgDn key to view the part of the list that's off the screen.

3 Press the Tab key to move from one command to another.

4 Press the Enter key to view information about the selected command. The syntax information screen appears. The syntax screen shows the proper way to type the command.

Select Notes or Examples for more information.

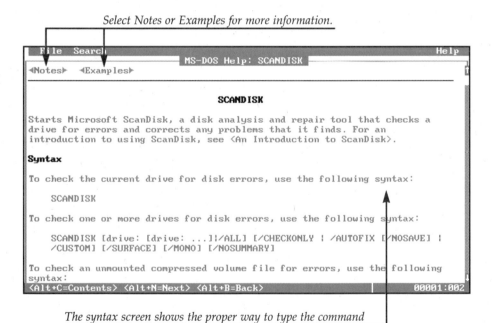

The syntax screen shows the proper way to type the command

5 Press the Tab key to view any syntax information that's not displayed in the window.

6 To view notes about the command, press Enter.

7 To view examples of how to enter the command, press ⏎Enter again. Note that each command has three help screens: syntax, notes, and examples. By pressing ⏎Enter, you move from one screen to the next.

8 To exit the Help system, press Alt+F, then type **X**.

More DOS Commands

The following list provides information about some more advanced DOS commands:

- If you have DOS version 5.0 or later, type **doskey** at the prompt, and press Enter. This makes it easier to edit commands. You can use the F3 key to recall a previous command, F7 to list previous commands, and the arrow keys to insert a command on the command line.

- Use the DISKCOPY command to create duplicate disks. (See Chapter 9.)

- Use MEM to check the amount of memory (RAM) installed on your system.

- If you have DOS 6.0 or later, type **msd** and press ⏎Enter to view information about your system.

Enter MSD at the DOS prompt to view information about your computer.

File Utilities Help			
Computer...	Gateway/Phoenix 486DX	Disk Drives...	A: C: E:
Memory...	640K, 7168K Ext, 4744K XMS	LPT Ports...	1
Video...	XGA, Paradise Paradise	COM Ports...	2
Network...	No Network	Windows...	3.10 Not Active
OS Version...	MS-DOS Version 6.22	IRQ Status...	
Mouse...	PS/2 Style Mouse 9.01	TSR Programs...	
Other Adapters...	Game Adapter	Device Drivers...	

Press ALT for menu, or press highlighted letter, or F3 to quit MSD.

Press the highlighted letter to view more specific information.

EXERCISE

Work through the following exercises to gain more experience with some harmless DOS commands:

1 Type **date** and press ⏎Enter.

```
C:\>date
Current date is Mon 08-22-1994
Enter new date (mm-dd-yy): 09-18-94
```

2 Type today's date in the displayed format, then press ⏎Enter.

3 Type **time** and press ⏎Enter.

4 Type the current time in the requested format, then press ⏎Enter.

5 Type **ver** and press ⏎Enter. VER stands for VERsion.

```
C:\>ver
```

The DOS version ⟶ `MS-DOS Version 6.22`

```
C:\>
```

6 Type **cls** and press ⏎Enter. CLS stands for CLear Screen.

7 Insert a formatted disk into drive A.

8 Type **a:** and press ⏎Enter.

9 Type **dir** and press ⏎Enter.

10 Type **c:** and press ⏎Enter.

CHAPTER DIGEST

Changing to a Disk Drive

Type the *drive letter*→Type :→Press ⏎Enter

Formatting a Floppy Disk

Insert unformatted disk in drive A→Type **format a:**→Press ⏎Enter
or
Insert unformatted disk in drive B→Type **format b:**→Press ⏎Enter

Changing to a Directory

Type **cd ***dirname*→Press ⏎Enter

Changing to a Subdirectory

Type **cd** *subdirname*→Press ⏎Enter

Viewing a List of Files

Type **dir**→Press ⏎Enter
or
Type **dir /p**→Press ⏎Enter
or
Type **dir /w**→Press ⏎Enter

Getting DOS Help

Type **help**→Press ⏎Enter→Tab to desired command→Press ⏎Enter

Copying File from Disk in Drive A

Change to drive and directory to which you want to copy the file→Type
copy *a:filename.ext*→Press ⏎Enter

Copying File to a Disk in Drive A

Change to the drive and directory that contains the file you want to
copy→Type **copy** *filename.ext a:*→Press ⏎Enter

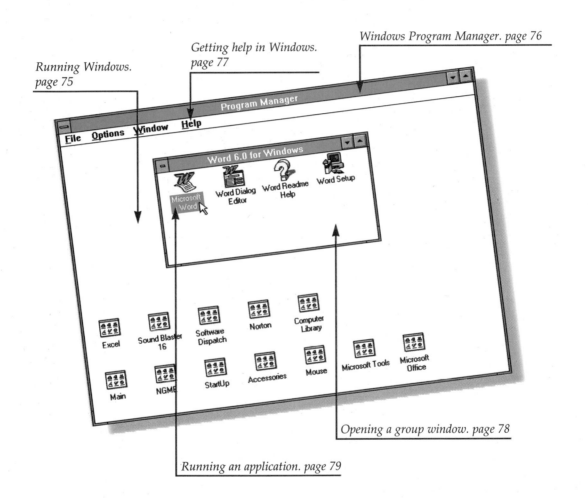

Running Windows.
page 75

Getting help in Windows.
page 77

Windows Program Manager. page 76

Opening a group window. page 78

Running an application. page 79

WORKING WITH MICROSOFT WINDOWS

7

M icrosoft Windows is a *graphical user interface* that runs on top of DOS and is designed to make your computer easier to use. With a graphical user interface, you don't have to type commands; instead, you select icons (small pictures that represent commands), and you choose commands from menus. In this chapter, you'll learn everything you need to know to get started in Windows.

RUNNING MICROSOFT WINDOWS

Before you can take advantage of Windows' ease-of-use, you have to start Windows from the DOS prompt. The following steps show you how to start Microsoft Windows.

1 Change to the drive that contains your Windows files. This is usually drive C.

2 Type **cd\windows** and press Enter.

3 Type **win** and press Enter. The Windows title screen appears for a few moments, then the Program Manager appears.

> *Tip: Graphical user interface is commonly abbreviated GUI and is pronounced "gooey."*

PARTS OF A WINDOWS SCREEN

The first time you start Windows, you'll see the Program Manager, which usually looks like the figure shown here (yours may look a little different). The Windows screen contains several unique elements you won't see in DOS. Here's a brief summary.

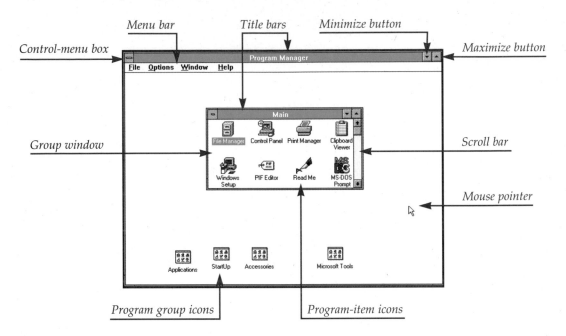

Mouse pointer   Allows you to point to and select items on-screen. Chapter 6 explains basic mouse moves.

Title bar   Shows the name of the window or application.

Group windows   Contain the program-item icons used to run applications (the programs that enable you to perform specific tasks).

Program-item icons   Small pictures that represent applications. To run an application, double-click on its icon with the mouse.

Minimize and Maximize buttons   Alter a window's size. The Minimize button shrinks the window to the size of an icon. The Maximize button expands the window to fill the screen.

Control-menu box   When clicked on, displays a menu that offers size and location controls for the window.

Menu bar   Contains the names of available pull-down menus. To display a menu, click on the menu's name in the bar.

Scroll bar   Allows you to see items that are not shown in the window. If a window contains more items or text than can be shown, a scroll bar appears. Click on an arrow at either end of the bar to view more.

> *Tip: If you skipped ahead and minimized the Program Manager or ran an application, the Program Manager window may have disappeared. To get it back, first press* Ctrl+Esc. *In the little window that appears, use the arrow keys to highlight Program Manager and then press* ↵Enter.

USING SCROLL BARS

If a window cannot display everything it contains, a scroll bar appears along the right side and/or the bottom of the window. You can use the scroll bar to bring the hidden contents into view using the following methods:

Scroll arrow   Scroll arrows appear on both ends of the vertical and horizontal scroll bars. Click once on an arrow to scroll incrementally in the direction of the arrow. Hold down the mouse button to scroll continuously in that direction.

Scroll box   The scroll box is a small box inside the scroll bar. Move the mouse pointer over the scroll box, hold down the mouse button, and drag the box to the area of the window you want to view. For example, to move to the middle of the window's contents, drag the scroll box to the middle of the bar.

Scroll bar   Click once inside the scroll bar, on either side of the scroll box, to move the view one screenful at a time. For example, if you click once below the scroll box, you will see the next windowful of information.

RUNNING THE WINDOWS TUTORIAL

One of the best ways to get a feel for Windows is to run the tutorial that comes with Windows. Here's how you do it:

 Click on Help in the Program Manager menu bar. The Help menu opens. (If the Windows Tutorial option is not there, either the Windows Help files were not installed or you don't have a VGA monitor.)

2 Click on Windows Tutorial. The tutorial starts.

3 Read and follow the on-screen instructions.

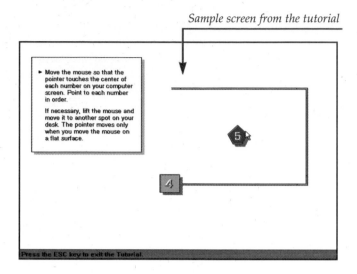

Sample screen from the tutorial

OPENING AND CLOSING GROUP WINDOWS

The Program Manager contains several group windows, each of which contains a set of related program-item icons. To open or close a group window, here's what you do:

- To open a group window, double-click on the group icon.

- To close a group window, double-click on the window's Control-menu box (in the upper left corner of the window).

Double-click on the Control-menu box to close the window.

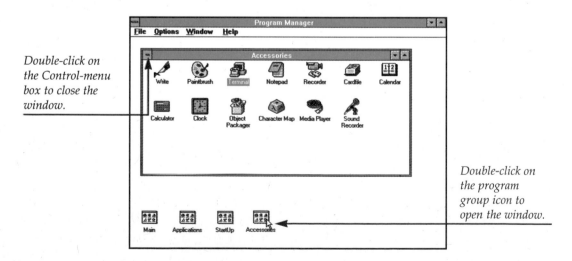

Double-click on the program group icon to open the window.

RUNNING APPLICATIONS

Windows comes with several applications (called accessories) that you can run by selecting their icons. In addition, whenever you install a Windows application, the installation program creates a program-item icon for that application. To run an application that has such an icon, perform the following steps:

1 Open the group window that contains the application's program-item icon.

2 Double-click on the application's program-item icon. Windows runs the application and displays its window.

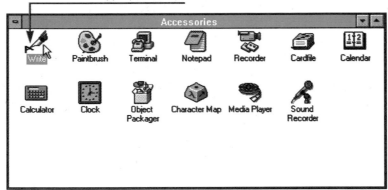

Double-click on a program-item icon to run an application.

If an application has no program-item icon, you can usually run the application by doing the following:

1 Click on File in Program Manager's menu bar.

2 Click on Run. The Run dialog box appears.

3 Type a complete path to the directory in which the application's files are stored, followed by the name of the file that executes the application.

4 Press *↵Enter* or click ___OK___ .

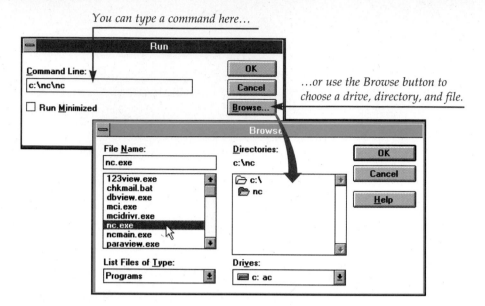

You can type a command here...

...or use the Browse button to choose a drive, directory, and file.

SWITCHING TO AN APPLICATION

With Windows, you can run two or more applications at the same time and switch from one application to another. You can switch to a different application in any of the following four ways:

- If part of the application's window is visible, click on any exposed part. The selected window moves to the front.

- Press (Ctrl)+(Esc), then double-click on the desired application in the Task List.

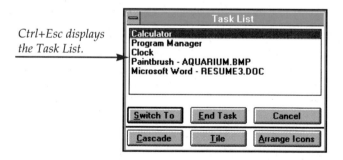

Ctrl+Esc displays the Task List.

- Click on the Control-menu box in the upper left corner of any application window, select Switch To, then double-click on the desired application.

- Hold down the (Alt) key and press the (Tab ⇄) key one or more times until the name of the desired application appears. When it does, release the Alt key.

MOVING AND SIZING WINDOWS

If you have more than one window open, you may want to arrange the windows so you can see them at the same time. You can then quickly switch to a window by clicking anywhere inside it. To move a window, perform the following steps:

1 Position the mouse pointer anywhere inside the title bar of the window you want to move.

2 Hold down the mouse button and drag the window where you want it. An outline of the window appears, showing its new location.

3 Release the mouse button.

To change a window's size, here's what you do:

1 Move the mouse pointer over one of the window's borders. Point to a side border to change only the width, the bottom border to change the height, or a corner to change both height and width. The mouse pointer turns into a double-headed arrow.

2 Hold down the mouse button and drag the window border to its new dimensions. An outline shows the new dimensions.

3 Release the mouse button.

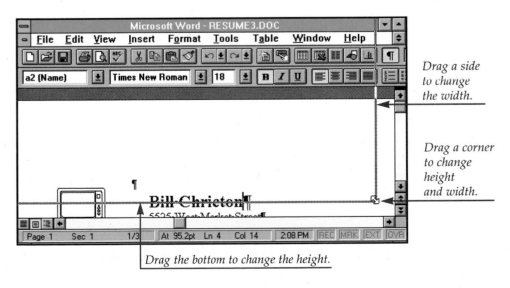

Drag a side to change the width.

Drag a corner to change height and width.

Drag the bottom to change the height.

Windows offers some faster ways to change the size of windows. In the upper right corner of any window, you will see two of the following three buttons:

Maximize   To expand a window so it takes up the full screen, click on the maximize button. The button is then replaced with the restore button.

Restore   To restore a window to its original size, click on the restore button. This button is then replaced by the maximize button.

Minimize   To shrink a window to icon size, click on the minimize button. You can then restore the icon to a window by double-clicking on the icon.

SELECTING COMMANDS FROM PULL-DOWN MENUS

Unlike DOS, which requires you to type commands, Windows allows you to select commands from pull-down menus. To select a command, you click on the menu's name to pull it down from the menu bar, then you click on the command you want to enter. Windows automatically executes some commands when you select them. However, for some commands, there's more to it. What happens next varies depending on the appearance of each command:

- **Dimmed commands** are not accessible. For example, if you try to select the Copy command but have nothing selected, the Copy command appears dim.

- **Command followed by an arrow** opens a submenu that contains additional commands.

- **Command followed by an ellipsis (...)** opens a dialog box that requests additional information.

- **Command preceded by a check mark** is an option that you can turn on or off. The check mark indicates that the option is on. Selecting the option removes the check mark and turns it off.

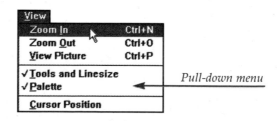

RESPONDING TO DIALOG BOXES

If you select a command followed by an ellipsis (...), a dialog box appears, requesting additional information. Each dialog box contains one or more of the following elements:

Tip: Notice that some commands are followed by a keyboard shortcut. For example, the Print command may be followed by Ctrl+P. *You can use these keyboard shortcuts to bypass the menus. Simply hold down the first key while pressing the second key. In this example, hold down the* Ctrl *key and press* P.

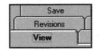

Tabs enable you to flip through the "pages" of options. Click on a tab to view a set of related options.

List boxes provide available choices. To select an item in the list, click on the item.

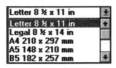

Drop-down lists are similar to list boxes, but only one item in the list is shown. To see the rest of the items, click on the down arrow to the right of the list box.

Text boxes enable you to type an entry. To activate a text box, click inside it. To edit text that's already in the box, use the arrow keys to move the insertion point, use the Del or Backspace keys to delete existing characters, then type your correction.

Check boxes enable you to select one or more items in a group of options. For example, if you are styling text, you can select Bold and Italic to have the text appear in both bold and italic type. To select an item, click on it.

Option buttons are like check boxes, but you can select only one option button in a group. Clicking on one button deselects any option that is already selected.

Spin boxes usually contain a numerical entry with up and down arrow buttons on the right. You can type an entry or click on the arrow buttons to change the value.

Command buttons finalize the entries, settings, or changes you have made in the dialog box. Most dialog boxes have three command buttons—one to give your final okay, one to cancel your selections, and one to get help.

MANAGING DISKS, DIRECTORIES, AND FILES WITH FILE MANAGER

In Chapter 5, you learned how to use DOS to format disks, make directories, and copy files. You can use the Windows File Manager to do all this and more. Here's what you do to run the File Manager:

1 Click on the ⊞ [Main] icon.

2 Double-click on the [File Manager] icon. The File Manager appears.

3 Use the icons and menus as shown to change drives and directories.

Click on a disk drive to activate it. Double-click on a drive letter to open a window for that drive.

Click on a directory to change to it; double-click on a folder to display subdirectories; double-click again to hide subdirectories.

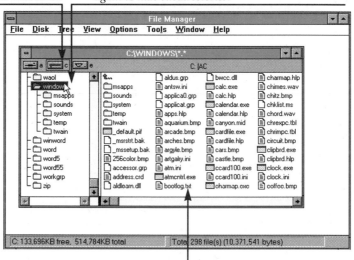

To select a file, click on it.

Here's a quick rundown of common things you can do using File Manager and general instructions on how to do them:

- **Format a disk.** Insert a blank disk in the floppy drive you want to use. Open the Disk menu and select Format Disk. From the Disk In drop-down list, click on the letter of the drive that contains the blank disk. From the Capacity drop-down list, click on the capacity of the disk. Click [OK].

- **Make a directory.** Click on the directory under which you want the new directory or click on the drive letter at the top of the directory tree. Pull down the File menu and select Create Directory. Type the name of the new directory in the dialog box. Click `OK` or press `⏎Enter`.

- **Select files.** Click on a single file to select it. To select two or more non-neighboring files, hold down the `Ctrl` key and click on each file. To select neighboring files, hold down the `⇧Shift` key and click on the first and last files in the group.

- **Copy files.** Select the files you want to copy. Move the mouse pointer over one of the selected files. Hold down the `Ctrl` key and the left mouse button, then drag the mouse pointer over the drive or directory icon to which you want the files copied.

- **Delete files.** Select the files you want to delete. Pull down the File menu and select Delete. Click `OK`, then click on Yes.

- **Move files.** Select the files you want to move. Move the mouse pointer over one of the selected files. Hold down the left mouse button and the Shift key, then drag the pointer over the drive or directory icon to which you want to move the files.

EXITING WINDOWS

When you are done with Windows, you can exit by performing the following steps.

> *Tip: A quick way to exit Windows is to press* `Alt`+`F4` *and press* `⏎Enter`. *You can also exit by double-clicking on the Control-menu box in the upper left corner of the Program Manager window.*

1 Use the File Exit command to exit any applications you have running.

2 Display the Program Manager window as explained earlier.

3 Open the File menu and select Exit Windows. The Exit Windows dialog box appears, asking for your confirmation.

4 Click `OK`. If you have any DOS applications running, or if you have work that you haven't saved, Windows displays a warning message.

5 Follow the on-screen instructions to exit Windows.

MORE WINDOWS TRICKS

So far, you learned the basics for moving around in Microsoft Windows. The following list contains some more advanced tips:

- To bypass the Microsoft Windows advertising screen when you start Windows, type **win :** and press ⏎Enter.

- To create icons for your DOS applications, open the Main group window and double-click on the Windows Setup icon. Open the Options menu and select Setup Applications.

- To have an application start automatically when you start Windows, drag its program-item icon into the StartUp program group.

EXERCISE

If this is your first encounter with Microsoft Windows, perform the following exercise to practice the basics:

1 Start Microsoft Windows.

2 Double-click on the Accessories group icon.

3 Double-click on the Paintbrush icon.

4 Click on the minimize button in the upper right corner of the Paintbrush window.

5 Double-click on the Notepad icon in the Accessories group window.

6 Press Ctrl+Esc.

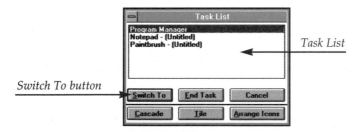

7 Double-click on Paintbrush in the Task List.

8 Drag the Paintbrush window's title bar to move the window.

9 Drag the lower right corner of the Paintbrush window to change its size.

CHAPTER DIGEST

Running Windows

Type c:→Press ⏎Enter→Type cd \→Press ⏎Enter→Type win→Press ⏎Enter

Running the Windows Tutorial

Press Alt+H→Press W

Opening Group Windows

Double-click on the program group icon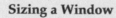

Running Applications with Icons

Double-click on an application's program-item icon

Running Applications Without Icons

Press Alt+F→Press R→Type the command to run the application→Press ⏎Enter

Switching to a Running Application

Press Ctrl+Esc→Press ↓ to get to the desired application→Press ⏎Enter

Sizing a Window

Drag a corner.

Moving a Window

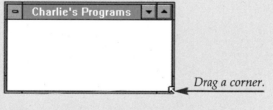

Drag the title bar.

Exiting Microsoft Windows

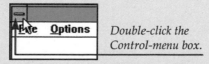

Double-click the Control-menu box.

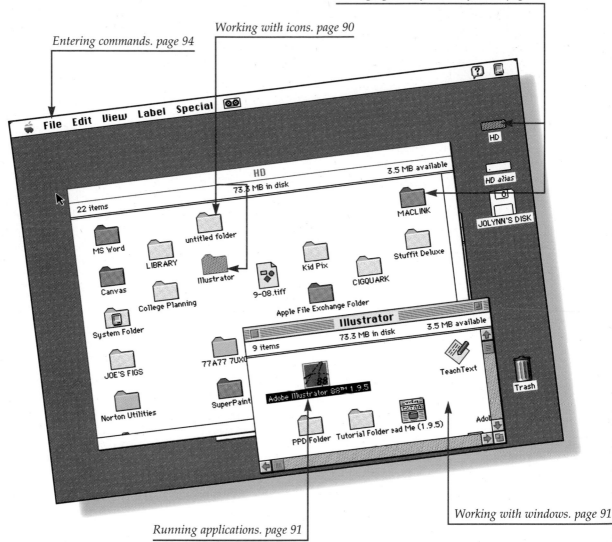

Managing disks, files, and folders. page 96

Working with icons. page 90

Entering commands. page 94

File Edit View Label Special

HD

73.3 MB in disk   3.5 MB available

22 items

MS Word

LIBRARY

untitled folder

MACLINK

Kid Pix

Stuffit Deluxe

Canvas

College Planning

Illustrator

9-08.tiff

CIGQUARK

System Folder

Apple File Exchange Folder

JOE'S FIGS

77A77 7UXO

Norton Utilities

SuperPaint

HD

HD alias

JOLYNN'S DISK

Trash

Illustrator

73.3 MB in disk   3.5 MB available

9 items

TeachText

Adobe Illustrator 88™ 1.9.5

PPD Folder   Tutorial Folder   ead Me (1.9.5)

Adob

Working with windows. page 91

Running applications. page 91

USING A MACINTOSH COMPUTER

Macintosh computers (Macs for short) are known for their simplicity. Instead of typing commands at a prompt, you select commands from menus or click on pictures (called icons) that represent various objects. Folders look like folders, documents look like sheets of paper, and disks look like disks. When you want to delete a file, you don't type a DELETE command (as you would on an IBM PC); instead, you drag the file icon over a Trash icon on-screen.

Although the Mac is easy to use, you do need to know some basics. In this chapter, you will learn the least you need to know to get around on a Mac.

UNDERSTANDING THE MACINTOSH DESKTOP

When you start up a Macintosh (see Chapter 3), the Macintosh Desktop (also called the Finder) appears. Why is it called a "desktop?" Because it is designed to work like a real-life desktop—you can open one or more files on the desktop and even overlap files, creating a stack. The desktop also contains a set of tools, including a calculator and a notepad, that you might find on a real desktop.

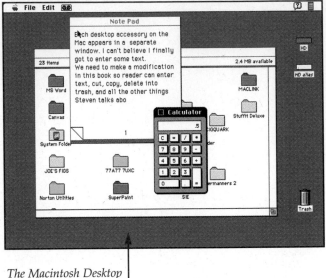

The Macintosh Desktop

WORKING WITH ICONS

Icons are small on-screen pictures that represent real objects. The icon's appearance varies depending on what it represents. Here are the types of icons you will encounter:

 Disk icons represent the disks that are currently in the Mac. Think of each disk as a filing cabinet: it can store applications or documents. To see what's on a disk, double-click on the disk's icon.

 Application icons represent the applications you can run. These are the applications you can use to write letters, draw pictures, and perform other real work. If you double-click on an application icon, the Mac runs the application.

 Folder icons represent collections of documents, applications, or other folders. Folders are used just as they would be used in a fil-ing cabinet— to create logical groups of documents and applica-tions. By double-clicking on a folder icon, you can see what is inside the folder.

Document icons represent memos, letters, pictures, and any other work you create using an application. If you double-click on a document icon, the Mac runs the application that was used to create the document and opens the document in that application.

 The **Trash icon** represents the trash can. If you no longer need a file, you can drag the file's icon to the Trash icon to delete the file. By double-clicking on the Trash icon, you can see what you have thrown in the trash, and you can then remove things from the trash.

To select an icon, click on it. The selected icon appears highlighted. To run an application, open a document, see what's in a folder, or open a window, double-click on the icon.

RUNNING A MACINTOSH APPLICATION

Once you know how to double-click on an icon, running an application is child's play. Here's how to do it:

1 Double-click on the disk icon for the disk that contains the application you want to run.

2 If the application's icon is in a folder, double-click on the folder to display the application's icon.

3 Double-click on the application icon. A window opens, allowing you to start using the application.

WORKING WITH WINDOWS

Whenever you double-click on an icon, a window opens. If you double-click on a disk icon, the window shows what is on the disk. If you double-click on an application icon, the window lets you start using the application. However, no matter what a window displays inside, its border (or frame) contains the following parts that let you control the window:

- **Title bar** at the top of the window displays the name of the disk, file, folder, or application that is currently using the window.

- **Close box** in the upper left corner of the window shrinks the window down to an icon and puts the icon back where it was on the Desktop. You can reopen the window by double-clicking on the icon.

- **Zoom box** in the upper right corner enlarges the window to full-screen size or takes a full screen and shrinks it to the previous size, which was set using the size box.

- **Scroll bars** allow you to view additional information that does not fit in the window. (If the window shows the entire contents, scroll bars will not appear.) To bring additional items into view, click on one of the arrows or drag the scroll box in the direction you want to view. You can scroll continuously by moving the mouse pointer over an arrow and holding down the mouse button.

- **Size box** in the lower right corner of the window lets you adjust the size of the window. To resize a window, simply drag the size box.

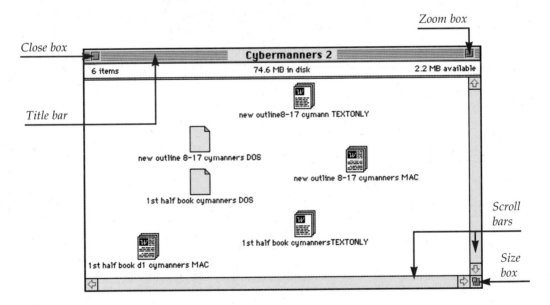

As you open more and more windows, the Desktop can become cluttered, and you may end up losing a window at the bottom. You may need to move some windows to get to the one you want. To move a window, perform the following steps:

1 Move the mouse pointer anywhere inside the title bar of the window you want to move.

2 Hold down the mouse button and move the mouse to drag the window to the desired location.

3 Release the mouse button.

Tip: Every window you open consumes some of your computer's memory. This may slow down some operations and make others impossible to perform. Try to keep the number of windows down to a minimum (four or five at most).

You can switch to a specific window on the Desktop by performing one of the following steps:

- If any portion of the window you want to switch to is visible, click anywhere inside the desired window.

- If no portion of the desired window is visible, find the original icon you clicked on to open the window, and click on it again.

- Click on the application menu icon in the upper right corner of the screen, then drag over the application you want to use.

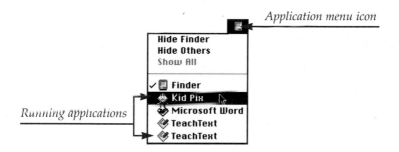

Application menu icon

Running applications

When organizing the Desktop to your liking, you may find you want to resize some of the windows. Here's what you do:

Tip: An easy way to organize your desktop is to make all the windows you are using very small. Use the Zoom box to enlarge only the window in which you are currently working.

1 Move the mouse pointer inside the size box for the window you want to resize.

2 Hold down the mouse button and drag the size box up and to the left to shrink the window, or down and to the right to expand it.

3 Release the mouse button.

ENTERING COMMANDS

When you start a Mac or any Mac application, a pull-down menu bar appears at the top of the screen or window. This bar contains the names of the menus you can open, and each menu contains a set of related commands.

Click on the menu name.

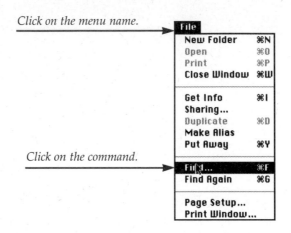

Click on the command.

Tip: *Notice the apple on the left end of the menu bar. If you point to the Apple and hold down the mouse button, the Apple menu opens. This menu lists the desk accessories that are installed on the Mac, including the Calculator, Notepad, and Alarm Clock.*

SELECTING A COMMAND FROM A PULL-DOWN MENU

Selecting a command from one of the pull-down menus is a two-step process: you *pull down* the menu, then you *drag* the pointer over the desired command and release the mouse button. Before you select a command, however, you should know about a few special cases you might encounter.

- **Dimmed commands** are unavailable. If you open the File menu when there is no file on-screen, the Print command will be dimmed (because you can't print what is not displayed).

- **A command followed by dots (...)** calls up a dialog box that requests additional information. The next section explains how to respond to dialog boxes.

- **A command followed by an arrow** displays a submenu that offers additional choices.

- **Check marked commands** allow you to turn an option on or off. A check mark indicates that the option is on; you can turn it off by selecting it again.

PART 2

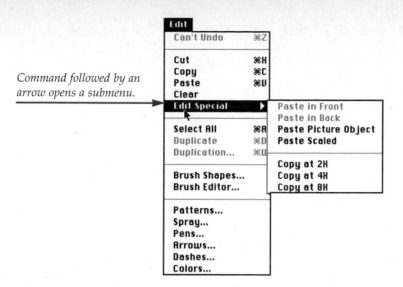

Command followed by an arrow opens a submenu.

Edit

Can't Undo	⌘Z
Cut	⌘H
Copy	⌘C
Paste	⌘U
Clear	
Edit Special ▶	
Select All	⌘A
Duplicate	⌘D
Duplication...	⌘U
Brush Shapes...	
Brush Editor...	
Patterns...	
Spray...	
Pens...	
Arrows...	
Dashes...	
Colors...	

Submenu:
- Paste in Front
- Paste in Back
- **Paste Picture Object**
- **Paste Scaled**
- Copy at 2H
- Copy at 4H
- Copy at 8H

RESPONDING TO DIALOG BOXES

If you select a command that is followed by a series of dots (an *ellipsis*), a dialog box appears, prompting you to enter additional information. Each dialog box contains one or more of the following elements:

- **List boxes** provide available choices. To select an item in the list, click on the item.

- **Pop-up menus** are similar to list boxes, but only one item in the list is shown. To select a different item or option, move the mouse pointer over the displayed item, hold down the mouse button, and drag the highlight over the desired item.

- **Text fields** allow you to type an entry. To change the displayed entry, move the mouse pointer inside the text box. The pointer changes to an I-beam. Position the I-beam where you want to move the insertion point (the vertical line or cursor) and click the mouse button. Use the Del or Backspace keys to delete existing characters, then type your correction.

- **Check boxes** enable you to select one or more items in a group of options. For example, if you are styling text, you can select Bold and Italic to have the text appear in both bold and italic type. To select an item, click on it. To turn off a selected item, click on it again.

> *Tip: Notice that some commands are followed by a keyboard shortcut. For example, the Print command may be followed by ⌘-P. You can use these keyboard shortcuts to bypass the menus. Simply hold down the first key and press the second key. In this example, hold down the ⌘ key and press P.*

CHAPTER 8

- **Radio buttons** are like check boxes, but you can select only one radio button in a group. Clicking on one button deselects any option that is already selected.

- **Command buttons** finalize any entries or choices you have made in the dialog box. Most dialog boxes have at least three command buttons—one to give your final OK, one to Cancel your selections, and one to get Help.

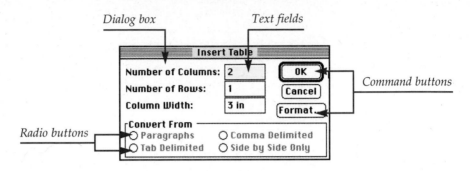

Dialog box   *Text fields*   *Command buttons*   *Radio buttons*

PREPARING A FLOPPY DISK TO STORE FILES

Before you can store files on a floppy disk, you must *initialize* the disk. (If you are familiar with IBM PCs, initializing is the same as formatting.) The initialization process divides the disk into storage areas and maps the storage areas so the Mac can find the data. Here's how you initialize a disk:

1 Insert a blank disk into the floppy disk drive. A dialog box appears, asking if you want to initialize the disk. If you insert a 1.4M disk, the dialog box gives you two options: Initialize and Eject. If you insert a 400K or 800K disk, the dialog box gives three options: One-Sided, Two-Sided, and Eject.

The Mac automatically asks if you want to initialize a blank disk.

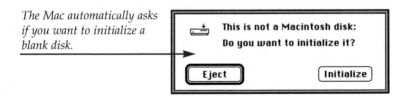

2 Click on Initialize if you inserted a 1.4M disk in the drive. Click on One-Sided if you inserted a 400K disk in the drive. Click on Two-Sided if you inserted an 800K disk in the drive. Click on Eject if you decide to not initialize the disk after all.

A dialog box appears, warning you that initialization will destroy any data on the disk.

> ⚠ **This process will erase all information on this disk.**
>
> [Cancel]   [**Erase**]

3 Click on Erase to start formatting, or click Cancel to quit. If you clicked on the Erase button, a dialog box appears, prompting you to name the disk.

4 Type a name for the disk (up to 28 characters) and press ⏎Enter. (You cannot use the colon (:) as one of the characters in the disk name.) The initialization process starts.

When initialization is complete, an icon for the newly formatted disk appears on-screen. You can now use the disk to store data.

VIEWING THE CONTENTS OF A DISK OR FOLDER

Once you have saved files to a disk (using a Mac application) or installed an application on disk, the disk contains files. To view the names of the files on a disk, first make sure the disk whose contents you want to view is in one of the disk drives, then double-click on the disk's icon. A window opens, showing you what is on the disk.

> *Tip: To eject a floppy disk from the disk drive, press* ⌘–E *or drag the icon for the disk to the Trash icon and release the mouse button.*

Note that the disk may contain applications, document files, and folders (which can contain more applications, document files, and folders).

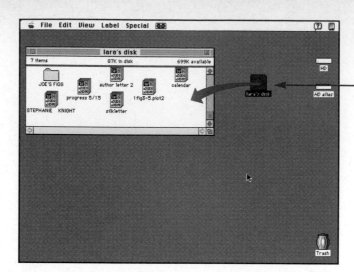

Click on a disk icon to see what's on the disk.

MAKING A FOLDER

Using folders, you can arrange related documents and applications in logical groups, just as you might use folders in a filing cabinet. To create a folder, perform the following steps:

1 Double-click on the disk icon or folder icon for the disk or folder in which you want the new folder created. A window opens for the original disk or folder.

2 Open the File menu, drag the pointer over New Folder, and release the mouse button; or press ⌘–N on the keyboard. A new folder named "Untitled Folder" appears in the window.

The Mac automatically names the folder for you, but you will probably want to change the name of the folder. Here's how you do it:

1 Click on the name of the folder you want to rename. (Don't click on the icon itself; click on the name below the icon.)

2 Type a new name for the folder. The old folder name disappears when you start typing.

3 Press ⏎Enter or click anywhere outside the folder icon. This finalizes the change.

98   Using an Operating System

COPYING AND MOVING FILES

You can copy or move files from one disk or folder to another. Here's what you do:

1 Make sure that some part of the disk or folder icon to which you want the file copied or moved is displayed. (If you are copying or moving to or from a floppy disk, make sure the floppy disk is in the drive.)

2 Double-click on the disk or folder that contains the file you want to copy or move.

3 Move the mouse pointer over the file icon, hold down the mouse button, and drag the icon over the destination disk or folder icon. (The disk or folder icon appears highlighted when you are on target.)

 At the destination, the icon appears highlighted.

4 Release the mouse button.

DELETING AND UNDELETING FILES

On a Mac, deleting a file or folder is as simple as throwing it into the trash... or Trash icon. Here's how you delete a file or folder:

1 Move the mouse pointer over the icon for the folder or file you want to delete.

2 Hold down the mouse button and drag the icon over the Trash icon. The Trash icon appears highlighted.

3 Release the mouse button. The Trash icon appears puffed out at the edges, indicating that it contains files.

> *Tip: To select more than one file, drag the mouse pointer so it draws a selection box around the files. Or, hold down the Shift key while clicking on each file icon. You can drag any file in the group to copy or move all the files to their destination.*

If you accidentally delete one or more files, you can get them back. Double-click on the Trash icon, and then drag the desired file out of the Trash window and into another window or over a disk or folder icon.

MORE THINGS YOU CAN DO WITH A MAC

In this chapter, you learned the basics of working on a Macintosh computer. The following list takes you beyond the basics.

- To learn more about the type of Macintosh computer you have, open the Apple menu and select About This Macintosh.

- The Alarm Clock option on the Apple menu enables you to turn on a clock that beeps you at a specified time.

- To get help on a Macintosh, click on the question mark in the menu bar and then select Show Balloons. Whenever you point to an object on-screen, a description of the object appears.

- To find a misplaced file or folder, open the File menu and select Find.

EXERCISE

If you're sitting in front of your Mac, get some practice by doing the following exercise:

1 Start the Mac.

2 Insert a floppy disk in the drive, and initialize it if necessary.

3 Drag the floppy disk icon over the Trash icon.

4 Open the Apple menu and select Note Pad.

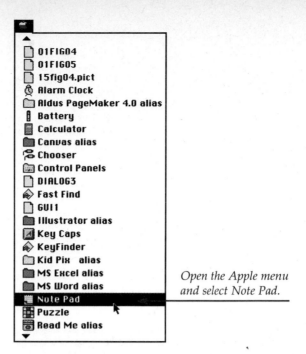

01FIG04
01FIG05
15fig04.pict
Alarm Clock
Aldus PageMaker 4.0 alias
Battery
Calculator
Canvas alias
Chooser
Control Panels
DIALOG3
Fast Find
GUI1
Illustrator alias
Key Caps
KeyFinder
Kid Pix alias
MS Excel alias
MS Word alias
Note Pad
Puzzle
Read Me alias

Open the Apple menu and select Note Pad.

5 Drag the title bar to move the window.

6 Drag the size box to change the window's size.

7 Click on the window's Close button.

8 Open the Special menu and select Shut Down.

CHAPTER DIGEST

Running a Macintosh Application

Double-click on the application's icon.

Initializing a Floppy Disk

Insert blank disk → Click on Initialize, One-Sided, or Two-Sided → Click on Erase → Type disk name → Press ⏎Enter

Copying or Moving a File

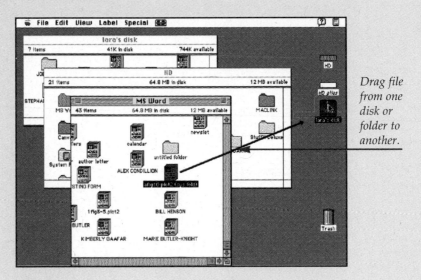

Drag file from one disk or folder to another.

Creating a Folder

Open File menu → Select New Folder → Click on folder name → Type new name → Press ⏎Enter

Deleting a File or Folder

Drag file icon over
Trash icon.

Drag folder icon over
Trash icon.

Undeleting a File

Double-click on Trash icon→Drag file from list over disk or folder icon→Release
mouse button

Ejecting a Disk

Drag disk icon over Trash icon.

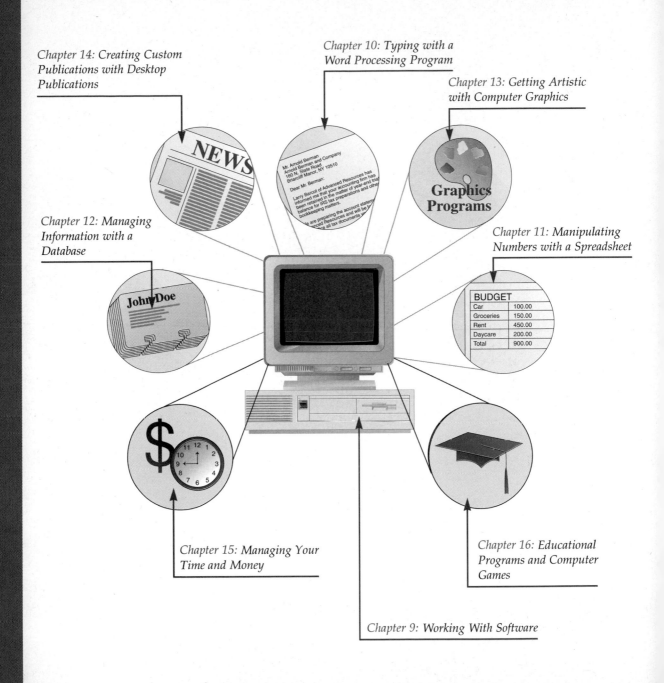

Chapter 14: Creating Custom Publications with Desktop Publications

Chapter 10: Typing with a Word Processing Program

Chapter 13: Getting Artistic with Computer Graphics

Chapter 12: Managing Information with a Database

Chapter 11: Manipulating Numbers with a Spreadsheet

Chapter 15: Managing Your Time and Money

Chapter 16: Educational Programs and Computer Games

Chapter 9: Working With Software

PART 3

APPLICATIONS: DOING SOME REAL WORK

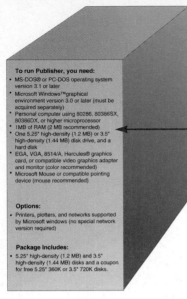

To run Publisher, you need:

* MS-DOS® or PC-DOS operating system version 3.1 or later
* Microsoft Windows™ graphical environment version 3.0 or later (must be acquired separately)
* Personal computer using 80286, 80386SX, 80386DX, or higher microprocessor
* 1MB of RAM (2 MB recommended)
* One 5.25" high-density (1.2 MB) or 3.5" high-density (1.44 MB) disk drive, and a hard disk
* EGA, VGA, 8514/A, Hercules® graphics card, or compatible video graphics adapter and monitor (color recommended)
* Microsoft Mouse or compatible pointing device (mouse recommended)

Options:

* Printers, plotters, and networks supported by Microsoft windows (no special network version required)

Package Includes:

* 5.25" high-density (1.2 MB) and 3.5" high-density (1.44 MB) disks and a coupon for free 5.25" 360K or 3.5" 720K disks.

Buying software. page 107

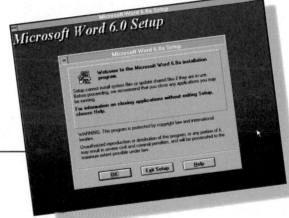

Installing software. page 111

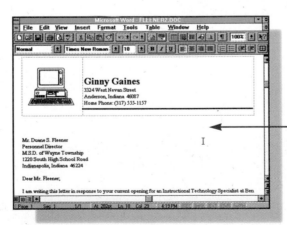

Using software. page 113

BUYING, INSTALLING, AND USING SOFTWARE

T he most important part of a computer is not all the components that make it up, but the *application software* (programs) that you can run on it. Applications enable you to use your computer to do something useful, such as type a letter, calculate your taxes, or create business presentations. In this chapter, you will learn how to select, install, and run most applications, and you'll learn about the general operations you perform in most applications.

SOFTWARE SHOPPING

If you just bought a new computer, chances are it came with some applications that you can use right away. However, you may soon find that those applications do not meet all your needs, and you will be in the market for some new software. As you shop, keep the following questions in mind:

- **What task do you want to perform?** In Chapter 1, you learned about the various types of software and what each type can do. Make sure you get the right software for the right job.

- **Is the application easy to use?** Ask friends and colleagues whether the application you are considering is easy to use. You might also try to find reviews of the application published in computer magazines.

- **Does the application offer all the features you need?** Check the features list (usually printed on the box). Check the features against those offered by comparable software. For example, one spreadsheet application may do three-dimensional graphs, whereas another can handle only two dimensions.

- **Can your computer run the application?** Check the hardware and software requirements printed on the box to make sure you have the equipment you need to run the application. Keep in mind that in most cases you can't run Macintosh software on an IBM computer, and vice versa.

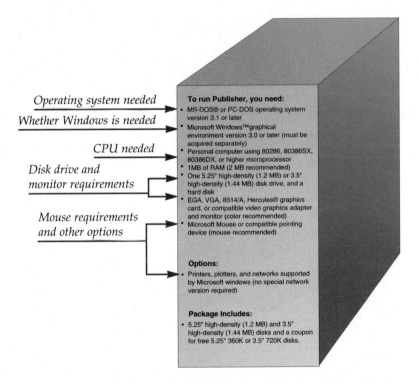

Operating system needed

Whether Windows is needed

CPU needed

Disk drive and monitor requirements

Mouse requirements and other options

To run Publisher, you need:

- MS-DOS® or PC-DOS operating system version 3.1 or later
- Microsoft Windows™ graphical environment version 3.0 or later (must be acquired separately)
- Personal computer using 80286, 80386SX, 80386DX, or higher microprocessor
- 1MB of RAM (2 MB recommended)
- One 5.25" high-density (1.2 MB) or 3.5" high-density (1.44 MB) disk drive, and a hard disk
- EGA, VGA, 8514/A, Hercules® graphics card, or compatible video graphics adapter and monitor (color recommended)
- Microsoft Mouse or compatible pointing device (mouse recommended)

Options:

- Printers, plotters, and networks supported by Microsoft windows (no special network version required)

Package Includes:

- 5.25" high-density (1.2 MB) and 3.5" high-density (1.44 MB) disks and a coupon for free 5.25" 360K or 3.5" 720K disks.

Tip: If you can't find a good price at your local computer store, check computer magazines for the names and phone numbers of mail-order software distributors. These companies usually offer speedy delivery and very reasonable prices.

- **Is the application in your price range?** Cost should be your last consideration. I have bought cheap applications and have been disappointed with them. Find the application that offers all you need, and then shop around for the best deal.

WHAT TO EXPECT FROM A SOFTWARE PACKAGE

When you get your software package home and open the box, it should include these elements (see the next figure): the disks that contain the application files, an instruction manual explaining how to use the application, and a registration card.

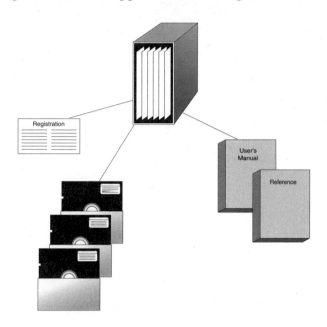

As soon as you open the software package, complete the registration card and mail it back to the manufacturer. This card lets the manufacturer know who owns a legal copy of the application. Software manufacturers offer several perks for returning the card. They may answer your questions over the phone, send free newsletters describing tips for using the application, and offer application upgrades (newer versions of the application) at greatly reduced prices.

PROTECT YOUR INVESTMENT: WRITE-PROTECT THE DISKS

Before you begin using the floppy disks included in the software package, protect the disks from damage by write-protecting them. When a disk is *write-protected*, your computer can read the disk files but cannot make changes to any information on the disk. To write-protect a 5.25-inch disk, cover the write-protect notch with a write-protect sticker. All 3.5-inch disks have a sliding write-protect tab. To write-protect these disks, slide the tab up so that you can see through the window.

Window

Write-protect tab

Write-protect notch | Write-protect sticker

Further Protection: Make Backup Copies

Never use the original program disks to perform your daily tasks. Always make copies of the original disks, and then use the copies to install or use the application. Store the original disks in a safe place, so you'll have them in case the copies get damaged.

To copy disks, first obtain a set of blank disks that are the same *size* and *density* (see Chapter 5) as the program disks you want to copy. You cannot copy low-density disks to high-density disks or 3.5" disks to 5.25" disks, or vice versa.

If you're copying Macintosh disks, initialize the blank disks (see Chapter 8) so they can hold the application files. If you're copying disks using DOS or Windows, formatting is unnecessary, although the operation will be slower with unformatted disks. Once you have the required disks, follow these steps to copy a disk using DOS (Macintosh steps are explained later):

Copying Disks with the DOS DISKCOPY Command

1 Type **diskcopy a: a:** (or **diskcopy b: b:**) and press ⏎Enter.

2 Insert the original program disk into the drive you specified (a: or b:), and close the drive door if it has a door.

3 Press any key on the keyboard. DOS reads the information from the disk and stores it in memory.

4 When DOS prompts you, insert one of the blank disks in the specified drive and press any key. DOS writes the information stored in memory onto the blank disk.

5 Follow the on-screen messages until you have created a copy of each program disk.

> *Tip: Copying disks in Microsoft Windows is easy. Run the File Manager, as explained in Lesson 6. Open the Disk menu and select Copy Disk. Follow the on-screen instructions to complete the operation.*

COPYING DISKS ON A MACINTOSH

1 Insert one of your blank, formatted disks into the floppy drive. An icon for the blank disk appears on-screen.

2 Press ⌘–E to eject the blank disk. The icon for that disk remains on-screen.

3 Insert the original program disk (the one you want to copy) into the floppy drive. An icon for the program disk appears on-screen.

4 Drag the program disk icon onto the blank disk icon and release the mouse button.

5 Follow the on-screen messages until the entire program disk is copied onto the blank disk.

6 Repeat this procedure until you have a copy of each program disk.

INSTALLING AND RUNNING APPLICATIONS

Before you can use an application, you usually have to perform two preliminary steps: *installing* the application (if you have a hard disk) and *running* it.

INSTALLING AN APPLICATION

If you have a hard disk, you must install the application before you can run it from your hard disk. Installation consists of copying the application files from the floppy disks to your hard disk. Although you can install some applications simply by copying the files from floppy disks to the hard disk, you usually have to run an installation program. Here's a quick overview of how to install most applications in DOS, in Windows, and on a Mac:

- **Windows.** Insert the first floppy disk in drive A or B. Open the Program Manager's File menu and select Run. Type **a:** or **b:**, depending on which floppy disk drive you're using. Click on the Browse button, select the Install or Setup file, and click on OK. Click on OK again, then follow the on-screen instructions.

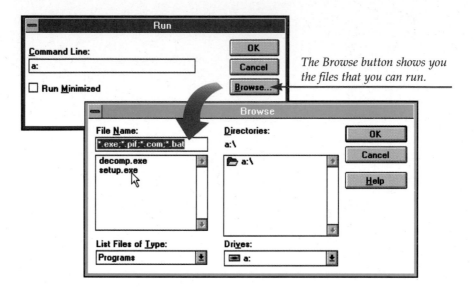

The Browse button shows you the files that you can run.

- **Macintosh.** Insert the first floppy disk into the drive, then double-click on the disk's icon. Double-click on the Install or Setup icon. Follow the on-screen instructions.

- **DOS.** Insert the first floppy disk into drive A or B. Type **a:** or **b:** at the DOS prompt and press Enter. Type **dir /w** and press Enter. Look for a file that starts with something like SETUP or INSTALL and ends with .BAT, .COM, or .EXE. When you find it, type the file's name and press Enter. Follow the on-screen instructions.

RUNNING THE APPLICATION

Running the application means starting it up to display a screen on which you can start working. The process of running an application varies depending on the computer, operating system, and application. For example, to run a DOS application on an IBM PC or compatible computer, you type the application's name (or an abbreviation of it), and press ⏎Enter. To run a Windows or Macintosh application, you double-click on the application's icon with your mouse. For details on running applications, refer to Chapters 6, 7, and 8.

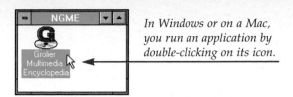

In Windows or on a Mac, you run an application by double-clicking on its icon.

WHAT YOU WILL SEE

When you start an application, it may take a while for the computer to read the program disk and load the application into RAM. How fast the application loads depends on the computer's speed and the application's complexity. When the computer is finished loading the application, you'll see an opening screen that usually contains a *menu bar* or *main menu* listing the commands you may want to use to begin.

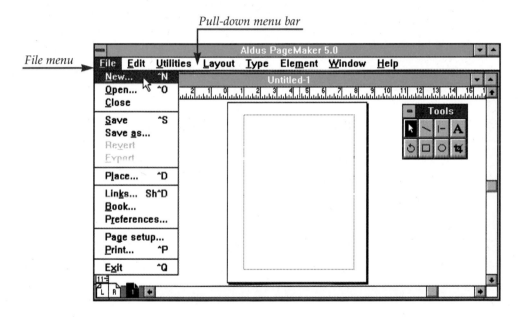

Pull-down menu bar

File menu

APPLICATION BASICS

The computer is a very literal beast: it understands only what you tell it. So you need to know how to talk to your computer—that is, which keys to press or objects to click on. To help you put the commands in some sort of context, the following sections introduce the most basic tasks you perform in any application.

CREATING AND SAVING FILES

Depending on the computer and application you're using, you may have to create a file before you can start working. This file then acts as a receptacle for your work (think of it as an envelope); whenever you save your work, it is saved to this file. In other applications, you can start working before you create a file. When you save your data for the first time (usually by opening the File menu and selecting Save), the application prompts you to name the file.

Type a file name in the text box.

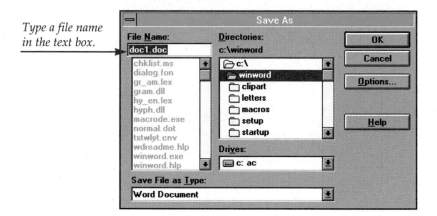

OPENING A FILE

Once you have saved a file on disk, you can open the file at any time to work on it. Opening a file consists of displaying the file's contents on-screen, where you can modify them. In most cases, you have to open the file in the application you used to create it. In some applications, however, you can open files created in other applications.

In most applications, you can call up a file by opening the File menu and selecting Open. A dialog box usually appears, asking you to specify the name and location of the file. After you supply this information and give your OK, the document appears.

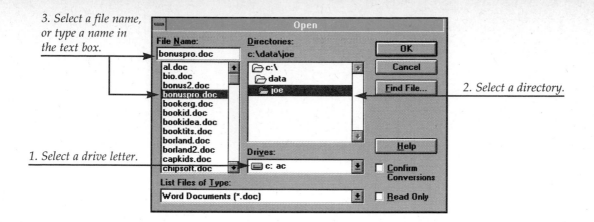

3. Select a file name, or type a name in the text box.

1. Select a drive letter.

2. Select a directory.

EDITING DATA

Once your work is displayed, you can edit it and change it as much as you want. Because your work is stored electronically in RAM, making changes is simple. Adding, deleting, or moving information is nothing more than an electronic version of cut-and-paste. You'll find the editing features to be the biggest timesavers associated with computers—and one of the most fun.

PRINTING DATA

As you edit a document or when you're done perfecting it, you can print the contents of your file on paper. Most applications give you complete control of the printing operation from your keyboard. You simply open the File menu and select Print. In most cases, a dialog box appears, asking you to specify which pages to print and how many copies to produce.

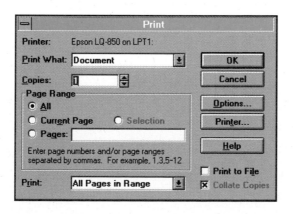

QUITTING AN APPLICATION

There are usually several ways to exit from an application. In Windows and on a Mac, you can exit by pulling down the File menu and selecting Exit or Quit. You can also exit by double-clicking on the box in the upper left corner of the application window. In some applications, you can exit by pressing one of the function keys (F7 in WordPerfect) or by pressing (Esc) (to escape). You can quit any Windows application by pressing (Alt)+(F4).

GETTING HELP

Most applications have a help system that can teach you how to perform tasks and use the various features. You simply open the Help menu and select the desired type of help. If the application you're using does not have a Help menu, try the following:

- **Press the F1 key.** The F1 key is the 911 of the computer industry. Most programs use this key to call up the help system.

- **Press the F3 key.** If you need help with WordPerfect, try pressing the F3 key. WordPerfect likes to buck the system.

- **Look for a Help button.** Some programs display a Help button in a button bar or in dialog boxes (it usually has a question mark on it). Click on the Help button.

MOVING AROUND WITH HYPERTEXT LINKS

No matter how you get into a program's help system, you need some way to get around in it once you're there. Most help systems contain *hypertext links* that enable you to jump from one topic to another. The hypertext link is a highlighted word or phrase that, once selected, displays a definition of or additional information concerning that word or phrase. You usually have to click or double-click on the hypertext link to display the additional information. Or you can tab to the link and press Enter.

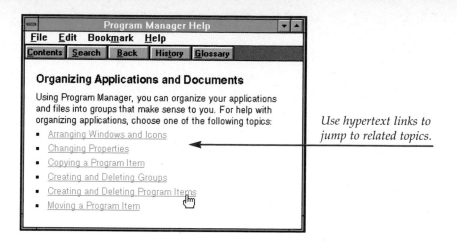

Use hypertext links to jump to related topics.

SEARCHING FOR A TOPIC

Advanced help systems usually provide a way for you to search for a specific topic. Here's what you do:

1 Open the Help menu and select Search, or enter the Search command in the help system.

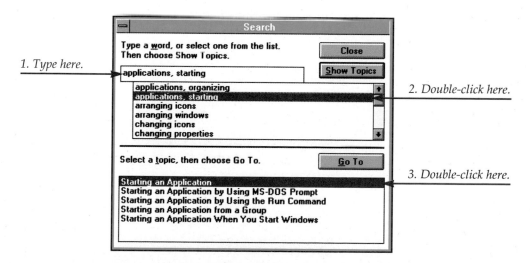

1. Type here.

2. Double-click here.

3. Double-click here.

2 Start typing the name of the term or topic. As you type, a list of available topics that match what you type scrolls into view.

3 When you see the desired topic, double-click on it, or highlight it and press ⏎Enter). A list of subtopics appears.

④ Double-click on the desired subtopic. A Help window appears, showing information that pertains to the selected subtopic.

MORE SOFTWARE TIPS

- If a popular program is being sold at a special price, that can mean two things: a newer version will be out soon (making this version obsolete), or this is the newest version and the manufacturer is offering a special introductory price. Be sure to ask around.

- When shopping, ask if you can try the application before you buy it. Many stores have computers set up and running.

EXERCISES

Before you go shopping for an application, you should know a little about your computer and operating system. The following exercises will lead you through the process.

LEARNING ABOUT YOUR PC-COMPATIBLE

① Type **ver** and press [↵Enter].

② If you have DOS 6.0 or later, type **msd** at the DOS prompt and press [↵Enter].

③ Write down the information. Or, open the File menu, select Print Report, make sure there is an X in each piece of information you want printed, and press [↵Enter].

④ If you have an earlier version of DOS, type **mem** and press [↵Enter]. Then type **chkdsk** and press [↵Enter].

⑤ Write down the amount of memory and free disk space your computer has.

LEARNING ABOUT A MAC

① Open the System menu.

② Select About This Macintosh.

③ Write down the information that's displayed.

CHAPTER DIGEST

Copying Disks with DOS

Insert disk in drive A→Type **diskcopy a: a:**→Press ↵Enter

Copying Disks with Windows

Insert disk in drive A→Double-click on [File Manager]→Open Disk menu→SelectCopy Disk→Select drive A as source and destination→Select OK

Copying Macintosh Disks

Insert a blank disk into the floppy drive→Press ⌘–E to eject the blank disk→Insert original program disk into floppy drive→Drag the program disk icon onto the blank disk icon and release the mouse button

Installing a DOS Application

Insert Disk 1 in drive A→Type **a:**→Press ↵Enter→Type **dir /w**→Press ↵Enter→Type **install** or **setup**→Press ↵Enter

Installing a Windows Application

Insert Disk 1 in drive A→Open File menu→Select Run→Type **a:setup** or **a:install**→Press ↵Enter

Installing a Macintosh Application

Insert Disk 1 in the floppy drive→Double-click on the disk's icon→Double-click on the Install or Setup icon

Running a DOS Application

Change to the drive and directory that contains the application's files→Type command to run application→Press ↵Enter

Running Applications in Windows or on a Macintosh

Double-click on application's icon

Adding graphics. page 132

Formatting text. page 127

BACCHUS CATERING
567 NORTH WINTHROP
CHICAGO, IL 60608

December 12, 1994

Ms. Carrie Klinker
1813 North Gamebridge Lane
Plymouth, Indiana 46785

Dear Ms. Klinker:

I'm sorry that you turned down our bid on your wedding feast. If you rejected our bid because of the price, please consider the fact that imported cognac and canary tongues do not come cheap. Many caterers offfer lower bids and then cut back on the quality of the celebration by using domestic canaries and what amounts to moonshine. Our offerings are premium.

Typing text. page 122

If you have not yet signed a contract with the other caterer, please reconsider our bid, keeping the following special items in mind:

1200 imported canary tongues	$600
50 bottles imported Russian cognac	$1250
300 bottles Classic burgundy	$3000

Checking for typos and spelling errors. page 126

With Bacchus, your wedding feast will be a meal to remember, a festibal, celebration, and carnival all rolled up into one grand party. And even if you can't remember it, free pictures are included in the cost of every party.

So, make the right decision, party with Bacchus.

Sincerely,

Printing a document. page 130

Amy Constantinople

Typing with a Word Processing Program

A word processing application essentially transforms your computer into a fancy typewriter that not only makes typing a lot easier, but can help you compose and perfect your work. It has an endless supply of electronic paper that scrolls past the screen as you type and allows you to cut and paste text on the screen. In addition, most word processing programs offer tools for checking your spelling and grammar and for enhancing your documents with graphics. In this chapter, you learn what you need to know to get started with word processing.

Four Steps to Creating Documents

Although word processing applications vary in complexity and in the number of features they offer, you must perform the same four basic steps when working with any of these applications:

- **Type** You need to type the first draft of your document.

- **Edit** Experiment with the information on-screen until it is just as you want it.

- **Format**   At any time, you can begin working on the appearance of the document. Set margins and line spacing, set tabs, change the way the text is aligned, and change type styles.

- **Print**   You finally get to see the document on paper. You can enter commands to change the type style of the entire document, merge two documents, and insert graphs and tables.

TYPING YOUR DOCUMENT

When you start a word processing application, the application usually displays a blank screen. You have two options. You can start typing to create a new document, or you can open a document you've created and edit it. To create a document, simply type. The cursor (or insertion point) moves from left to right across the screen, leaving characters in its wake.

Information about your document and the location of the insertion point.

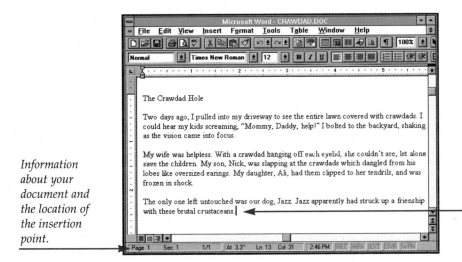

Cursor (or insertion point) shows where the next character you type will appear.

The first time you type in a word-processing application, you may feel a little awkward. To help you get up to speed, keep the following points in mind:

- Press Enter only to end a paragraph. The program automatically *wraps* text from one line to the next as you type.

- You can't move down if there is no text to move down to. Pressing the Enter key will move the insertion point down by creating new paragraphs.

- Text that floats off the top of the screen is NOT gone. Use the Page Up key or the scroll bar to view the text.

- To delete text, use the Del or Backspace key. Del deletes characters to the right; Backspace deletes characters to the left.

- You can usually type in two modes: insert or overtype. Insert mode adds text without deleting existing text. In overtype mode, existing text is replaced with the text you type. You usually change modes by pressing the Ins key.

> *Tip: When an application starts in a certain mode, that mode is referred to as the default mode. Because you have not yet specified a setting, the application defaults to a particular setting, usually the safest or most common setting.*

EDITING YOUR TEXT

The biggest timesaving feature of computers is that you never have to retype. You can edit, cut, and paste the text to perfect your document. The following sections explain the basics of editing in any word processing application.

MOVING AROUND IN A DOCUMENT

Before you can edit text, you need some way to move the cursor to the text you want to edit. The easiest way to move is to use a mouse: move the mouse pointer where you want the insertion point placed, and click. You can also use the following cursor movement keys:

← → ↑ ↓	The arrow keys let you move one line up or down or one character left or right. Ctrl+ → or ← usually moves the cursor one word at a time.
PgDn or PgUp	Use the PgDn key to see the next screenful of text or the PgUp key to see the previous screenful.
Home	The Home key usually moves the insertion point or cursor to the beginning of a line. Many programs use Home in combination with other keys to move to the beginning of a paragraph or the top of the document.

[End] The End key usually moves the insertion point or cursor to the end of a line. Used in combination with other keys, End may move to the end of a paragraph or the beginning of a document.

If you have a long document, you may find it more efficient to use the scroll bars to move from one place to another. You can scroll up or down a page, flip pages, and even jump around inside the document.

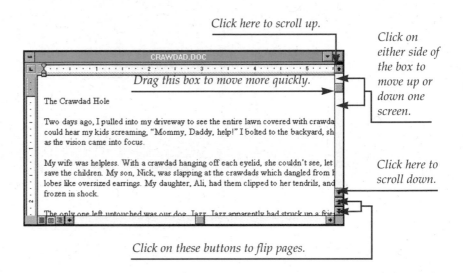

Click here to scroll up.

Click on either side of the box to move up or down one screen.

Drag this box to move more quickly.

Click here to scroll down.

Click on these buttons to flip pages.

COPYING AND MOVING TEXT

Usually, revising a document is not a simple matter of changing a word here or there or correcting typos. You may need to delete an entire sentence or even rearrange the paragraphs. To help with these tasks, most word processing applications have tools for selecting, cutting, copying, and pasting text. Nine times out of ten, here's what you'll do:

Tip: Many word processing applications offer a feature called drag and drop. To drag and drop, you select the text, and then you drag it to where you want it inserted. In most Windows applications, you hold down the [Ctrl] key while dragging to copy the text. To move the text, you drag without pressing Ctrl.

1 Mark or select an area of text (the block) to work with. To mark a block, you usually drag the mouse pointer over the text you want to mark. If you don't have a mouse, try holding down [⇧Shift] and using the arrow keys to stretch the highlight over the text. The block you select appears highlighted.

2 Open the Edit menu and select Cut or Copy. Cut removes the selected text and places it in a temporary storage area in memory. Copy places a duplicate of the selected text in the storage area.

3 To paste the text somewhere else, move the cursor or insertion point to where you want the text inserted.

4 Open the Edit menu and select Paste.

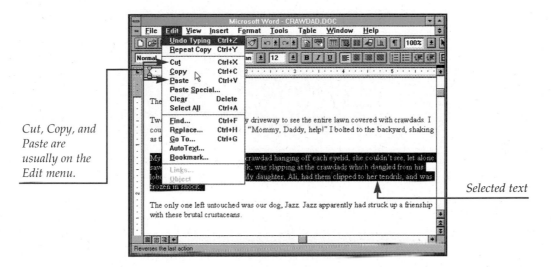

Cut, Copy, and Paste are usually on the Edit menu.

Selected text

UNDOING YOUR CHANGES

For minor editing mistakes, such as accidentally deleting a line or a paragraph, most applications have a safety buffer that lets you undo the most recent change. Many newer applications enable you to undo any of several changes, assuming you know which one to select from the list.

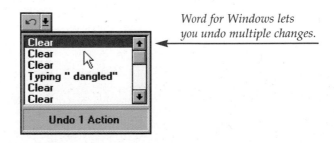

Word for Windows lets you undo multiple changes.

CHAPTER 10

CHECKING FOR TYPOS AND SPELLING ERRORS

Many word processing applications include dictionaries of various sizes that can check your document for spelling errors, typos, repeated words (such as the the), and incorrect capitalization (tHe).

If a spell checking application finds a word that doesn't match one of the words in its dictionary, it stops and waits for you to enter a correction or give your okay. These applications may offer suggestions for correct spellings. If the word is okay, and you don't want the spell checker to stop on the same word again, you can enter the word into the application's dictionary.

A spell checker can help you proofread your work.

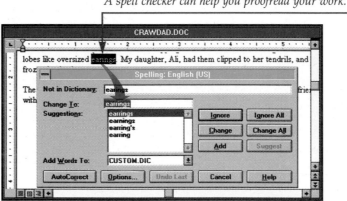

USING AN ONLINE THESAURUS

If you can't think of the right word, simply press a button to open the *thesaurus*. Enter the best word you can come up with, and your word processing application displays a list of synonyms.

Selected word

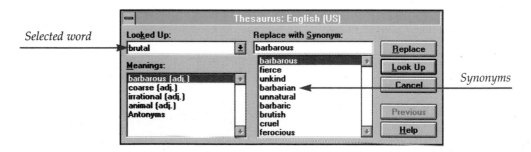

Synonyms

FORMATTING: CHANGING THE LOOK OF YOUR TEXT

Once you have the content of your document under control, and you've fixed all your typos and misspellings, you can start working on the appearance of your document (how you want it to look on paper). For example, you might decide to change the margins, use a different type style, or set the text in columns (as in a newspaper). The following sections explain the various page and text formatting options.

PAGE FORMATTING

Page formatting options control the overall positioning of text on the page. Most word processing applications offer the following page formatting options. (See the application's Help system or documentation for more information.)

- Set left/right margins
- Number pages
- Align the text (left, center, or right)
- Center a word, line, or block of text
- Adjust the line spacing
- Control page length
- Set top/bottom margins
- Create headers and footers
- Create multiple columns

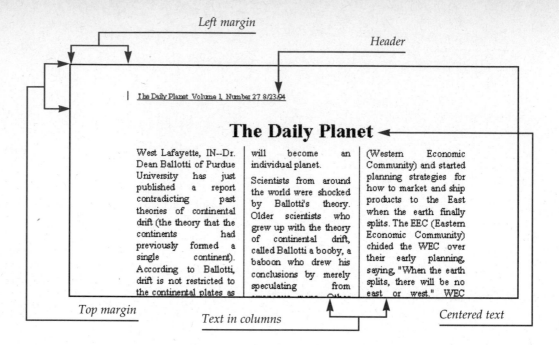

Left margin

Header

The Daily Planet Volume 1, Number 27 8/23/94

The Daily Planet

West Lafayette, IN--Dr. Dean Ballotti of Purdue University has just published a report contradicting past theories of continental drift (the theory that the continents had previously formed a single continent). According to Ballotti, drift is not restricted to the continental plates as

will become an individual planet.

Scientists from around the world were shocked by Ballotti's theory. Older scientists who grew up with the theory of continental drift, called Ballotti a booby, a baboon who drew his conclusions by merely speculating from

(Western Economic Community) and started planning strategies for how to market and ship products to the East when the earth finally splits. The EEC (Eastern Economic Community) chided the WEC over their early planning, saying, "When the earth splits, there will be no east or west." WEC

Top margin

Text in columns

Centered text

Tip: To see the results of your formatting, look for an application that offers WYSIWYG (What-You-See-Is-What-You-Get, pronounced "wizzy-wig"). With WYSIWYG, the application displays your document as it will appear in print.

To emphasize key words and phrases, word processing applications provide various fonts and type styles from which you can choose. A *font* is any set of characters of the same *typeface* (design) and *type size* (measured in points). For example, Helvetica 12-point is a font; Helvetica is the typeface, and 12-point is the size. (Just for reference, there are 72 points in an inch.) A *type style* (or *enhancement*) is any variation that enhances the existing font. For example, boldface, italics, and underlining are all type styles; the character's design and size stay the same, but an aspect of the type is changed.

Cheltenham 12 pt
Dom Casual 12 pt..
Futura 12 pt.
Letter Gothic 12 pt.
MACHINE 12 PT.
Revue 12 pt.
Tekton 12 pt.

ADVANCED FORMATTING TOOLS

In addition to standard page and text formatting options, many applications offer formatting tools that can help ensure consistent formatting and make it easier to apply specific formats. Here are a couple of advanced tools you are likely to encounter:

- **Styles**   To save time formatting, you can save several format settings as a style and apply the style to various blocks of text (usually with a single keystroke). If you change a format setting in a style, that setting is changed for all the text formatted with that style.

- **Format painter**   A format painter allows you to copy the formats of selected text to other text. You select the text whose format you want to copy, click on the format painter button, and then select the text to which you want to apply the formats.

- **Templates**   Templates are preformatted documents for common documents, such as letters, memos, and reports. You select a template and then type the content. The template controls the formatting for you.

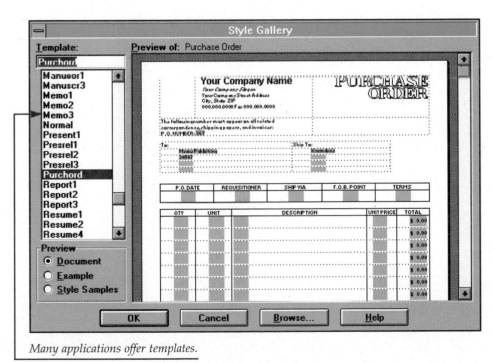

Many applications offer templates.

PRINTING YOUR DOCUMENT

You've done all the hard work—the writing, editing, formatting, and reformatting. All you need to do now is print your final creation to have all those electronic characters transferred to paper.

Before you can print, you usually have to install a *printer driver*, a file that tells the application how to communicate with your specific printer. You usually pick a driver when you install the application. When you are ready to print the document, perform the following steps:

1 Make sure your printer has paper and is turned on, and that its On Line light is lit, not blinking.

2 Open the document you want to print.

3 Open the File menu and select Print. The Print dialog box appears, prompting you to enter instructions.

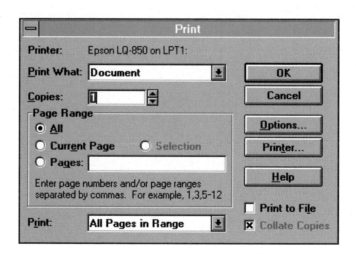

4 In the Print Range section, select one of the following options:

All prints the entire document.

Selection prints only the selected portion of the document, assuming you dragged over some text before selecting the Print command.

Pages prints only the specified pages. If you select this option, type entries in the From and To boxes to specify which pages you want to print.

5 Click on the arrow to the right of the Print Quality option, and select the desired quality. (High prints sharply but slowly; Low prints faintly but fast.)

6 To print more than one copy of the document, type the desired number of copies in the Copies text box.

7 Click OK . The application starts printing the document.

Although printing usually proceeds trouble-free, you may run into some problems. When that happens, check the following:

- **Is the printer turned on, does it have paper, and is the On Line light lit?** A printer won't even go through the motions unless all these conditions are met.

- **Is the printer printing strange symbols?** If so, chances are you picked the wrong printer driver for your printer. The application is sending codes to your printer that your printer does not understand.

- **Is the correct printer port selected?** If you just set up your printer, and it is not working, maybe you selected the wrong printer port. If your printer is on port LPT2, and LPT1 is selected, the printed document will never reach the correct destination.

- **Are you having problems in only one application?** If you can print from other applications, the error is in the printer setup of the problem application.

Special Word Processing Features

Most of the features discussed so far in this chapter are fairly common. There are other features that make your work even easier. You might want to keep the following helpful features in mind when you're out shopping.

- **Automatic backups and autosave** The automatic backup feature creates a backup file whenever you save the file to disk. Autosave saves the file every specified number of minutes; so if you experience a power outage, you lose little of your work.

- **Windows** With a windows feature, you can divide the screen into two or more parts and open a different document in each window. You can then cut and paste text between the two documents.

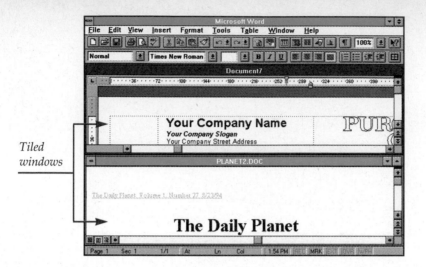

Tiled windows

- **Graphics support**   Graphics support enables you to insert a picture you created in another application or simple graphic elements (lines, shading) into your document. Some word processing applications come with a collection of clip art that you can use to enhance your documents.

- **Indexing**   With an indexing feature, you mark each occurrence of a term you want to index, and the application takes care of the rest, creating a list of indexed words complete with the page numbers on which they appear.

- **Macros**   A *macro* is a record of several commands, assigned to a two-key keystroke or an on-screen button.

- **Basic math**   To add a column of numbers contained in a report, a word processing application may offer mathematical capabilities that can add, subtract, multiply, or divide numbers.

- **Outlining**   With some word processing applications, you can create an outline heading and type a paragraph beneath the heading. When you move the heading within the outline, all text that appears under the heading moves with the heading.

- **Tables**   You can create a table with tabs in any application. But it's even easier when an application offers special formatting elements to keep the entries separate and make table editing more convenient. Some word processing applications combine the table feature with the math feature to provide a basic spreadsheet. In WordPerfect, for example, you can use the table to add a column of numbers.

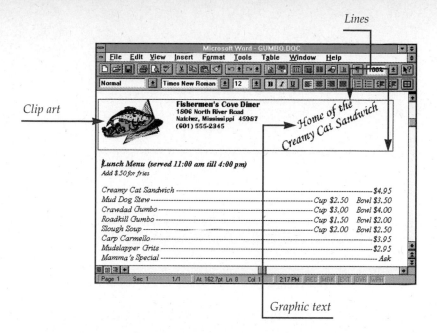

Lines

Clip art

Graphic text

- **Grammar Checker** Grammar checkers will scan your documents for common grammatical errors, including overuse of the passive voice, subject/verb disagreement, wordy sentences, overly long sentences, incomplete sentences, and more.

Expenses (November)	
Auto Insurance	660
Homeowner's Insurance	356
Groceries	879
Car Repairs	45
Daycare	375
Gradeschool Tuition	250
Entertainment	450
Gas and oil	78
Utilities	250
Total	$3,343.00

MORE YOU CAN DO WITH WORD PROCESSING

Once you master word processing basics, apply your skills to the following projects:

- Use your word processing application to create a résumé. You can quickly customize the résumé for each application to highlight your best qualities for the job.

- Type your phone list and use the sorting feature to alphabetize the list.

- Use the tables feature to catalogue your possessions (for insurance purposes). In the first column, name the item; in the second column, estimate its worth.

```
┌─────────────────────────────────────┐
│ Possessions Log                      │
├─────────────────────────────────────┤
│ Computer              2598           │
│ TV                    450            │
│ Bed                   1400           │
│ Lounge Chair          250            │
│ CD Player             987            │
│ Cds                   2300           │
│ Entertainment System  3200           │
│ Sofa                  1400           │
│ Camcorder             450            │
│ RCA Satellite Dish    2500           │
│ Total                 $15,535.00     │
└─────────────────────────────────────┘
```

EXERCISES

Although each word processing application has its own way of doing things, the following exercises work for most Windows and Macintosh applications.

TYPING TEXT

1 Start your word processing application.

2 Type three lines of text without pressing the Enter key.

3 Use the arrow keys to move up, down, left, and right.

4 Delete a few characters with the Del key.

5 Move the cursor between text and start typing.

COPYING AND PASTING

1 Select some text.

2 Enter the Copy command.

3 Move the cursor or insertion point to where you want the text inserted.

4 Enter the Paste command.

Enhancing Text

1 Select some text.

2 Change the type size.

3 Change the typeface.

4 Add bold and italic.

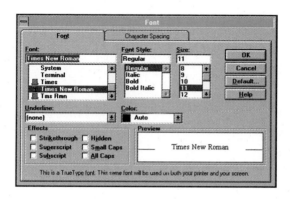

Printing a Document

1 Open the File menu and select Print.

2 Enter your printing instructions.

3 Press Enter.

CHAPTER DIGEST

Moving in a Document

Press ← or → to move one character left or right

Press ↑ or ↓ to move one line up or down

Press `PgDn` or `PgUp` to move one screen up or down

Press `Home` to move to beginning of line

Press `↵Enter` to move to end of line

Selecting Text

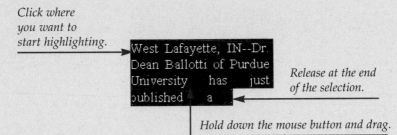

Click where you want to start highlighting.

Release at the end of the selection.

Hold down the mouse button and drag.

Copying or Cutting Text and Pasting Text

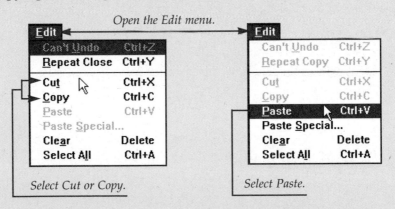

Open the Edit menu.

Select Cut or Copy.

Select Paste.

Undoing Changes

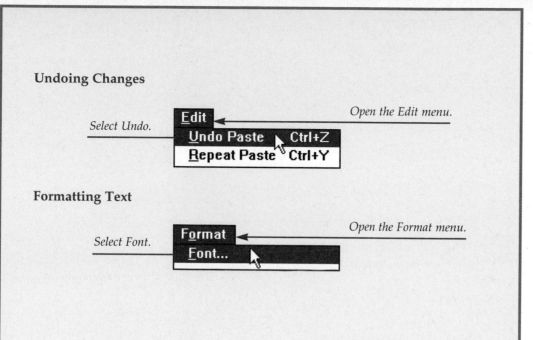

Select Undo.

Open the Edit menu.

Edit	
Undo Paste	Ctrl+Z
Repeat Paste	Ctrl+Y

Formatting Text

Select Font.

Open the Format menu.

Format
Font...

IRTHGO's Retirement Savings Plans

Enhancing a spreadsheet. page 145

Rows, columns, and cells. page 140

Cell addresses. page 140

Entering formulas. page 143

Low-Risk Option				High-Risk Option	
Annual Deposit	$ 1,200.00			**Annual Deposit**	$ 1,200.00
Interest Rate	6%			**Interest Rate**	10%
Year	**Savings**	**Interest**		**Savings**	**Interest**
0	$ -			$ -	
1	$ 1,200.00	$ 72.00		$ 1,200.00	$ 120.00
2	$ 2,472.00	$ 148.32		$ 2,520.00	$ 252.00
3	$ 3,820.32	$ 229.22		$ 3,972.00	$ 397.20
4	$ 5,249.54	$ 314.97		$ 5,569.20	$ 556.92
5	$ 6,764.51	$ 405.87		$ 7,326.12	$ 732.61
6	$ 8,370.38	$ 502.22		$ 9,258.73	$ 925.87
7	$10,072.61	$ 604.36		$ 11,384.61	$ 1,138.46
8	$11,876.96	$ 712.62		$ 13,723.07	$ 1,372.31
9	$13,789.58	$ 827.37		$ 16,295.37	$ 1,629.54
10	$15,816.95	$ 949.02		$ 19,124.91	$ 1,912.49
11	$17,965.97	$1,077.96		$ 22,237.40	$ 2,223.74
12	$20,243.93	$1,214.64		$ 25,661.14	$ 2,566.11
13	$22,658.57	$1,359.51		$ 29,427.25	$ 2,942.73
14	$25,218.08	$1,513.08		$ 33,569.98	$ 3,357.00
15	$27,931.16	$1,675.87		$ 38,126.98	$ 3,812.70
16	$30,807.03	$1,848.42		$ 43,139.68	$ 4,313.97
17	$33,855.46	$2,031.33		$ 48,653.64	$ 4,865.36
18	$37,086.78	$2,225.21		$ 54,719.01	$ 5,471.90
19	$40,511.99	$2,430.72		$ 61,390.91	$ 6,139.09
20	$44,142.71	$2,648.56		$ 68,730.00	$ 6,873.00

Investment Options (20 years)

High-risk option

Low-risk option

Savings axis: $-, $10,000.00, $20,000.00, $30,000.00, $40,000.00, $50,000.00, $60,000.00, $70,000.00

Years axis: 0, 3, 6, 9, 12, 15, 18

Savings / **Years**

If you plan on keeping your money in the program, the high-risk option can provide high returns with compounding interest!

Graphing data. page 146

MANIPULATING NUMBERS WITH A SPREADSHEET

I f you've ever balanced a checkbook, figured averages for students' grades, or kept track of product inventory, you know how time-consuming it is to key in the numbers and perform the required calculations. In this chapter, you'll learn how spreadsheets can help you perform these same tasks more quickly and with fewer errors.

The Parts of a Spreadsheet

The Seven Steps for Making a Spreadsheet

Entering Formulas and Functions

Adding Lines and Shading

Generating Graphs

Sample spreadsheet   *Values*

	A	B	C	D	E	F	G
1			*Hokey Manufacturing*				
2							
3	*Income*	*1st Qtr*	*2nd Qtr*	*3rd Qtr*	*4th Qtr*		
4	*Wholesale*	$55,000.00	$46,000.00	$52,000.00	$90,900.00		
5	*Retail*	$45,700.00	$56,500.00	$42,800.00	$57,900.00		
6	*Special*	$23,000.00	$54,800.00	$67,000.00	$45,800.00		
7	*Total*	$123,700.00	$157,300.00	$161,800.00	$194,600.00		
8							
9	*Expenses*						
10	*Materials*	$19,000.00	$17,500.00	$18,200.00	$20,500.00		
11	*Labor*	$15,000.00	$15,050.00	$15,500.00	$15,400.00		
12	*Rent*	$1,600.00	$1,600.00	$1,600.00	$1,600.00		
13	*Misc.*	$2,500.00	$2,550.00	$3,000.00	$1,500.00		
14	*Total*	$38,100.00	$36,700.00	$38,300.00	$39,000.00		
15						*Total Profit*	
16	*Profit*	$85,600.00	$120,600.00	$123,500.00	$155,600.00	$485,300.00	

PROFIT.XLS

Sheet1 / Sheet2 / Sheet3 / Sheet4 / Sheet5 / Shee

If you change a value, the spreadsheet recalculates the results.

Formulas total the value and determine the averages.

PARTS OF A SPREADSHEET

Look across the top of any computer spreadsheet, and you'll see the alphabet (A, B, C, and so on). Each letter stands at the head of a *column*. Along the left side of the spreadsheet, you'll see numbers representing *rows*. The place where a column and row intersect forms a box, called a *cell*. The cell is the basic unit of any spreadsheet. You will type text, values, and formulas in the cells to make your spreadsheet.

To keep track of cells, the spreadsheet uses *cell addresses*. Each cell has an address made up of its column letter and row number. For example, the cell that's formed by the intersection of column A and row 1 has the address A1.

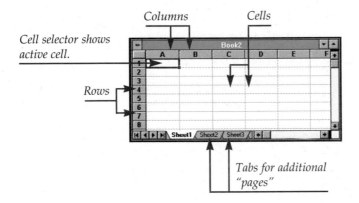

Cell selector shows active cell.

Columns

Cells

Rows

Tabs for additional "pages"

MOVING AROUND IN A SPREADSHEET

When you first start your spreadsheet application, look in the upper left corner of the spreadsheet, and you'll see a cell that has a thick box around it. This thick box is the *cell selector*; it shows you which cell you're on.

To jump from one cell to the next, you can click on the desired cell with the mouse, or you can use the arrow keys or the Tab key (press ⌊Tab⌉ to move to the next cell to the right; press ⌊⇧Shift⌉+⌊Tab⌉ to move left). When the cell selector is on a cell, the contents of that cell are usually displayed in the *input box* at the top of the screen. By modifying the cell's contents in the input box, you can edit the existing entry or type a new entry.

CREATING A SPREADSHEET

Although a spreadsheet can be fairly large and complex, consisting of hundreds of cells and formulas, the process for creating a spreadsheet is fairly simple.

1. Think about how you want the spreadsheet structured.

2. Label the columns and rows.

3. Enter your data: numbers and dates.

4. Enter the formulas and functions that the spreadsheet will use to perform calculations.

5. Perform a test run to make sure the spreadsheet works.

6. Format the cells. For example, you can display values as dollar amounts, shade cells to emphasize their contents, and add lines to help read across a row or down a column.

7. Print the spreadsheet.

STEP 1: DESIGNING YOUR SPREADSHEET

Before you begin, plan the basic structure of your spreadsheet. If you have a form that you want the spreadsheet to look like, lay the form down by your keyboard and use it as a model. For example, if you're going to use the spreadsheet to balance your checkbook, use your most recent bank statement or your checkbook register as a model. If you want to calculate student grades, use your current grade book.

STEP 2: LABELING YOUR COLUMNS AND ROWS

When you have some idea of the basic structure of your spreadsheet, you're ready to enter *labels*. Labels are common-sense names for the columns and rows. To enter a label, move to the cell where you want it to appear, type the label, and press ⏎Enter.

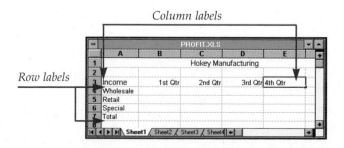

Column labels

Row labels

STEP 3: ENTERING VALUES AND DATES

Once you have labeled your rows and columns, you're ready to enter your raw data: the values and/or dates that make up your spreadsheet. Simply type your entries as you typed your labels, keeping the following in mind:

- **Don't enter dollar signs or percents.** You can have the application add these symbols for you when you format the cells. Type only the number.

- **Type dates in the proper format.** In most applications, you must type the date in the format mm/dd/yy (02/25/94) or dd-mmm-yy (02-FEB-94).

- **Don't worry about long entries.** If a value you type is too wide to fit in a cell, the application may display a series of asterisks instead of the value. Don't worry— your entry is still there. You can click on the cell to see the entry in the input line, and if you widen the column later, the application displays the entire value.

STEP 4: CALCULATING WITH FORMULAS AND FUNCTIONS

Tip: To enter values or labels quickly, many applications let you copy entries into one or more cells or fill selected cells with a series of entries. For example, in Excel, you can type January in one cell, and then select the Fill command to have Excel insert the remaining 11 months in 11 cells to the right.

At this point, you should have rows and columns of values. You need some way to total the values, determine an average, or perform other mathematical operations. That's where formulas and functions come in. They do the calculations for you... once you set them up.

WHAT ARE FORMULAS?

Spreadsheets use *formulas* to perform calculations on the data you enter. With formulas, you can perform addition, subtraction, multiplication, or division using the values contained in various cells.

Formulas generally consist of one or more cell addresses and/or values and a mathematical operator, such as + (addition), – (subtraction), * (multiplication), or / (division). For example, if you wanted to determine the average of the three values contained in cells A1, B1, and C1, you would use the following formula:

(A1+B1+C1)/3

ENTERING FORMULAS IN YOUR SPREADSHEET

To enter a formula, move to the cell in which you want the formula to appear, type the formula, and press ⏎Enter). Most applications require you to start the formula with a mathematical operator, such as an equal sign (=) or plus sign (+).

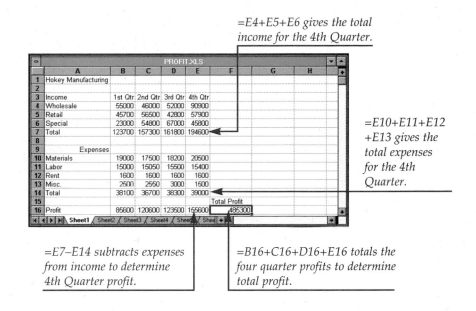

=E4+E5+E6 gives the total income for the 4th Quarter.

=E10+E11+E12 +E13 gives the total expenses for the 4th Quarter.

=E7–E14 subtracts expenses from income to determine 4th Quarter profit.

=B16+C16+D16+E16 totals the four quarter profits to determine total profit.

You can usually enter formulas in either of two ways. You can type the formula directly into the cell in which you want the result inserted, or you can use the mouse to point and click on the cells whose values you want inserted in the formula. You still have to type the mathematical symbols (+ – * and /), but you save time by selecting the cell addresses instead of typing them.

USING READY-MADE FUNCTIONS FOR FANCY CALCULATIONS

Creating simple formulas (such as one for adding a column of numbers) is easy. But creating a formula for the one-period depreciation of an asset using the straight-line method is a chore. To help you in such cases, many applications offer predefined formulas called *functions*.

Functions are complex ready-made formulas that perform a series of operations on a specified *range* of values. For example, to determine the sum of a series of numbers in cells A1 through H1, you can enter the function @SUM(A1..H1), instead of entering +A1+B1+C1+ and so on. Every function consists of three elements:

- The @ or = sign indicates that what follows is a function.

- The *function name* (for example, SUM) indicates the operation to be performed.

- The *argument* (for example A1..H1) gives the cell addresses of the values the function will act on. The argument is often a range of cells, but it can be much more complex.

Some common types of functions are explained in the following table. If you're working with statistical process control, statistical functions are a must. Special accounting applications, such as DacEasy and Peachtree Complete, provide an exhaustive repertoire of financial functions.

Functions	What Kinds of Things They Calculate
Mathematical	Arithmetic calculations, absolute values, logarithms, square roots, and trigonometric equations.
Statistical	Averages, maximum and minimum values, standard deviations, and sample variance.
Financial	Compounding periods, internal rate of return, straight-line depreciation allowance, and number of payment periods in an investment.

STEP 5: PERFORMING A TEST RUN

When your spreadsheet is complete, perform a test run to verify that the spreadsheet works. Most spreadsheets automatically calculate formulas as you enter them, but some spreadsheets require that you enter a Calculate command. After you enter the Calculate command, look for the following problems:

- **Crazy results**   If your formulas or functions produce results that you know can't be correct, make sure you entered the formulas correctly and that the cell addresses refer to the right cells.

- **Narrow columns**   If a column is too narrow, you may end up with a label that is chopped short or a value that appears as a series of asterisks. Change the column width to accommodate the longest label or value.

- **Wrong order of operations**   Make sure each formula performs its calculations in the right order. You can change the order of calculations by using parentheses. For example, if you entered =C3+C4+C5/3 to determine the average of C3+C4+C5, the application will divide the value in C5 by 3 and then add it to C3+C4. The formula =(C3+C4+C5)/3 would give you the correct result.

- **Forward references**   If you use formulas that rely on other formulas for their calculations, make sure that no formula uses the formula in a later cell. In other words, a formula cannot use a value that has not yet been calculated.

- **Circular references**   A circular reference occurs when a formula uses its own results as part of a calculation. The spreadsheet goes around in circles trying to find the answer, but never succeeds.

If something doesn't work, go back and correct it; then perform another test run until the spreadsheet works.

STEP 6: ENHANCING THE SPREADSHEET'S APPEARANCE

Once you have the basic layout of your spreadsheet under control, you can *format* the cells to give the spreadsheet the desired "look."

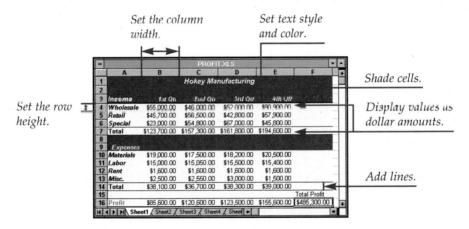

Many newer applications have an autoformat feature that allows you to select the look you want your spreadsheet to have. The application then applies the lines, shading, and fonts to give your spreadsheet a makeover, as shown here.

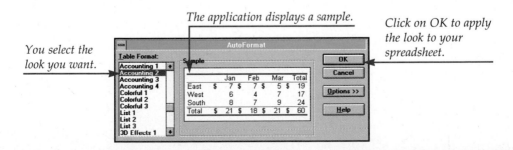

Step 7: Printing Your Spreadsheet

When you finally have all your numbers entered and the spreadsheet has performed the calculations, you may want to print the spreadsheet to send to someone else or to file with your records.

The biggest problem you'll face when printing most spreadsheets is that the spreadsheet is too wide for the paper. If you print a spreadsheet that's too wide, you end up with several pages that you have to tape together. Most spreadsheet applications offer various ways to solve this problem:

- **Automatic font reductions**   You can tell some applications to fit the spreadsheet on the page no matter how small it has to make the type.

- **Landscape printing**   You can print your spreadsheet sideways on a page to fit more columns across the page. However, you must have a printer that can print in landscape mode.

- **Partial printing**   You can select the section of the spreadsheet you want to print and then print only that section.

- **Hiding columns**   You can enter a command to hide some of the columns in the spreadsheet. When you print the spreadsheet, the hidden columns are omitted.

Instant Graphs

People like to look at graphs. They want to see immediately how the numbers stack up. Most spreadsheet applications offer a graphing feature that transforms the values you enter into any type of graph you want: bar, line, pie, area, or high-low (to analyze stock trends). Here are the steps for creating a graph:

1 Drag over the labels and values that you want to include in the graph. (Labels are used for the axes.)

2 Enter the Graph or Chart command. (This command varies from application to application.)

3 Select the type of graph you want to create.

4 Select `OK`. The application transforms your data into a graph and inserts it into the spreadsheet, as shown on the following page.

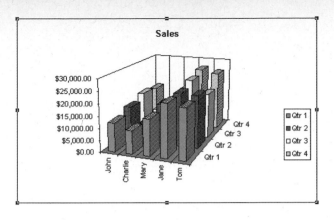

MORE YOU CAN DO WITH SPREADSHEETS

Once you master the spreadsheet basics, try creating spreadsheets that can perform the following tasks:

- **Amortizing loans**   Use functions to determine how much you'll pay on a loan or how much interest you'll pay over the life of the loan. You can play with the percentages and terms to find out which loan is best for you.

- **Setting goals**   To save for your children's education or plan for your own retirement, use the spreadsheet's goal setting feature to see how much money you need to set aside at a given interest level to meet your goals.

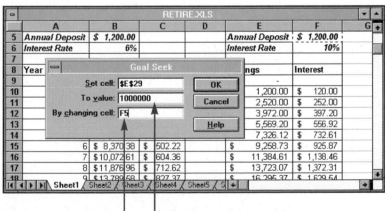

The spreadsheet will determine how much money you must set aside per year to reach your goal.

If you want to retire with a million bucks, set your goal.

- **Creating schedules**   Spreadsheets are not just for number crunching. You can use spreadsheets to plan and schedule your projects.

CHAPTER 11

EXERCISE

The best way to learn how to use spreadsheets is to convert one of your existing paper ledgers into a spreadsheet, as in the following exercise:

1 Open your checkbook's balance book.

2 Start your spreadsheet application.

3 Type the column labels in row 1.

4 In the Balance column in row 2, type the current balance.

5 Starting in row 3, type at least three rows of data from your checkbook, leaving the Balance column blank.

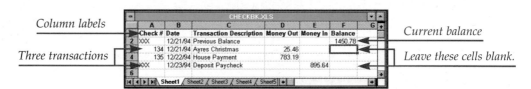

Column labels —
Three transactions —

Current balance —
Leave these cells blank.

6 In the Balance column, type a formula that adds the value from the deposit cell and subtracts the value from the payment cell from the previous balance cell.

	A	B	C	D	E	F
1	Check #	Date	Transaction Description	Money Out	Money In	Balance
2	XXX	12/21/94	Previous Balance			1450.78
3	134	12/21/94	Ayres Christmas	25.46		1425.32
4	135	12/22/94	House Payment	783.19		
5	XXX	12/23/94	Deposit Paycheck		895.64	

CHECKBK.XLS

=F2–D3+E3

7 Copy the formula into the balance cell for all subsequent rows.

When you copy the formula, the spreadsheet automatically changes the formula's addresses.

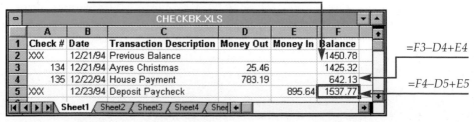

=F3–D4+E4

=F4–D5+E5

CHAPTER DIGEST

Creating a Spreadsheet

Type row and column labels. → ← Enter values and dates.

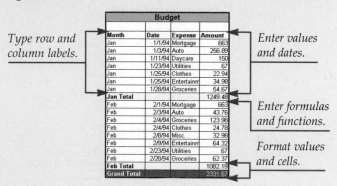

Enter formulas and functions.

Format values and cells.

Graphing Spreadsheet Data

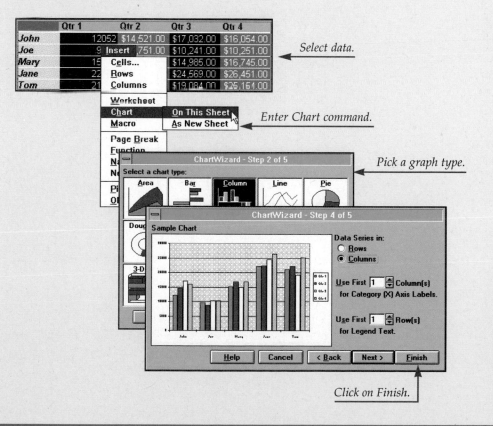

Select data.

Enter Chart command.

Pick a graph type.

Click on Finish.

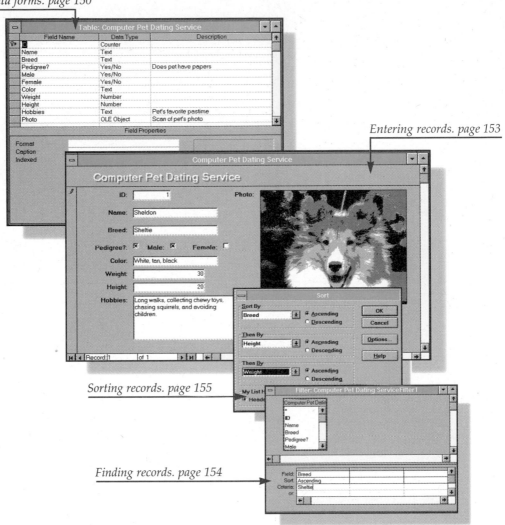

Creating data forms. page 150

Entering records. page 153

Sorting records. page 155

Finding records. page 154

Managing Information with a Database

You probably come in contact with databases every day of your life without ever realizing it. For example, say you want to find all the bookstores in your area. You flip through the phone book to the Bookstore section and scan the list for familiar addresses or locations. When you do this, you are using a database in its most primitive form—a paper database.

If the phone book were on your computer, you could look up the information much more quickly simply by entering a command that tells your computer to look for "Bookstore." You might even narrow the search by specifying a ZIP code, to find only those bookstores in your area. In this chapter, you'll learn how computerized databases work and how you can create a database to manage your own information.

Creating a Database

Although creating a database can be a complicated operation, the process consists of two steps:

1. **Create a fill-in-the-blanks form.** Forms simulate, on the computer screen, the paper forms you fill out with a pen or pencil,

such as an insurance claim, a tax return, or a Rolodex card. To create a form, you must enter *field names* to indicate where each piece of information should be typed. These names are equivalent to what you see on paper forms: Last Name, First Name, MI, SSN, and so on.

2 **Fill in the blanks.** Once you have a form, you can fill in the blanks with information (or put an ad in the paper for a data-entry operator). The blanks in this case are referred to as *fields*. By entering information into the fields, you create a *record*, as shown in this picture. A database file is a collection of records.

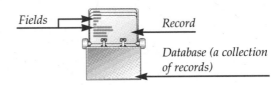

Fields

Record

Database (a collection of records)

MAKING A BLANK FORM

The first step in creating a database is to make a blank form. Refer to the paper system you're currently using—your Rolodex, phone book, calendar, list of employees, accounts receivable, or inventory list. Assign field names for each piece of information you'll need. Weed out any unnecessary information.

When you have a general idea of the form you want to use, run your database application and set up your form. As you create the form, keep a few guidelines in mind:

- **Use bite-size entries.** For example, if you need to record a name, create a separate field for the person's title (Mr./Ms./Mrs.), first name, last name, and middle initial. This will help later when you search for records or extract bits of data.

- **Add form numbers.** If you're using the database to store information such as invoices or purchase orders, include a field that gives each record a unique number. This makes it possible for you to sort and find records easily. In most database applications, you can add a code that automatically numbers the records as you create them.

- **Be logical.** Your form should present information in a natural flow from left to right and top to bottom, in the order that you use it.

- **Use brief field names.** Keep field names just long enough to explain the entry that follows. Long field names take space away from your entries.

- **Set brief but realistic field lengths.** By limiting the size of entries, you can limit the amount of disk space and memory the database consumes. However, don't set a limit that's too small, or you may not be able to type all the characters of an entry.

- **Specify a data type.** When you create a field, you usually must specify a data type, such as text, number, or graphic. This prevents you from entering the wrong type of information in the field.

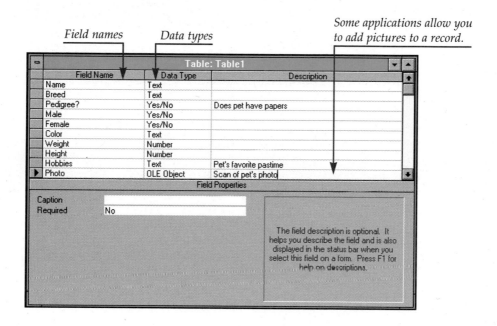

When you're done creating the fields for your form, you usually save the form or choose a command for entering data. In either case, the database application displays the form you created, and the field names appear, showing you the information you must enter.

FILLING IN THE BLANKS

Typing field entries is the least challenging, most time-consuming part of creating a database. Here's where you enter all the information that you want to include in the database—names, addresses, company contacts, part numbers, prices, and other data. You're simply filling out the form. You don't have to enter information into every field; however, if you don't enter information into a field, and you use the database to search for a record according to what's entered in that field, you're out of luck.

To type field entries, move the cursor from field to field and type the required information. To move from one field to the next, you typically press ⌈Tab⁚⌉ or ⌈↵Enter⌉. To move back one field, press ⌈⇧Shift⌉+⌈Tab⁚⌉. If the application offers mouse support, you can move to a field by clicking inside it.

Fill in the blanks.

SAVING EACH RECORD SEPARATELY

Once you've entered all the information you have for a record, save the record. This usually consists of selecting a single command as indicated on your screen. The application saves the information you entered and displays a blank form, ready for you to enter information for the next record. Continue filling out forms until you have entered all your information.

> *Tip: Many database applications save records automatically when you display the next blank form. In these applications, you don't have to worry about saving the file regularly.*

SEARCHING FOR RECORDS

The biggest timesaving feature your database offers is its capability to find records quickly. Most applications give you at least three methods of searching for records:

• **Browsing**   You can flip through the records just as if you were flipping pages in a book.

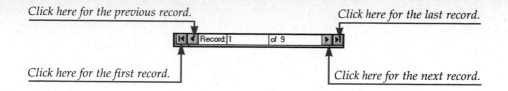

Click here for the previous record.

Click here for the last record.

Click here for the first record.

Click here for the next record.

- **Listing the records** Instead of displaying each record on a single screen, the list option displays the records in a list. You can then scan the list to find the desired record.

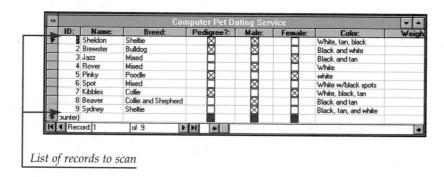

List of records to scan

- **Searching for a specific record** This is the fastest way to find a specific record or group of records. In most databases, you enter a search command, and then enter search instructions specifying the field to search and the entry to find.

Finds all records that have a breed entry of Sheltie

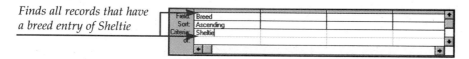

SORTING YOUR RECORDS

To sort a database, first decide which field to sort on. For example, you can sort an address by Name or by City—or by Name within City within State. Each of these sort fields is considered a *key*.

You can usually use up to three keys when sorting your database. The first key in the above example would be Name; City would be the second; State would be the third. You can sort your database in ascending order (1 to 10 or A to Z) or descending order (10 to 1 or Z to A).

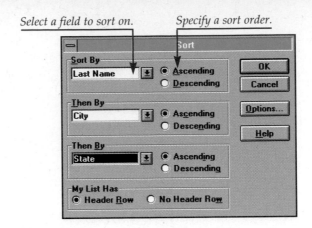

Select a field to sort on.　　Specify a sort order.

GENERATING FORM LETTERS, REPORTS, AND MAILING LABELS

You've seen how much power the field names give you in searching and sorting your records, but that's not the half of it. You can also use the field names to pull information out of your records and consolidate it in a single location:

- **Form letters**   Create a generic letter and type field names surrounded by *delimiters* (such as curly braces {}) where you want to insert information. Then merge your letter with your database. The merge process looks up the field names in your database and inserts them in the form letter, creating a separate letter for each selected record in the database.

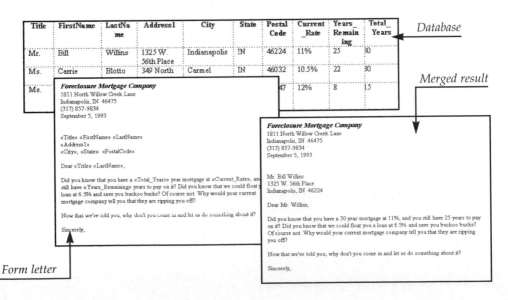

Database

Merged result

Form letter

- **Reports and analyses**   Set up a report that arranges the field names in your database in the order in which you want the information printed. The report inserts information from the database into the specified locations to create a comprehensive report that can often reveal important trends and patterns.

Report arranges data in a meaningful presentation

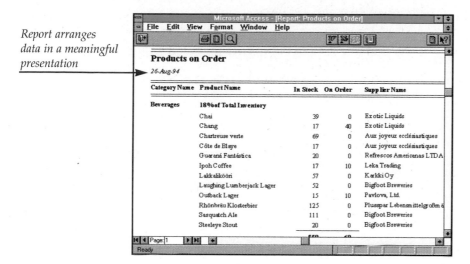

- **Mailing labels**   Create a single mailing label that consists of field names in the place of actual names and addresses. Merge the label with your database to print an entire roll or sheet of mailing labels in a matter of minutes. Some database applications have predefined label templates that are designed for various sizes of mailing labels.

CHOOSING THE RIGHT DATABASE FOR YOU

Database applications vary in how they structure the database and what special features they offer. That's not to say that one is better than the other. You just need to find the one that's right for your needs and budget. You can choose from three types of databases.

A *free-form database* mimics the random pile of notes you might find cluttered on a desk. When you search for data, the application searches the entire database—not just a specified field. Some popular free-form databases include MemoryMate and Info Select.

A *flat-file database* works like a Rolodex. Each record in the file contains the same type of information entered in standard fields, such as names, addresses, and telephone numbers. Some popular flat-file databases include Q&A, FileMaker Pro, PC-File, Reflex, and RapidFile.

A *relational database* is the most powerful type of database because it can use two or more database files and combine them into a new, separate file. For example, you can create one database for inventory and another for invoices. Whenever you create an invoice that charges a customer for an inventory item, the inventory database is updated to show that the item was removed. Popular relational databases include dBASE IV, FoxPro, Oracle, Paradox, Microsoft Access, and 4th Dimension.

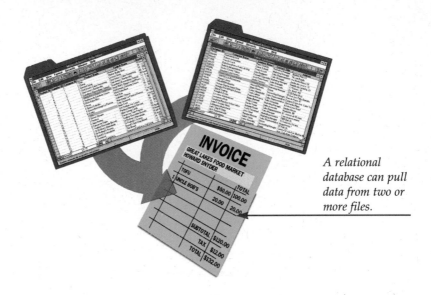

A relational database can pull data from two or more files.

SPECIAL FEATURES

In addition to the different structures of the various databases, some offer many special features that make them easier to use.

- **Automatic Field Length Adjustment**   One of the most difficult parts of setting up a form is guessing how long the longest field entry will be. To help in these cases, some applications offer fields that you can stretch when you need more room. Even though all the information isn't displayed, the field holds all the information you need.

- **English Language Assistance**   Many databases offer a special English language assistant. Instead of typing cryptic commands to the database like "2FIND Name = Smith and Salary > $25,000," you can type the sentence, "Find me all the Smiths who make more than $25,000 a year." Q&A by Symantec Corporation is one of the most popular flat-file databases offering this feature.

MORE YOU CAN DO WITH DATABASES

In addition to helping you organize and retrieve data, databases can help with other practical tasks.

- **Analyzing sales figures**   Sort the records for your sales force to determine who's selling the most goods.

- **Following up on late payments**   Sort invoices by balance, so you can find out who owes you the most money.

- **Saving on postal rates**   Print out form letters grouped by ZIP code to take advantage of bulk rates.

- **Creating rosters**   Print out a list of clients by phone number to create telemarketing lists. Find out which clients haven't placed an order recently to target your calling.

EXERCISE

Microsoft Windows comes with a simple flat-file database that you can use to record names, addresses, and phone numbers. Try the following exercise to create an electronic phone book.

1   In Program Manager, double-click on the ⊞ Accessories icon.

2   Double-click on the 📇 Cardfile icon.

3   Open the Card menu and select Add.

4   Type a person's name, and click **OK**.

5   Type the name, address, phone number, and any other information you want to appear on the card.

```
Bill Crullers
Bill Crullers
1807 North Michigan
Chicago, IL  60601

(312) 474-8797

Birthday: 02/20

Likes doughnuts
```

6 Repeat steps 3 through 5 to create additional cards.

7 Save the file.

8 Click on the arrows to flip through the cards.

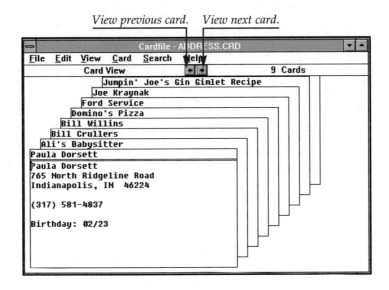

View previous card.   *View next card.*

CHAPTER DIGEST

Creating a Form

Type a field name.   Select a data type.   Type an optional description.

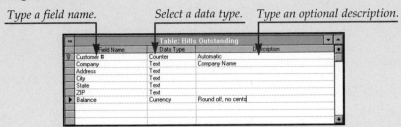

Entering Data

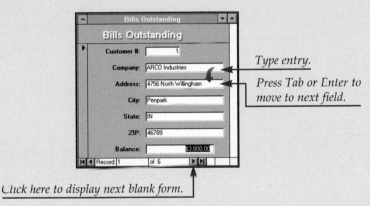

Type entry.

Press Tab or Enter to move to next field.

Click here to display next blank form.

Sorting a Database

Select desired field to use for sort.

Select sort order.

Use additional fields for tie-breakers.

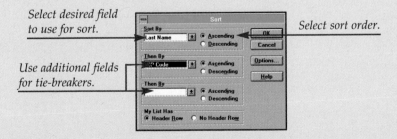

Searching a Database

Select the field to search.

Select the entry to find.

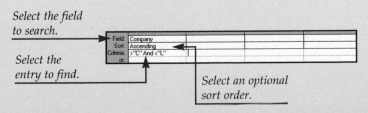

Select an optional sort order.

Creating slide shows. page 164

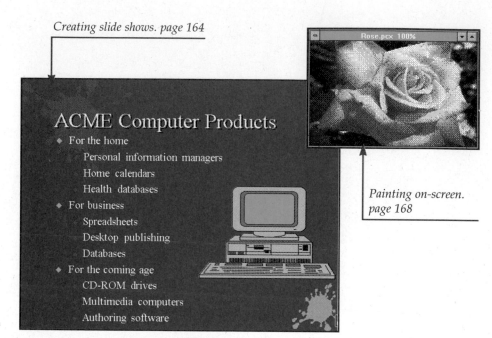

Painting on-screen. page 168

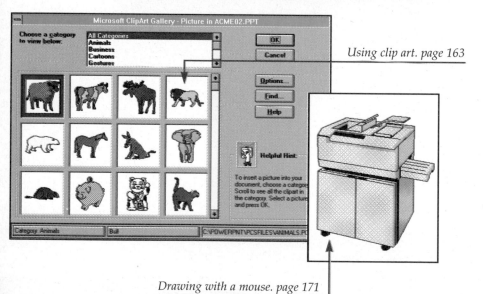

Using clip art. page 163

Drawing with a mouse. page 171

GETTING ARTISTIC WITH COMPUTER GRAPHICS

N o matter how good you are with words, you often need
pictures to illustrate your ideas. For example, graphs can
help you display complicated financial or scientific trends
so your audience can quickly grasp the relationships. In addition,
drawings, illustrations, and predrawn art can help accent and clarify
your presentations and reports. In this chapter, you will learn about
the applications you can use to create illustrations and other graphic
elements.

USING PREDRAWN ART: CLIP ART

Say you're creating a newsletter or brochure, and you want to spruce
it up with some pictures. Although you might be able to draw the
pictures yourself, you can add the art more easily by using *clip art—*
predrawn images that come on disks.

Some applications (including most business presentation graphics,
word processing, and desktop publishing applications) come with a
collection of clip art on-disk. You can also purchase clip art libraries
separately, just as you would purchase an application. These graphic
libraries usually include hundreds or thousands of clip art images
that are broken down into several categories.

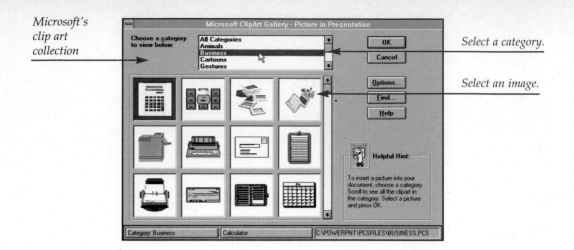

Microsoft's clip art collection

Select a category.

Select an image.

To insert a clip art image into a document, you enter a command telling the application to import or insert an image. You pick the desired piece of clip art and click ▭OK▭ to insert it. The application usually inserts the image in the upper left corner of the screen or at the current cursor position. You can then drag the image where you want it and resize it to fit.

MAKING SLIDE SHOWS, OVERHEAD TRANSPARENCIES, AND HANDOUTS

Tip: Before you buy a clip art library, make sure you have an application that can use the clip art. For example, if you have a word processing application that cannot use .PCX files (art created using an application called PC Paintbrush), do not buy a clip art library that consists of .PCX images.

Even if you are not in sales or marketing, you have probably seen a business presentation sometime in your life—probably on TV or in a movie. A sales or marketing representative stands up in front of the board of directors or some other group and shows a series of slides that pitch a new product or show how profitable the company is. How did that person create this presentation? Probably by using a presentation graphics application. Most presentation graphics applications enable you to create presentations in various forms:

- **On-screen slide shows** You can create a slide show that is displayed on a computer screen. If you have the right equipment, you can project the on screen slide show onto a projector screen or wall.

- **35mm slide shows** You can transform your presentation file into 35mm slides for viewing with a slide projector.

- **Overhead transparencies** Most printers will print your slide show on special transparency sheets instead of paper (or you can send them out to have them done). You can then display them with an overhead projector.

- **Audience handouts** Many business people use presentation graphics applications to create audience handouts, which can be used alone or in conjunction with slide shows.

WHERE DO I START?

Presentation graphics applications are not all alike. With some applications, you first select the type of chart you want to use: pie chart, organizational chart, bar graph, and so on. The chart becomes the central element on the slide. You can then add other elements, such as titles, labels, and pictures.

With other presentation graphics applications, you start with an overall look. For example, you might select the colors and layout you want to use for all the slides in the slide show. You can then add a chart, bulleted list, title, picture, and other elements to each slide you create. The step-by-step approach described in the following sections applies to most presentation graphics applications, and shows you in general how it's done. Depending on the application, the sequence of steps may differ.

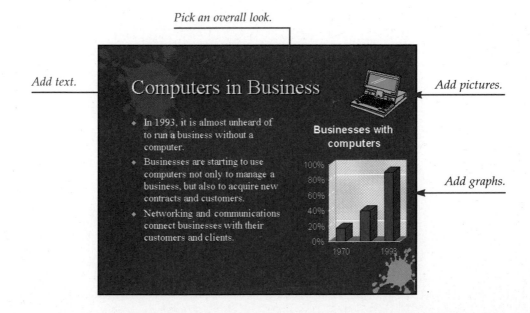

STEP 1: PICKING AN OVERALL LOOK

You usually start a presentation by picking the colors and layout you want to use for all the slides in your presentation. Most applications come with a collection of professionally designed *templates*. By selecting a template, you ensure that all the slides in your presentation will have a consistent look, and that no colors will clash.

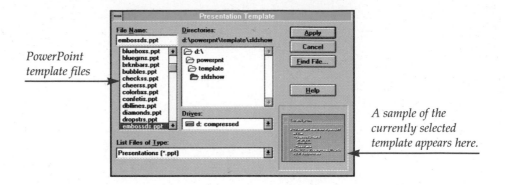

PowerPoint template files

A sample of the currently selected template appears here.

STEP 2: ADDING PICTURES, GRAPHS, AND TEXT

Once you have set the look for your slide show, you can start concentrating on individual slides. In most applications, you can add one or more of the following elements to a slide: graphs, titles, bulleted lists, organizational charts, flow charts, and clip art (or your company logo).

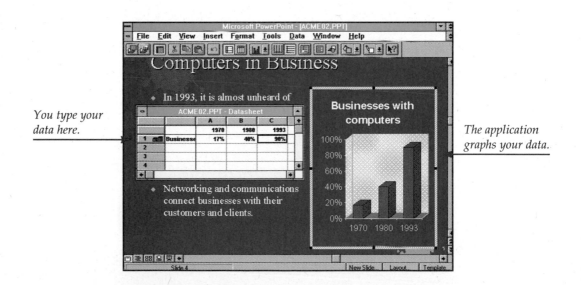

You type your data here.

The application graphs your data.

Step 3: Arranging the Slides

Although you will probably create your slides in sequential order, you may need to rearrange the slides for a more logical flow. Usually, the application can display the slides in miniature view, so you can rearrange them. You just drag the slides around wherever you want them.

Drag the slide where you want it.

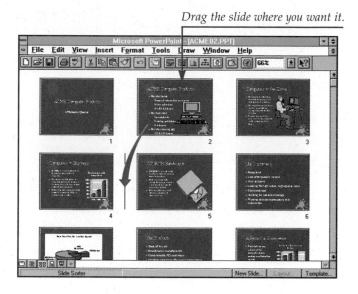

Step 4: Adding Special Effects

If you're creating an on-screen slide show, you may be able to add some special effects, such as sounds and transitions. For example, if your computer has a sound board (such as SoundBlaster), you can plug in a microphone and record your voice, music, or other sounds that will play when you move from one slide to the next. Some applications can create an animated effect, called a *transition*, that controls the movement from one slide to the next. For example, the current slide may open like vertical blinds, revealing the next slide.

Step 5: Outputting Your Slide Show

After you've created your slides, you need to transfer your creation into some usable form. The form you choose depends on the presentation. You may want to include your charts in an annual report, create overheads, or develop a slide show. Because business presentations can take so many forms, business presentation applications offer a number of ways to output the slides:

- **Printer** Output the slides to your printer. Although this seems old fashioned, this is what most businesses do.

- **Plotter** Draw the slide using a special drawing device called a plotter.

- **Film recorder** Print the slides on photographic film to create your own slides.

- **Slide show** Display your slides one by one onscreen, just as if you were using a slide projector. There are special devices that project the on-screen slide show onto a projector screen.

- **Note cards** Print a series of note cards to carry with you to the presentation.

- **Slide show list** Print a list of the slides included in your presentation to help you keep track of them.

Tip: If you're interested in creating slide shows or overhead presentations but you don't have the right equipment, you can usually send the files to an outside vendor to have the work done. Many vendors offer overnight service.

CREATING ORIGINAL ART

Up to this point, you have seen ways of making your presentations and documents graphical without demanding any artistic talent on your part. In the following sections, you'll learn about a couple types of applications that enable you to create original art and require some artistic talent: painting and drawing applications.

USING A PAINTING APPLICATION

Your computer screen is essentially a canvas made up of 150,000 to 700,000 tiny lights called *pixels*. You can use a painting application to turn these pixels on or off or to change their color in order to create an illustration or painting on-screen. When you save your illustration, the application saves a complete map of the pixels, including their status (on or off) and color.

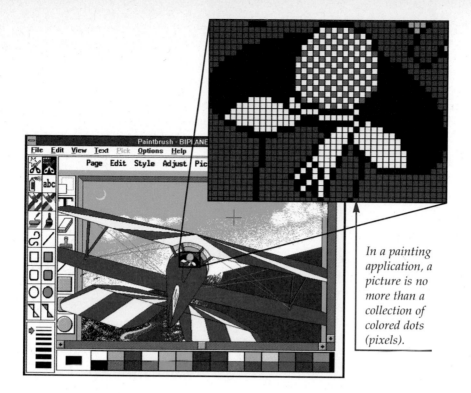

In a painting application, a picture is no more than a collection of colored dots (pixels).

When you start a painting application, the application displays a set of painting tools that give you complete control over the pixels. Most painting applications come with the following tools to help you manipulate the thousands of on-screen pixels:

 Spraypaint tool The spraypaint tool acts like a can of spraypaint. You hold down the mouse button and drag the tool across the screen to create a band of paint. Drag the tool fast, and the paint goes on light. Drag it slowly, and the paint goes on thick.

 Paintbrush tool The paintbrush tool spreads "paint" evenly across the screen. When you drag the tool across the screen, you get a smooth, uniform ribbon of color.

> *Tip: The one essential item that you must purchase for use with painting and drawing applications is a mouse. Although in a few applications you can create simple drawings using the keyboard arrows, doing so is like starting a fire with two sticks of wood.*

Basic shapes All painting applications come with a set of shapes: rectangles, circles, lines, and other tools to draw irregular shapes. With these tools, you can stretch a shape to any size and dimensions you desire. For example, you can create a small circle or a large oval.

Fill tool The fill tool enables you to fill a shape with color. You pick the color and then pour it into the shape. The color fills the shape to its outer boundaries.

Color palette The color palette lets you select the color you want to use for the various tools. For example, if you choose red and then use the spraypaint tool, the paint comes out red.

Thickness palette The thickness palette allows you to select the width of the line created by the selected tool. For example, you can choose to use a wide paintbrush or a narrow one.

Eraser The eraser works like a chalkboard eraser. You drag it across the screen to remove any unwanted dots. You can zoom in on a portion of your drawing to erase individual dots. (This takes some patience.)

Although the procedure for using the tools may vary from application to application, you can use the following steps in most applications:

1 Select the tool you want to use 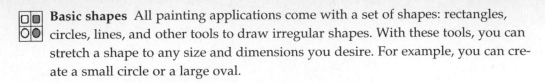.

2 Select a color from the color palette .

3 Select a line thickness from the thickness palette 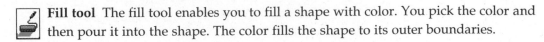.

4 Using the mouse (or some other drawing device) position the mouse pointer where you want the shape or line to begin, and press the mouse button. (This beginning point is called the *anchor point*.)

5 Hold down the mouse button and drag the mouse away from the anchor point. As you drag the mouse pointer away from the anchor point, the object is stretched out between the anchor point and the mouse pointer.

6 Release the mouse button.

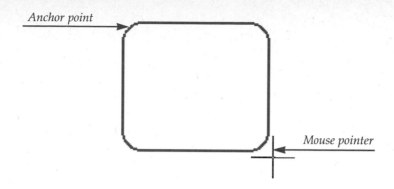

Anchor point

Mouse pointer

USING A DRAWING APPLICATION

With a drawing application, you can create drawings by putting together a bunch of shapes. For example, you might draw a cityscape by putting together several rectangles of various sizes and dimensions.

Completed monitor

Shapes, shades, and lines comprising the monitor

Like a painting application, a drawing application displays a blank screen and a set of shapes and line-drawing tools you can use to start drawing. You place a shape on the screen the same way you would in a painting application:

1 Select the desired shape and line thickness.

2 Using the mouse (or other drawing device) position the mouse pointer where you want the shape or line to begin.

3 Press and hold down the mouse button. (This beginning point is called the *anchor point*.)

4 Drag the mouse pointer in the direction in which you want to stretch the line or shape. As you drag the mouse pointer away from the anchor point, the object is stretched out between the anchor point and the mouse pointer.

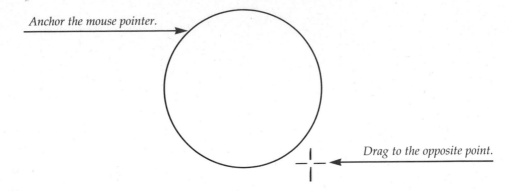

Anchor the mouse pointer.

Drag to the opposite point.

Once you've drawn an object, handles appear around it. You can then drag the object anywhere on-screen or change its shape, size, or orientation without affecting surrounding objects. If you don't see handles around the object, click on it to display the handles.

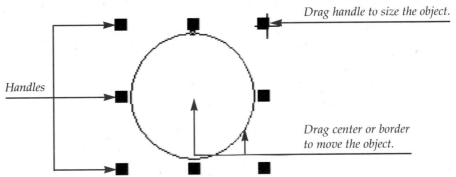

Drag handle to size the object.

Handles

Drag center or border to move the object.

Unlike shapes in a painting application, drawn objects retain their own identities. If you lay a circle on top of a square, you can later pull the circle off the square just as if you had drawn it on a separate piece of paper. However, you can treat several objects as a group in a drawing application. You can then move, copy, or delete the group of objects as if they were a single object.

WHICH IS BETTER: PAINTING OR DRAWING?

Because painting applications give you control over individual pixels, they are especially useful for drawing irregular lines and for using fine grades of shading. This makes painting applications useful for creating freehand sketches and realistic-looking images. Popular IBM painting applications include PC Paintbrush and Publisher's Paintbrush.

Drawing applications are useful for creating simple or complex drawings consisting of basic geometric shapes and straight lines. This makes drawing applications especially useful for technical illustrations, advertisements, and logos. Popular drawing applications include CorelDRAW! and Windows Draw.

> **Tip:** *Painting applications handle text as a series of pixels, making the text very difficult to edit. Drawing applications offer much more flexibility when dealing with text. The text is contained in a separate box; you can edit the text just as if you were using a word processing application.*

WHAT ABOUT TEXT?

Although painting and drawing applications are not designed to handle huge blocks of text, you can add labels and draw arrows to point out important areas of an illustration.

USING SCANNED PHOTOS AND FIGURES

If you have a photograph or a drawing on paper, and if you have the right equipment, you can turn your existing photos into pixel versions. To do this, you need a digitizer or a scanner that converts the image into a series of dots and stores it on a disk. You also must have a graphics application that supports a scanner (the scanner usually comes with an application). Once the image is in your system, you can edit it in your favorite painting or photo enhancement application.

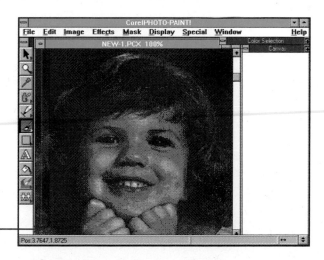

Scanned image

MORE YOU CAN DO WITH GRAPHICS

Tip: Some drawing applications offer an outline feature that can convert the scanned pixel image into a group of drawn objects. You can then edit the image in the drawing application. However, I've never seen an outline feature that works very well.

In addition to the major graphics applications, you can purchase applications for the following types of special tasks (to name a few):

- **Photo enhancement** If you scan and use photographs, you can purchase photo editing and enhancement software to improve the quality of the scanned photo.

- **Home and landscape design** If you want to design your own home or home improvement, or draw up plans for your yard, you can purchase special home and landscape design programs to simplify the process. Many applications include clip art for furniture, windows, doors, and appliances, so you don't have to draw them yourself.

- **Morphing** You may have seen commercials in which a car magically transforms into a tiger. That special effect is called morphing, and you can purchase applications that can morph for you.

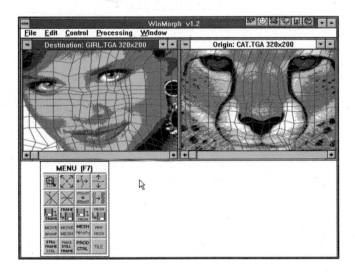

- **Flow charting** If you often compose procedures for your business, you may save time by using a flow charting application to create organizational charts and to illustrate processes and procedures.

EXERCISE

If you have Microsoft Windows, you have a graphics application called Paintbrush that you can use for practice.

1 Double-click on the ▦ Accessories icon.

2 Double-click on 🎨 Paintbrush icon.

3 Click on ▣, click on red, and click on a medium line thickness.

4 Drag the mouse around in the picture area to paint your name on the screen.

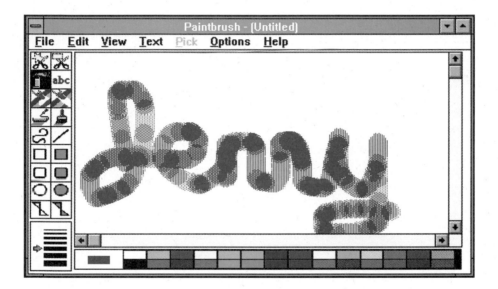

5 Click on ◩ and use it to erase your name.

6 Click on one of the shape tools, and drag the mouse to place some shapes on-screen.

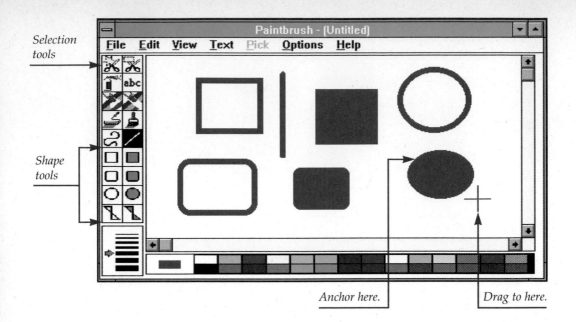

Selection tools

Shape tools

Anchor here.   Drag to here.

7 Click on , click on your favorite color, and then click inside one of the shapes to fill it with color.

8 Use the selection tools and the Cut and Paste commands to cut some areas from the screen and paste them elsewhere.

CHAPTER DIGEST

Drawing Objects

1. Click on a drawing tool 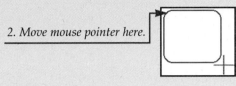.

2. Move mouse pointer here.

3. Hold down mouse button while dragging mouse here.

Sizing Objects

Drag top or bottom handle to change only the height.

Drag side handle to change only the width.

Drag corner handle to change height and width.

Moving Objects

Drag line to move object.

Sometimes you can drag from the center.

Layering Objects

Click on Move To Front.

Click on Move To Back.

Click on the object.

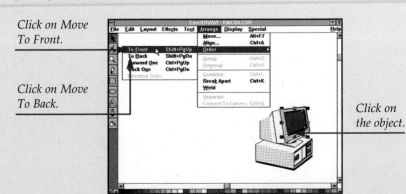

CHAPTER 13

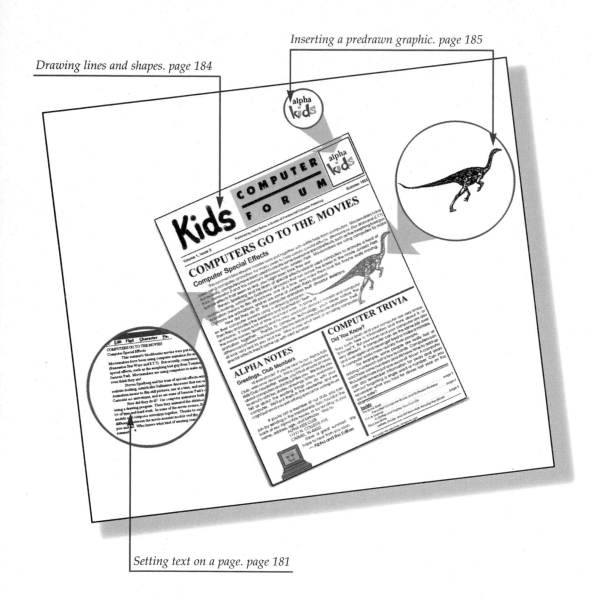

Inserting a predrawn graphic. page 185

Drawing lines and shapes. page 184

Setting text on a page. page 181

CREATING CUSTOM PUBLICATIONS

W ith desktop publishing, you can use your computer to create custom brochures, newsletters, sales pamphlets, greeting cards, and other publications. In this chapter, you learn how to use a desktop publishing application to combine text and graphics on a page, how to style text, and how to enhance your publications.

UNDERSTANDING DESKTOP PUBLISHING

Desktop publishing (DTP) applications are designed to work with word processing (see Chapter 10) and graphics applications (see Chapter 13). The word processing application creates the text, the graphics application creates the graphics, and the desktop publishing application combines the text and graphics to create illustrated publications.

Starting with a Blank Page

When you start a desktop publishing application, it displays a blank screen that represents a blank sheet of paper. Your job is to "paste" text and graphics on the blank page, just as if you were creating a collage. To help, desktop publishing applications display a set of on-screen tools that usually includes the following:

- **Paste-up board** You can use the space around the page to temporarily store scraps of text and pictures. For example, if you want to move a picture from one page to the next, you can drag the picture off the page and set it on the paste-up board. Turn to the page on which you want the picture to appear, and then drag the picture from the paste-up board onto the page.

- **Rulers** Horizontal and vertical rulers appear around the perimeter of the paste-up board. You can use the rulers to help you align text and graphics more precisely. Some applications let you drag the rulers right where you are aligning objects.

- **Toolbox or toolbar** In addition to the standard menu commands, an on-screen toolbox may offer shortcuts for placing pictures, lines, and shapes on a page.

- **Pull-down menus** Use the pull-down menus to enter commands that do not appear as buttons or tools.

- **Page buttons** With the page buttons, you can flip from page to page in your publication.

- **View settings** Sometimes you want a bird's-eye view of a page. Other times you want to see a close-up view of a given area. You can use the View buttons or View commands to zoom in or zoom out on a page.

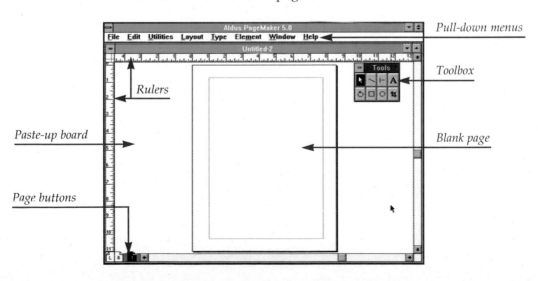

PUTTING TEXT ON THE PAGE

Although you can type text directly into most desktop publishing applications, you may save time by typing the text first in your word processing application. By doing this, you can use the advanced features of your word processing application (such as the spell checker and search and replace) to edit the text. You can then *import* the text into your desktop publishing application.

> **Tip:** *Most desktop publishing applications can use files created by the more popular word processing applications—WordPerfect, Microsoft Word, and WordStar. If you are using a less popular application, you can save the document as an ASCII file (a plain-text file).*

To import text, you usually click on a text box button, drag the text box to its desired size and dimensions on the page, and then enter a command to import a text file. After you specify the drive, directory, and file name of the text file, the application inserts the text inside the text box. If you make an empty text box, you can start typing inside the box.

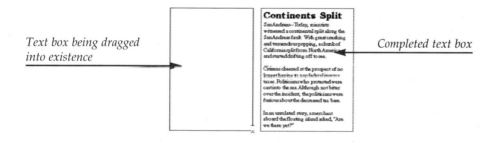

Text box being dragged into existence

Completed text box

Once the text box is on the page, you can drag it (to move it), squeeze it to make a column of text more narrow, or stretch it to make the column wider. When you click on the text box, handles appear around it. You can then drag the text box to move it, or drag a handle to resize it. In addition, you can usually shade inside the box, add a line (*border*) around the box, or add a drop-shadow that makes the box look as though it is lifted above the page.

> **Tip:** *If the text does not fit inside the text box, some of the text may not be shown, or the application will give you the option of spilling the text that won't fit into another text box. In either case, don't worry if you can't see part of the text; it's still there.*

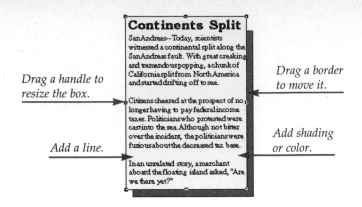

Continents Split

SanAndreas--Today, scientists witnessed a continental split along the SanAndreas fault. With great creaking and tremendous popping, a chunk of California split from North America and started drifting off to sea.

Citizens cheered at the prospect of no longer having to pay federal income taxes. Politicians who protested were cast into the sea. Although not bitter over the incident, the politicians were furious about the decreased tax base.

In an unrelated story, a merchant aboard the floating island asked, "Are we there yet?"

Drag a handle to resize the box.

Drag a border to move it.

Add a line.

Add shading or color.

CHANGING THE LOOK OF YOUR TEXT

When you bring text into a document, it looks fairly drab—nothing like the fancy print you see in magazines or newspapers. In order to bring the text to life, you must *format* the text. Here's a quick list of the formatting you can apply to your text:

- **Fonts**   A *font* is any set of characters of the same *typeface* (design) and *type size* (measured in points). For example, Times Roman 12-point is a font: Times Roman is the typeface, and 12-point is the size. (There are 72 points in an inch.) You can use different fonts to emphasize text or set headings apart from the body text. Here are some examples of fonts:

  ## Century Schoolbook 18-point

  ### Helvetica 12-point

  `OCR/B 10-point`

  Times 9-point

- **Enhancements**   Unlike fonts, which control the essential quality of text, enhancements act as text make-up. When you apply an enhancement, the typeface and size remain the same, but the look of the text changes. Some common enhancements are:

Bold	*Italic*	Shadow
Condensed	Overstrike	~~Strikethrough~~
Superscript^P	Subscript$_B$	<u>Underline</u>
SMALL CAPS		

- **Color**   If you have a color printer, you can color your text to create full-page color ads or brochures.

Applications: Doing Some Real Work

- **Alignment**   You can center your text, align it left or right, or fully justify it (so it looks like the text in newspaper columns).

- **Line spacing and leading**   You can set line spacing at single or double spacing and increments thereof. (Spacing is determined by the text size you are using.) You can add space between lines of text (called leading) to control spacing more precisely. For example, if your résumé is coming up short, you might want to add 2 points of leading between all the lines.

- **Kerning**   Kerning helps you close up the space between two characters. For example, if you have a headline that says "Washington's New Tax Bill," the Wa in Washington may appear to be farther apart than other character pairs. You can kern the characters to remove the extra space.

In most applications, you apply font formatting by selecting the text and then entering the Font command. You'll get a dialog box, like the one shown here, through which you apply all the character formatting at once. (To change text alignment, leading, or kerning, you usually have to enter additional commands.)

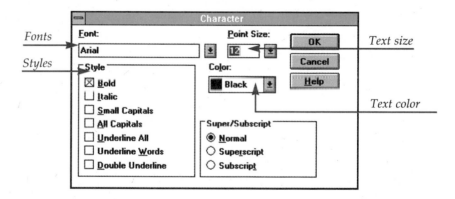

FAST FORMATTING WITH STYLES

Desktop publishing applications, like word processing applications, often use styles to simplify the task of formatting the text of a document. A *style* is a name assigned to a collection of formatting settings.

HOW STYLES WORK

To understand styles, consider the following example. You are creating a book and each chapter title is to be set in 24-point New Century Schoolbook font, set in italic, and indented five spaces from the right margin. Rather than change the font, style, point size, and indentation each time you type a chapter title, you can create a style called

Chapter Title. This style would contain all the specified format settings. The next time you need to format a chapter title, you highlight the chapter title and choose the Chapter Title style.

QUICK REFORMATTING WITH STYLES

Another advantage of using styles is that you can quickly change the formatting of all the text formatted with a particular style. Continuing with the Chapter Title example above, suppose you decide that the chapter title should be larger, say 36-point type. Because you formatted all the chapter titles with the Chapter Title style, you can edit the style, changing the point size from 24 to 36. When you are finished editing, all the chapter titles that were formatted with the Chapter Title style are changed to 36-point type.

WHAT ABOUT GRAPHICS?

Although you will spend most of your time working with text, the real power of a desktop publishing application is that it lets you place graphic elements on the page, as well. What kind of graphic elements? The following list explains some common graphic elements you might paste on a page:

- **Pictures created in a graphics application**   If you have a painting or drawing application (see Chapter 13), you can create an illustration and import it into your document.

> *Tip: Most desktop publishing applications can use any files that have been saved in a standard graphics format. For IBM applications, the most common file formats are .PCX, .TIFF, and .BMP. For a Macintosh, common file formats include MacPaint and PICT. If your desktop publishing application does not support a particular format, you can not import a file that has been saved in that format.*

- **Clip art drawings**   Many desktop publishing applications come with a collection of clip art that you can use to accent your publications. You can also purchase clip art separately.

- **Scanned images**   If you have a scanner, you can scan an image or photo from paper, save it as a file, and import the scanned image into your document.

- **Lines, circles, and rectangles**   Most desktop publishing applications have tools for drawing basic shapes, such as lines, circles, and rectangles. You can use these objects effectively as visual devices for dividing the text on a page.

PUTTING A PICTURE ON THE PAGE

Although you can create basic graphic elements, such as lines and boxes, from within the desktop publishing application, you cannot create the complex illustrations that you can scan in or generate with a drawing or painting application. Because of that, you will likely import existing pictures into the desktop publishing document.

To place a picture on a page, enter the Insert Picture or Import Picture command (the command will vary from application to application). You'll get a dialog box asking which graphics file you want to import. Select the drive, directory, and name of the graphics file you want to import. (You may also have to specify a file format.) Click OK. The application sets the picture somewhere on the screen; you can move it later.

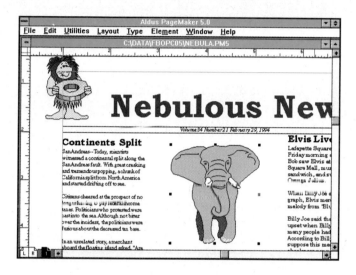

RESIZING THE PICTURE

Once you have your picture on-screen, you can resize it or move it. When you select the image, handles appear around it, just as with a text box. You can drag the handles or drag a side of the box to reshape or move the box. Most applications allow you to change the shape of the box without messing up the dimensions of the picture.

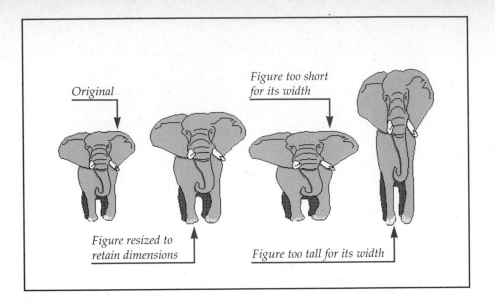

Original

Figure too short for its width

Figure resized to retain dimensions

Figure too tall for its width

LAYERING GRAPHICS AND TEXT

When you place the graphic element on some text, the application automatically wraps (shifts) the text, so it flows around the picture. In some cases, however, you may want the text to overlap all or part of the picture. Most applications allow you to do this.

STACKING AND UNSTACKING OBJECTS

When you place objects on a page, you eventually get overlapping objects, like a stack of papers. With sheets of paper, you can't work with the one on the bottom unless you move it to the top or move the other sheets off it. The same is true with text and graphics objects on a page. If you try to click on an object that's on the bottom of the stack, you end up selecting the object on top.

To help in such cases, most DTP applications contain commands that let you move an object to the front, move it to the back, or move it up one level in the stack.

GETTING SOME HELP WITH PAGE LAYOUT

Many desktop publishing applications offer the following features to help you lay out pages more consistently and accurately and to help you design commonly used publications:

- **Templates**   Some applications come with *templates* for common publications, such as greeting cards, brochures, newsletters, and business cards. You simply open the template, type in your own information, change the pictures used in the template, then print.

- **Master pages**   A *master page* contains a collection of elements (company logo, page number, chapter title) that will appear on every page in the publication. When you print the publication, these elements are printed on every page in the same location. If you do not want the text or graphics from a master page to appear on all pages, you can turn it off for certain pages.

- **Grids**   A *grid* is like a transparent piece of graph paper that allows you to align text and graphics precisely on a page. Many applications include a *snap-to* grid. When you move text or graphics on the grid, the snap-to feature snaps the object to the nearest grid line for consistent alignment (hence the name).

DESKTOP PUBLISHING APPLICATIONS— ARE THEY ALL THE SAME?

Desktop publishing applications differ most in the number of features they offer. Some applications are great for designing single pages for brochures and newsletters, but they lack the comprehensive features required for publishing long documents with repetitive page layouts, such as books.

When looking at different applications, decide what types of publications you need to produce. If you want to create greeting cards, résumés, newsletters, business cards, and other short publications, applications like PFS: First Publisher, Microsoft Publisher, and Express Publisher offer enough basic features to get the job done without overwhelming you with complexity.

For more intensive work, an application like PageMaker, Ventura Publisher, or QuarkXPress provides more features for refining the appearance of your pages.

DO YOU NEED A DESKTOP PUBLISHING APPLICATION?

If you don't want to invest the time and money learning to use a desktop publishing application, try a full-featured word processing application, such as WordPerfect for Windows, Microsoft Word for Windows, or Ami Pro. These advanced word processing applications support several fonts and typestyles, allow you to import graphics, let you preview pages, and provide line drawing tools for accenting your documents.

Although you won't have the same amount of control over text and graphics as you'll find in a desktop publishing application, you will still be able to get the job done.

MORE YOU CAN DO WITH DESKTOP PUBLISHING

You can use desktop publishing applications to create a variety of publications.

- **Greeting cards** Applications such as Print Shop Deluxe are designed to enable you to create your own greeting cards in a snap.

- **Banners** Special banner applications help you create your own banners for special occasions. Advanced text controls enable you to style and twist the text to your liking.

- **Calendars** Create your own decorative calendars and mark any special dates.

EXERCISE

If you have a desktop publishing application, perform the following exercise for practice:

1 Start the application and display a blank page.

2 Insert a blank text box on the page, then type some text.

3 Change views so you can read the text.

> Typing text in a desktop publishing application can be a chore. Before you change views, you may not even see the characters you are typing. Sometimes, it is a good idea to zoom in before you start typing.

4 Change views so you can see the full page.

5 Insert a piece of clip art or other graphic on the page.

6 Resize the picture so it takes up one fourth of the page.

7 Set the picture next to the text box.

8 Insert a border around the graphic box.

9 Click on the text box and shade it.

> In Microsoft Publisher, you can shade a text box and add a fancy border.

CHAPTER DIGEST

Placing a Text Box

Select the text tool 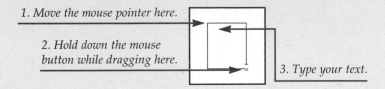.

1. Move the mouse pointer here.

2. Hold down the mouse button while dragging here.

3. Type your text.

Styling the Text

1. Drag over the text.

2. Select Format/Character.

3. Select a font.

4. Select a size.

5. Select a color.

6. Select an enhancement.

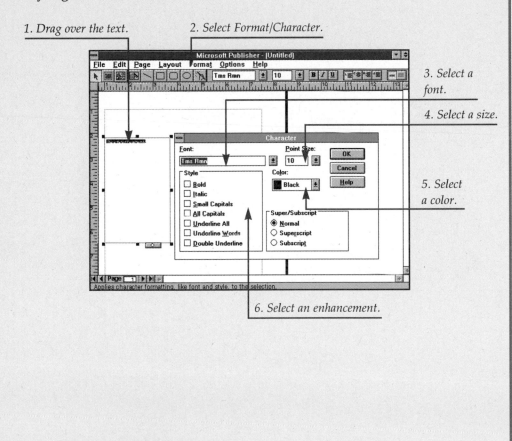

Resizing an Object

1. Click on the object.

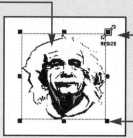

2. Drag a side, top, or bottom handle to change one dimension.

3. Drag a corner handle to change two dimensions.

Moving an Object

1. Click on the object.

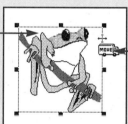

2. Drag the object to move it.

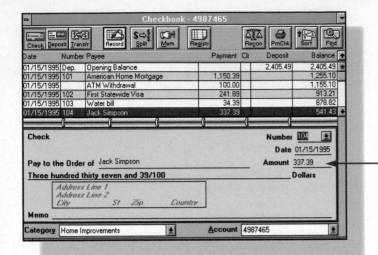

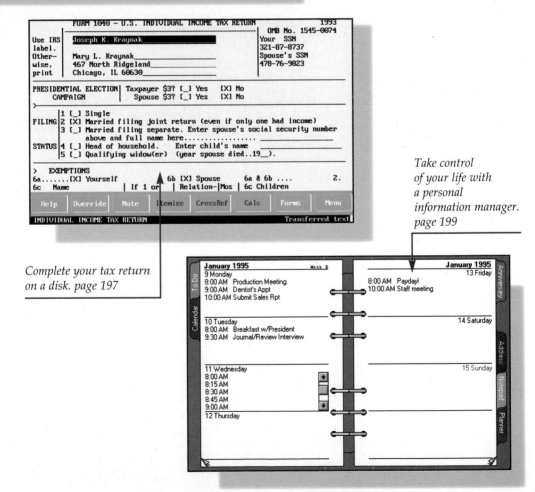

Balance your checkbook electronically. page 194

Take control of your life with a personal information manager. page 199

Complete your tax return on a disk. page 197

Managing Your Time and Money

Computers are naturals when it comes to accounting and date-keeping. In this chapter, we look at how the following types of software can help you manage your time and money:

- **Personal finance applications** can help you balance your checkbook and manage a budget.

- **Tax applications** can help you fill out your tax return and can offer important tax saving advice.

- **Accounting applications** can help you manage money in a business setting.

- **Personal information managers (PIMs)** can keep track of important dates, appointments, and upcoming projects.

Personal Finance Applications

Personal finance applications are also known as *check-writing* applications because their main purpose is to automate the check-writing process. You type the information that you want to appear on the check, and the application prints the check, records the transaction in the check register, and figures the balance. Because you enter the information only once (on the check), you perform fewer steps and avoid introducing errors. And because the process is computerized, you have a neater, more organized checkbook to look back on.

WRITING CHECKS AND RECORDING TRANSACTIONS

When you write a check by hand, you have to write the date on the check, the name of the person or business the check is for, and the amount of the check (both numerically and spelled out). Then, you flip to your check register and enter all the same information again, hopefully without making a mistake.

With a personal finance application, your computer automatically enters the date. You enter the name of the person or business the check is for, the check amount (only once), and a memo telling what the check is for. The application spells out the check amount on the check and enters the following information in the check register:

- The current date

- The check number

- Any address or memo you typed on the check

- The amount of the check

- The current balance

BALANCING AN ELECTRONIC CHECKBOOK

Back in the old days, balancing a checkbook was an exercise in frustration. You calculated and recalculated till you started seeing double. With a check-writing application, you simply mark the checks that have cleared, mark the deposits on the bank statement, and enter any service charges. The application takes care of the rest, determining the total according to the register.

If the total on your register does not match the total on the bank statement, the application lets you know. If you have to correct an entry in the register, the application automatically recalculates the total, saving you the time of doing it over.

The application enters the check amount in the register and determines the new balance.

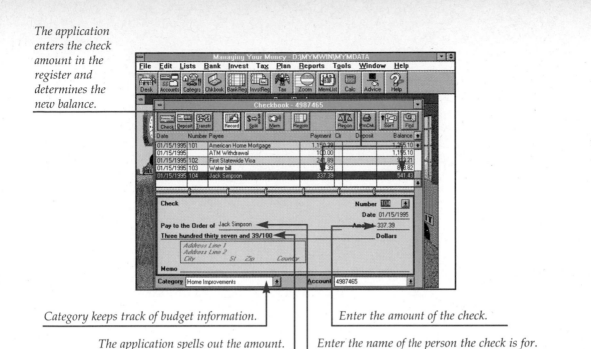

Category keeps track of budget information.

The application spells out the amount.

Enter the amount of the check.

Enter the name of the person the check is for.

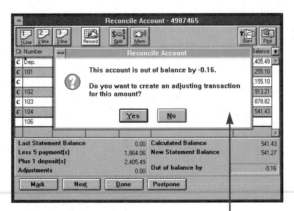

The application lets you know if your checkbook does not balance.

MONTHLY BUDGETS

Before you can take control of your finances, you have to figure out where all your money is going. For instance, you won't be able to decide if you are spending too much money on auto-repair bills unless you know exactly how much you are spending. Would you save money by buying a new car instead? With accurate budget information, you can make a financially sound decision.

With most personal finance applications, you can have the application keep track of each expense for you. Whenever you write a check, you specify the category of the expense. At the end of the month, you tell the application to generate a budget report.

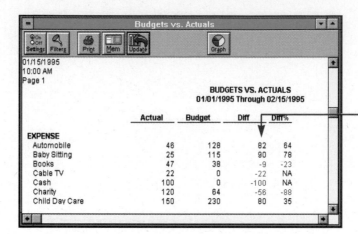

The application shows if you are over budget or under budget for each item.

ADVANCED PERSONAL FINANCE FEATURES

Check writing and budget reports are the bread and butter of any personal finance application. However, several applications offer additional features that you might find useful:

- **Recurring entries**   If you have a monthly bill that is the same each month (a mortgage payment, rent, or budgeted utility payment), a recurring entry feature can save you some time and prevent errors. The application issues the same payment according to the specified schedule.

- **Bill planning**   You enter the information for all the bills you have to pay for the month and then mark the bills you currently plan to pay. The application compares the total amount with your current checking account balance to determine whether you have enough money. You can then prioritize your bills.

- **Electronic bill paying**   If your computer has a modem, you may be able to pay your bills without writing a check. You must subscribe to a service that connects you to your mortgage company, bank, utility company, and others that you have to pay. If you owe money to a person who is not connected to the system, the service will issue the person a paper check.

- **Reminders**   A reminder feature will automatically tell you when a bill is due. You specify the number of days in advance you want to be notified. When you start your computer, the application displays a message letting you know if any bills are due.

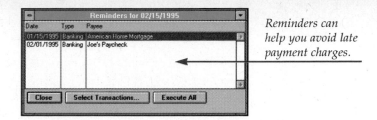

Reminders can help you avoid late payment charges.

- **Income tax estimator**   Compare how much you are actually paying in taxes to how much you should be paying to determine whether you are on track for the year.

- **Investment manager**   Now that you have a budget and are saving loads of money, you may decide to invest that money. If you do, an investment manager feature can help you keep track of how your investments are doing.

- **Net worth calculator**   A net worth calculator compares your total assets to your total liabilities to determine your net worth. If you apply for a loan, your banker will probably ask you to produce a net worth statement to prove that you are financially solvent.

- **Financial advice**   Some personal finance applications, such as WealthStarter, offer financial advice to help you make such determinations as whether or not you need life insurance and how much you should be saving each month to send Junior to college.

DOING YOUR TAXES ON A COMPUTER

Speaking of personal finances, you can also get applications for doing your taxes. In TurboTax, for example, you enter your name, the amount of money you made, the number of deductions you can claim, and so on. The application determines which forms you need to fill out and how much money the IRS owes you or how much money you owe the IRS. And because all the forms are linked, you enter a piece of information only once; TurboTax copies the information to the appropriate forms. For example, you enter your name and social security number only once, and it is placed at the top of every form and schedule.

Popular tax applications include TurboTax, RapidTax, TaxCut, Easy Tax, and CA-Simply Tax. I've done taxes both ways, and this is the only way to go. (Because tax laws change from year to year, you'll need to get an updated copy of the application each year. Plan to spend about 40 bucks.)

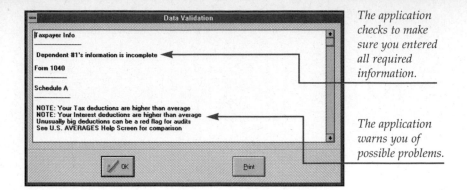

The application checks to make sure you entered all required information.

The application warns you of possible problems.

BUSINESS ACCOUNTING APPLICATIONS

Although personal finance applications are useful for individuals, they cannot offer the powerful features required for a business, including invoicing, inventory control, and payroll. If you work in an accounting department or if you are expanding your small business, you may need to know the basics of business accounting applications.

To handle the complexities of a business, most business accounting applications use a series of interconnected *modules*, including the following:

- **Invoicing**   You send invoices to customers to tell the customers how much money they owe you for products or services. The invoice module also helps you keep track of payments received and is linked to the inventory module so that items sold are deducted from inventory.

- **Fixed assets**   This module helps you keep track of the stuff your company uses to make money but does not sell to customers, including machinery and computers. The fixed assets module performs depreciation calculations and prepares reports for tax time.

- **Job cost**   This module adds up the cost of parts and labor used to produce a product and subtracts it from the amount the product is sold for to determine whether you are making or losing money on a product.

- **Purchase order**   You use this module to order parts or services from vendors or suppliers. When you fill out a purchase order, any products you purchase are recorded in the inventory module, and the cost is deducted from the accounts payable module.

- **Payroll**   This module prepares and prints checks for your employees and prepares quarterly and year-end reports.

- **Accounts payable**   This module keeps track of all the checks you write to vendors for products and services purchased, and sends necessary information to the job cost module.

- **Accounts receivable**   This module keeps track of all incoming money (including payments from customers), and updates balances, past-due payments, and finance charges.

- **General ledger**   The general ledger acts as a manager, making sure that the information entered in one module is transferred to all other modules that are affected. For example, say you send a shipment of refrigerators with an invoice to a customer. When you post the invoice, you want the application to notify the inventory module that a certain number of refrigerators were taken out of inventory. In turn, you want the inventory module to notify the purchase order module that you need to purchase more parts.

PERSONAL INFORMATION MANAGERS (PIMs)

PIM stands for *personal information manager* and is not to be confused with PDA, which stands for Personal Digital Assistant. A PIM is an application that runs on your PC and allows you to keep track of appointments, contacts, and projects. A PDA is a little hand-held computer that you use to do basically the same things.

The Calendar shows important dates and meetings.

Lotus Organizer is a popular PIM.

Click on a tab to go to it.

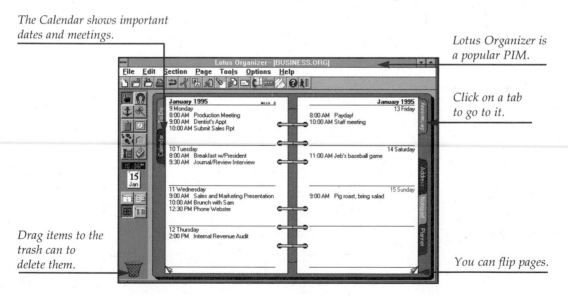

Drag items to the trash can to delete them.

You can flip pages.

There are several PIMs on the market. My personal favorite is Lotus Organizer. Organizer is set up as a book that's divided into six sections:

To Do provides you with an area in which to keep a list of tasks you must perform and to prioritize the tasks.

Calendar displays the days of the month. When you click on a day, you get to see a list of appointments for that day. In the calendar, you can also set alarms that notify you of upcoming meetings.

Address acts just like the paper version of an address book. You can store names, addresses, and phone numbers for relatives, friends, and business associates.

Notepad is a scratch pad in which you jot things down as you think of them.

Planner is a project planner in which you keep track of the various stages of projects, vacation time, meetings, and anything else that fills up your days.

Anniversary enables you to keep track of important days, including birthdays, anniversaries, and holidays.

In addition to these separate features, most PIMs allow you to cross-reference the sections so that all the information you need is linked. For example, you may link an appointment with the name and phone number of the person you are meeting and with some notes you are keeping in the notepad.

MORE YOU CAN DO

Once you have learned the basics of using time and money management software, try some of the following advanced features:

- **Financial calculators.** Many personal finance applications come with a loan calculator. You enter the principal of the loan (how much money you want to borrow), the annual interest rate, and the term. The calculator figures out the payment.

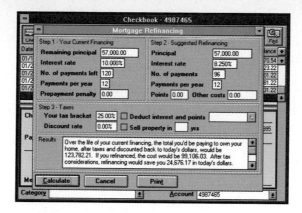

- **Using a modem to dial phone numbers.** If you have a modem hooked up to your computer, and your phone is hooked up to the modem, you can have your PIM dial phone numbers from the address book.

- **Filing taxes over the phone.** Some tax applications offer a service that enables you to file your tax return electronically for faster processing. You can send the return using a modem or on a floppy disk. The service forwards the return to the IRS.

EXERCISE

If you have Microsoft Windows, you have a computerized calendar that you can use to set appointments. Try the following exercise:

1 Double-click on the Accessories icon.

2 Double-click on the Calendar icon.

3 Select the day of the appointment.

4 Click on the time for which you want to set the appointment.

5 Type a description of the appointment.

6 To have an alarm ring at the appointment time, open the Alarm menu and select Set.

```
 ┌────────────────────────────────────────┐
 │ ─         Calendar - [Untitled]    ▼ ▲  │
 │ File  Edit  View  Show  Alarm  Options  Help │
 │ ┌──────────┬───┬───────────────────────┐ │
 │ │10:42 AM  │ ◆ ◆│ Friday, January 20, 1995│ │
 │ │      7:00 AM                          │▲│
 │ │      8:00                             │ │
 │ │      9:00                             │ │
 │ │     10:00                             │ │
 │ │     11:00                             │ │
 │ │     12:00 PM                          │ │
 │ │      1:00                             │ │
 │ │ △    2:00      Weekly meeting         │ │
 │ │      3:00                             │ │
 │ │      4:00                             │ │
 │ │      5:00                             │ │
 │ │      6:00                             │ │
 │ │      7:00                             │ │
 │ │      8:00                             │▼│
 │ └───────────────────────────────────────┘ │
 │                                          │
 └────────────────────────────────────────┘
```

Bell indicates alarm is on.

7 To have the alarm ring before the appointment time, open the Alarm menu, select Controls, type the number of minutes in advance you want the alarm to ring, and click on OK.

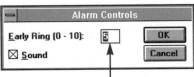

Alarm will ring 5 minutes in advance of appointment.

8 To change calendar views, open the View menu and select the desired view: Day or Month.

CHAPTER DIGEST

Writing a Check

6. *Click on Record.*

1. *Application inserts date.*

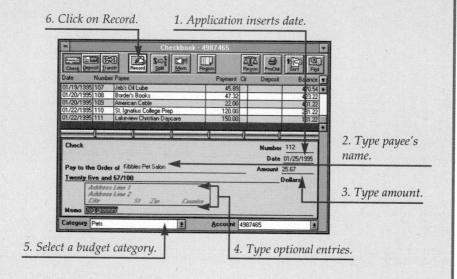

2. *Type payee's name.*

3. *Type amount.*

5. *Select a budget category.*

4. *Type optional entries.*

Entering an Appointment

1. *Specify an appointment time.*

2. *Type a description.*

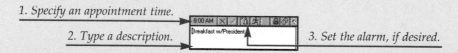

3. *Set the alarm, if desired.*

Computer games. page 205

Educational programs. page 209

STEAM POWER

3 MPH/4.8 KPH

SLOW   FAST

The steam engine works
by heating water beyond
the boiling point and
channeling the steam
into a cylinder, in which
a piston is driven down
by the force of the
steam. The first
vehicles to move under
steam power were built
by a Swiss engineer,
working for the French

EDUCATIONAL PROGRAMS AND COMPUTER GAMES

I n Chapters 10 through 15, you learned about programs that are business related or that can help you perform some task. However, a computer isn't all business. As you will see in this chapter, you can use a computer to play a wide variety of games—everything from chess and solitaire to arcade games and flight simulators. This chapter will also introduce you to programs that can help you (and your kids) learn various subjects such as reading, math, music, and even foreign languages.

HAVING FUN WITH COMPUTER GAMES

In the old days, "computer game" was synonymous with "adventure game." The program would ask you a question about what you wanted to do. For example: "You come to a door. Do you want to enter the room or walk down the hallway?" You would press a key to make your selection, and then the program would describe the consequences of your choice.

Nowadays, computer games are much more diverse and sophisticated. Sure, you can get adventure games, but the new adventure games let you see what's going on. If you look around a room for weapons, you may find a battle axe on-screen. If you enter a room and encounter a three-eyed monster with bad breath, you will see that monster. And computer games are not limited to the action/adventure categories of old. You can now get computerized sports games, arcade games, and even games that allow you to plan a city or control the world!

ACTION/ADVENTURE GAMES

Although computer games have recently become more diverse, action/adventure games are still very popular. In action/adventure games, you usually take on the persona of some hero, maybe Mario or Indiana Jones. You are then sent on some mission, such as stopping the Nazis from obtaining a new secret weapon, or saving a kingdom from destruction.

Star Trek: Judgment Rites lets you command the Enterprise.

ARCADE STYLE GAMES

In addition to adventure games, you can get arcade style games for your computer, including pinball, PacMan, and Super Tetris. These games have the same look and feel as their arcade room or Nintendo counterparts, although the actual controls you use to move around on-screen may differ.

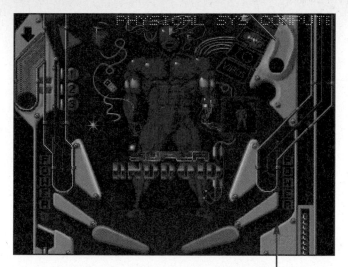

Epic Pinball transforms your computer into a pinball machine.

SPORTS GAMES

You may be familiar with sports games on Nintendo or Sega Genesis. Well, similar games are available for PCs and Macs. For example, in Front-Page Sports Football (for PCs) and NFL Challenge (for Macs), you get to play head coach for your favorite football team. Pick your players, and call your own offensive and defensive plays.

You can purchase programs for almost any sport ranging from individual sports, such as golf and tennis, to team sports, such as baseball and basketball. For Macs, you can even get a program that simulates skiing over 20 different slopes.

PLANNING A CITY

Ever wonder what it's like to plan a city? In SimCity, you get to do just that when the citizens of SimCity elect you mayor. You lay out roads and highways, attract professional ball clubs to your city, and create zoning laws for industrial plants and recreational areas. See the effects of your decisions on such problems as crime, pollution, and inflation. If the citizens of your fair city are happy with your decisions, you can sit back and watch them prosper. However, if you make the wrong decisions, they leave your city—and you have no city to govern.

> *Tip: A game similar to SimCity called Capitalist Pig lets you play CEO of a large corporation. You get to steer your company through difficult financial times to prosper or collapse as a result of your decisions.*

CHAPTER 16

In SimCity 2000, you must build and manage a booming metropolis.

War Games

Whether you like to fight by land, air, or water, you can find a war game designed for you. For example, in The Perfect General, you engage the enemy in various ground battles to prove your superiority in up to three difficulty levels.

In Aces of the Pacific, you play a World War II fighter pilot, attacking the enemy from the air. In order to survive, you must outfly and outshoot the enemy as he tries to defend himself from land and air.

Playing the All Powerful

If you think being a god would be easy, you should try to play Populous. In Populous, you become a deity and try to guide your chosen people as they encounter, and hopefully defeat, an enemy population.

In Populous, you have several tools at your fingertips, including the power to raise and lower land (to help your people fortify their positions). And you can make life hell for the enemy by creating floods, swamps, volcanoes, and earthquakes. You can even unleash a killer plague that may wipe out the entire population of earth (including your chosen people).

LEARNING TO FLY WITH A FLIGHT SIMULATOR

If you have ever wondered what it's like to fly an airplane, to deal with the instrument panel inside a cockpit, or to fly in formation, you can try it out with a flight simulator. In Microsoft Flight Simulator, for example, you can climb into the cockpit of a Cessna 182 or a Gates Business Jet, and try your hand at the controls.

You can take off from the runway of any of 118 different airports, including O'Hare and Kennedy. Fly over the famous Chicago skyline, the Statue of Liberty, or even the Golden Gate Bridge.

Strike Commander combines flight simulation and war action.

HELPING KIDS LEARN THE BASICS

With the proper software and approach, you can use your computer to help your children (or someone else's children) learn the basics of reading, writing, and arithmetic. There are many programs on the market that can help children learn while they play. The following sections provide a small sampling of what's out there.

> *Tip: Before you buy an educational program, ask your kids what they want. Take them to the store with you; they might get to try out the program before you buy it. Kids won't learn anything from a program that they won't play with.*

EARLY LEARNING IN THE PLAYROOM

The Playroom is a good program for preschoolers, kindergarteners, and slightly older kids who have little experience using a computer. (Kids who know a little about computers may get bored.)

When the child starts the program, he is placed in the playroom. The child is not given any instructions; it is up to him to explore the room in order to find out what's in it. When the child clicks on an object in the playroom, the object comes to life or the child is lifted to another room where he can play games that help him develop the following skills: telling time, number recognition, matching, counting, story telling, and reciting the alphabet.

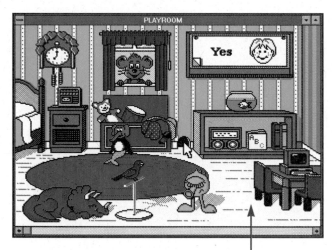

In The Playroom, your child is free to explore.

GETTING A JUMP ON READING

One of the greatest pleasures of parenthood is watching your child start to read. However, it is a very frustrating experience as well, because you don't know what kind of exercises your child needs, and even when you do know, you may not have the patience to work through those exercises as often as necessary. To help, you can purchase any of several reading and reading readiness programs for your child.

Two of the more popular reading programs on the market are Reader Rabbit and Reader Rabbit 2, which contain several games to help develop early reading skills, including phonics. In Reader Rabbit 2, for example, the child can play four games to help acquire and sharpen his reading skills.

LEARNING GEOGRAPHY IN THE '90S

Chances are you have heard reports about the average high-school student not being able to point out Washington D.C. on a United States map and how the country is going to rot because of it. If you're overly concerned that your kids may not be able to pinpoint Washington D.C. or Baghdad, consider getting them a game called Where in the World Is Carmen Sandiego?.

Carmen Sandiego makes learning geography fun by making you solve a mystery. At the beginning of the game, Carmen or one of her fellow V.I.L.E. agents has committed a crime. It's up to you to solve the crime and find and arrest the criminal. Throughout the game, you receive clues from various people. For example, a bank teller may say, "I last saw the culprit driving away in a limousine flying a red and green flag." Or "The person you are looking for exchanged all the dollars for rubles." You must make the connection between the clue and where on the globe that clue refers to.

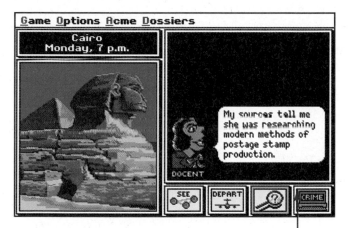

In Where in the World Is Carmen Sandiego,
you learn geography by solving a mystery.

MASTERING MATH

Most beginning math programs on the market are designed to help kids learn counting, equalities and inequalities, and the four mathematical operations: addition, subtraction, multiplication, and division. What differentiates these programs, however, are the games they use to teach the basics.

One of my favorite beginning math programs is Math Blaster, which offers four games. One of the

Tip: Although most commercial math programs focus on basic math for younger kids, there are programs for older kids. For example, Alge Blaster Plus can help high school students hone their algebra skills.

more interesting games makes you choose the correct answer for the problem that's shown at the top of the screen. You have to shoot the little rocket man into the right spaceship to score.

Math Blaster uses video arcade techniques to teach math.

DEALING WITH THE MORE CREATIVE SIDE

Although there are computer programs for almost every academic subject a child might encounter in school, there are also programs for the more creative, less academic subjects, such as creative writing and art. One of the most popular programs to help kids channel their creative energies is KidPix.

KidPix lets kids freely combine graphics and text.

COLLEGE AND CONTINUING EDUCATION

Young children are not the only ones who can benefit from educational programs. College students and adults who want to improve their minds can benefit as well. In the following sections, you will learn about programs that can help you prepare for tests, learn how to type, learn a foreign language, and even brush up on your knowledge in a certain field.

PREPARING FOR STANDARDIZED TESTS

If you are in college, trying to get into college, or even trying to get out of high school by passing a standardized test, you may need some help preparing for such tests. There are several programs on the market that you can use to prepare yourself for the ACT, SAT, GRE, GMAT, LSAT, and college boards. Once you have worked through the sample questions, you'll be more comfortable and confident when it comes to taking the real thing.

LEARNING HOW TO TYPE

If you don't know how to type or if your typing skills are rusty, consider purchasing a typing program, such as Mavis Beacon Teaches Typing or Typing Tutor. These programs will teach you the basics—where your fingers should rest when you are not typing and which fingers should press which keys. In addition, typing programs lead you through exercises that help you hone your skills and can even drill you on keys you are having trouble with.

Typing Tutor comes with an arcade style typing game. In this game, words fall from the sky to crush your beautiful planet. Type the word correctly before it hits your planet, and you destroy the word.

Type the word before it crushes a part of the scenery.

Learning a Foreign Language

Foreign languages are tough, and you can't fully master a language unless you converse with native speakers on a regular basis. However, there are several programs on the market that can help drill you on vocabulary, sentence structure, verb tenses, and the other basics you'll need to become fluent.

Foreign language programs can help you learn vocabulary.

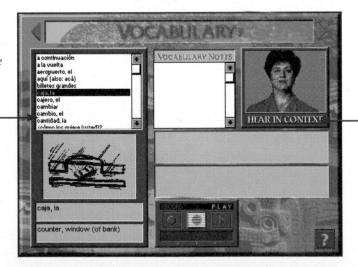

With a sound board, you can hear the word pronounced by a native speaker.

BRUSHING UP ON SCIENCE AND TECHNOLOGY

Because the computer is pegged as a breakthrough in science and technology, you would think that there would be several programs on the market to help you learn biology, chemistry, physics, and engineering. However, there are surprisingly few programs to help you learn those disciplines.

The most popular programs you can find are marketed by Software Publishing Corporation: AutoWorks, Chemistry Works, Bodyworks, Orbits, and Computer Works. These programs make incredible use of graphics and animation as teaching tools. For example, in AutoWorks, the program shows you the parts of a car in action.

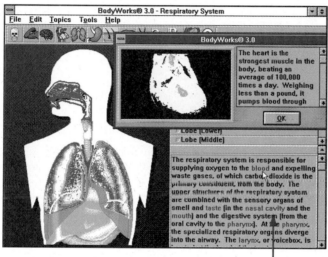

Science programs can show you how things work.

ENCYCLOPEDIAS AND OTHER REFERENCE MATERIALS

How would you like to have a 26-volume set of encyclopedias on a single disc? What about an encyclopedia that could play snippets of Mozart's symphonies, show full color pictures on your screen, and let you look up an article just by typing a portion of its name? How about a world atlas that provides a view of the globe along with information about each country? Or maybe you would like a book of mammals that lets you hear lions roar and monkeys chatter and lets you view the animals moving in their natural habitats? You can get all this and more with a CD-ROM player and the right discs. Chapter 17 discusses the details.

BEFORE YOU BUY A GAME OR EDUCATIONAL PROGRAM

Shopping for computer games and educational programs may be the most frustrating computer activity you will encounter. The box might show monsters and spaceships lunging at you from the sales rack. When you get the program home, your screen shows monsters that look like they're built out of Legos. The best way to shop for a game is to try it out first. If that's not an option, use the following checklist:

> *Tip: Before purchasing any software product, ask the dealer about the store's return policy. Many stores offer a no-questions-asked policy that allows you to return software for any reason within three or four days of the purchase.*

- **Video**   If you have a VGA or SVGA monitor, make sure the program supports that monitor. If you buy a program that offers only CGA support, the on-screen pictures will look blocky.

- **Sounds**   If you have a sound board and you want a program that creates nifty sounds, make sure the program includes sounds, and that it supports the type of sound board you have. Many educational programs offer verbal feedback that can reinforce learning.

- **Controls**   Some programs do not work with a joystick. If your computer is equipped with a joystick, look for comparable programs that support joystick use.

- **CD-ROM**   Because compact discs can store gobs of data, programmers can add all sorts of neat sounds, animation, and video clips to CD-ROM software to bring it to life. If you have a CD-ROM drive, look for CD versions of your favorite programs. (Chapter 17 talks about CD-ROM drives and multimedia in detail.)

MORE GAMES AND EDUCATIONAL PROGRAMS

Once you've mastered a couple of computer games, you may yearn for a bigger challenge. To test your game expertise, try the following:

- **Two-player games over the phone.** Some games enable two people to play against each other over the phone lines. In order for you to play these games, both computers must be equipped with modems (see Chapter 18).

- **Online service games.** Many online services have trivia games and other games you can play. See Chapter 19 for more information about online services.

EXERCISES

If you have Microsoft Windows 3.1, you have a couple of computer games on your computer. Here's how you play them.

PLAYING SOLITAIRE

1 Double-click on the Games icon.

2 Double-click on the Solitaire icon.

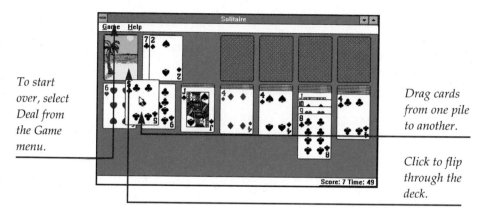

To start over, select Deal from the Game menu.

Drag cards from one pile to another.

Click to flip through the deck.

PLAYING MINESWEEPER

1 Double-click on the Games icon.

2 Double-click on the Minesweeper icon.

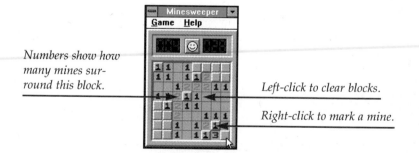

Numbers show how many mines surround this block.

Left-click to clear blocks.

Right-click to mark a mine.

CHAPTER 16

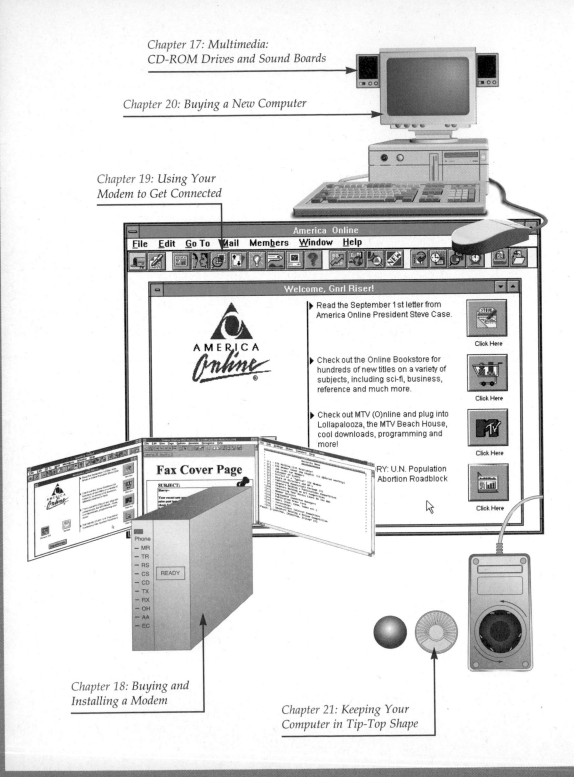

Chapter 17: Multimedia:
CD-ROM Drives and Sound Boards

Chapter 20: Buying a New Computer

Chapter 19: Using Your
Modem to Get Connected

Chapter 18: Buying and
Installing a Modem

Chapter 21: Keeping Your
Computer in Tip-Top Shape

PART 4

BECOMING A
POWER USER

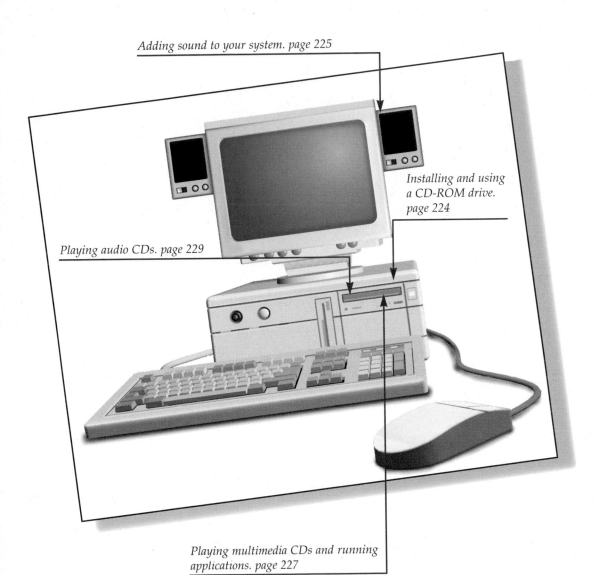

Adding sound to your system. *page 225*

Installing and using a CD-ROM drive. *page 224*

Playing audio CDs. *page 229*

Playing multimedia CDs and running applications. *page 227*

MULTIMEDIA: CD-ROM DRIVES AND SOUND BOARDS

Chapter 17

I f you bought a computer recently, you probably bought a multimedia computer—a computer with a CD-ROM player and sound card. These two devices enable the computer to run applications from compact discs (CDs); to use multimedia products, such as electronic encyclopedias and computer games (complete with sound); and to play audio CDs, including music CDs. In this chapter, you'll learn how to use your multimedia PC to do all this and more.

If your computer does not have a CD-ROM drive or a sound card, this chapter will teach you how to shop for and install these devices in your computer, so that you, too, can experience multimedia.

THE EQUIPMENT YOU NEED

If you have a multimedia computer, you probably have most of the equipment you need to play CDs complete with sound, and you can skip this section. If you're attempting to upgrade your computer to multimedia, here's what you will need:

- 386 or better microprocessor and at least 4 megabytes of RAM. A 486 with 8 megabytes of RAM is better.

- Microsoft Windows 3.1 and Windows-compatible software.

- 200 MB or larger hard drive.

- Super VGA monitor (to display all the pretty pictures and video clips). You can get by with a VGA monitor.

> *Tip: If you have an old computer and don't have the disk space, memory, and monitor you need to run multimedia CDs efficiently, it may be less expensive to buy a new computer than it is to upgrade.*

- Double speed (or faster) CD-ROM drive. Double speed means that the drive can kick into high gear and read some CDs twice as fast.

- Sound card (make sure it can handle both digitized and synthesized sounds). 16-bit is better than 8-bit.

- Speakers and a microphone (the microphone is optional, but you'll probably want to record something).

SHOPPING FOR A CD-ROM DRIVE

If you're in the market for a CD-ROM drive, don't look only at the price tag. Consider the following options as well:

- **Internal or external?** If you have the room inside your computer for an internal CD-ROM drive, buy an internal drive. Internal drives are typically faster than external drives and take up less space on your desk.

- **Double speed or faster?** Newer CD-ROM drives are double-speed, triple-speed, or quadruple-speed. Don't settle for anything slower than double-speed, no matter how inexpensive the drive is. *Minimum transfer rate:* 150 (at single-speed) to 300 kilobytes (at double-speed) per second or faster. *Maximum access time:* 200 milliseconds or less.

- **On-drive cache?** To help the drive deliver information to the computer more quickly, the drive should have a disk cache of 64 kilobytes or more.

- **Compatible with sound board?** Make sure the drive can work with the sound board you decide to purchase. For example, if you plan to use the CD-ROM drive with a SoundBlaster Pro board, make sure the two devices are compatible.

- **Other compatibility issues.** Make sure the drive is compatible with the following standards: High Sierra and ISO-9660, which enables you to play some CDs on a

Mac and IBM PC; Kodak Photo CD (or XA Mode 2), which reads Kodak CDs containing your photos (more about this later); CD-Audio, which plays music CDs; and MPC 2.

- **Bundled discs.** When comparing two CD-ROM drives of the same quality, compare the discs (if any) that come with the drive.

SHOPPING FOR A SOUND BOARD

Shopping for a sound board is a little easier than shopping for a CD-ROM drive. Consider the following list of factors:

- **Compatible with CD-ROM drive?** Most CD-ROM drives are compatible with Sound-Blaster or AdLib, so those cards are pretty safe. However, you should check the CD-ROM drive's specifications to make sure. You should also check the requirements of the software you want to run.

> *Tip: Don't expect much from the dinky speakers that come with a sound board. They're usually about as good as a set of headphones you get with a walkman. Special computer speakers with built-in amplifiers are better.*

- **8-bit or 16-bit?** 8-bit sound cards produce low-quality sound. Make sure you get a 16-bit card.

- **Digital signal processor (DSP)?** Some sound cards have their own processor that can handle some of the work required to play complex sounds. This can help increase the overall speed of your system.

- **Input and output connectors?** Make sure the sound card has connectors to handle the following input and output: input from your CD-ROM drive; input from a microphone; MIDI (musical instrument digital interface) to handle input from optional musical devices; output to speakers.

- **Additional equipment and software?** Some sound boards come with speakers, a microphone, cables for connecting your CD-ROM drive to the sound board, and software that you can use to record and play back sounds. When comparing prices, take these extras into account.

OTHER MULTIMEDIA DEVICES

Although most people experience multimedia only through premade CDs, some like to go a bit further and create their own. If you're one of these people, you can purchase additional equipment for inserting movie clips, recording and composing music, and creating animations.

To capture video clips, you need a special video capture board. You can connect a camcorder, VCR, or laserdisc player to the board and play your video clips into the board. The board digitizes the images and saves them in a file on your hard disk.

For recording and composing music, you need a special MIDI (musical instrument digital interface) musical device that can connect to the MIDI input port on your sound card. You also need special software that can record the music and enable you to edit and mix music clips using your computer.

SETTING UP YOUR CD-ROM DRIVE

The procedure for installing a CD-ROM drive varies depending on whether the drive is internal or external. For an external drive, you use a cable to connect the drive to a port (usually the serial port) on the system unit, and you plug the drive into a power source. You then must run an installation program that came with the drive.

Installing an internal drive is more difficult. You must mount the drive inside the system unit, plug a controller board into the motherboard, and connect the drive to the controller board. In addition, you must connect the drive to the power source. If you have never installed an internal drive before, get help from someone who has.

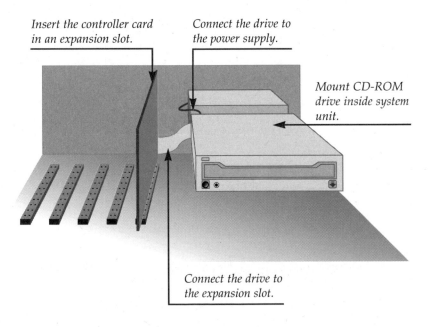

Insert the controller card in an expansion slot.

Connect the drive to the power supply.

Mount CD-ROM drive inside system unit.

Connect the drive to the expansion slot.

INSTALLING A SOUND BOARD

A sound board is a circuit board that you plug into a slot inside the system unit. The procedure is not very difficult, but if you have never installed an expansion board before, get help from a more experienced person the first time you try. When installing any expansion board, make sure the computer is off, touch a metal part of the system unit before you touch the board (to discharge static), and hold the board only by its edges.

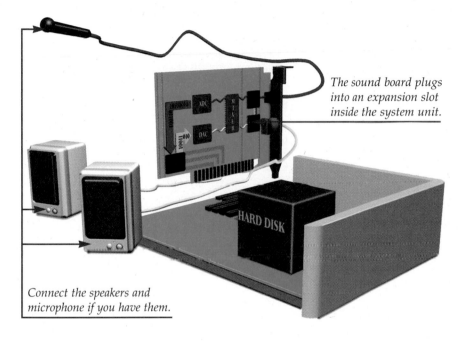

The sound board plugs into an expansion slot inside the system unit.

Connect the speakers and microphone if you have them.

Once you get the board in place (and the cover back on your system unit), you have a couple of options concerning how you want your speakers connected:

- **CD-ROM to sound board connection**   To have all your sounds come out of the same set of speakers, connect the output jacks on the CD-ROM controller board to the input jack on the sound board. Then connect the sound board output jack to the speakers.

- **CD-ROM with no sound board**   Most CD-ROM drives have a headphone jack. If you have no sound board, you can still hear CD-ROM sounds and listen to audio CDs by plugging a set of headphones into this jack.

- **Sound board to speakers or amplifier** You can connect the sound board output to a set of small speakers or headphones. You can then use the volume control on the sound board (and on some speakers). Or, you can connect the sound board output to the input jacks on your stereo system, and use the controls on your stereo for high-quality sound.

INSTALLING THE CD-ROM AND SOFTWARE DRIVERS

Whenever you install a hardware device, such as a sound board or a CD-ROM drive, you must install software drivers that tell the computer how to use the device. These drivers come on disk. Read the instructions that came with the device to install the drivers. It's usually as easy as running a Setup or Install program for an application.

After you install the necessary drivers, you must reboot your computer to run the drivers. You can then use your CD-ROM drive and sound board to proceed through this chapter.

PLAYING COMPACT DISCS

Once you have managed to install the necessary hardware, you can start using your CD-ROM player to play compact discs. In the following sections, you'll learn how to install applications from CDs, run multimedia and game CDs, and play audio CDs (such as music CDs).

INSTALLING APPLICATIONS FROM CDS

Many software manufacturers are starting to market and distribute their products on CD. In addition, new computers commonly come with a CD that contains copies of all the files on the computer's hard disk. That way, if anything happens to the hard disk files, you can reinstall them from the CD. You install an application from a CD the same way you do from a floppy disk, but without the disk swapping. Refer to "Installing an Application" in Chapter 9 for more information.

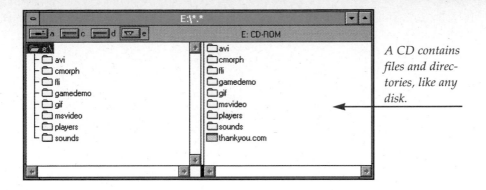

A CD contains files and directories, like any disk.

Running Multimedia and Game CDs

Most multimedia and game CDs contain much more data than you would want to copy to a hard disk. With CDs such as these, you usually run the application directly from the CD. The procedure varies depending on whether the CD is designed for DOS or Windows.

- With DOS multimedia and game CDs, you generally enter a command to run the CD, just as if you were running an application from your hard disk. Refer to Chapters 6 through 8.

- With Windows CDs, you usually run an installation or setup program first. The installation program creates a program group window and a program-item icon that you can use to run the CD. Simply double-click on the icon to start the application.

Tip: You can shop for software using a CD. Some companies, such as Software Dispatch (phone: 1-800-289-8383), send out a CD with several applications on it. You can read information about the applications, view a demonstration, and even try the application. If you decide to purchase an application, you can call the company for a code that unlocks the application you want. The cost of the application is then charged to your credit card.

With CDs for Windows, the setup program adds an icon for the application.

CHAPTER 17

Playing Music CDs

If you purchased a CD-ROM player that can also play audio CDs, you can use it to listen to music as you work. Before you can play music CDs, however, you may need to install some additional software:

- **CD-ROM audio driver**   If you want to play a CD in Windows, you need a driver that enables the CD player to play sounds. Windows 3.1 comes with a file called MCICDA.DRV that works with most CD-ROM players. To install the driver, read the instructions below.

- **Audio CD program**   You need a special program for playing CDs that provides you with a control panel for selecting songs, stopping and ejecting a disc, and so on. You usually get such an application with your CD-ROM drive.

Installing a CD-ROM Audio Driver in Windows

To use most hardware devices in Windows, you must have the proper driver installed. The driver tells Windows how to play the device. To install the Windows CD-ROM driver, do the following:

1 Run Windows and double-click on [Control Panel] .

2 Double-click on [Main] .

3 Double-click on [Drivers]. The Drivers dialog box appears, showing a list of installed drivers.

4 Select Add... from the Drivers dialog box. A list of available drivers appears.

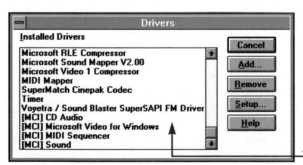

Available drivers

5 Select [MCI] CD Audio from the List of Drivers. If you don't see [MCI CD] Audio in the List of Drivers, you need to install the MCICDA.DRV. See the instructions on the next page.

6 Select [OK].

7 Follow the on-screen instructions to complete the operation.

If you don't see [MCI CD] Audio in the List of Drivers, you need to install the MCICDA.DRV file. Look for a file on your Windows installation disks named MCICDA.DR_; you can use the Windows File Manager to find the file, as explained in Chapter 7.

Use File Manager to find MCICDA.DR_.

With the disk in the floppy drive (A or B), open the File Manager's File menu, select Run, then type

> **expand a:mcicda.dr_ c:\windows\system\mcicda.drv**

or

> **expand b:mcicda.dr_ c:\windows\system\mcicda.drv**

Press [↵Enter] or click [OK]. You can now perform the steps given previously to install the driver.

PLAYING AN AUDIO CD

Once you have your system set up to play audio CDs, you simply run the audio CD application and then use its controls to play songs and other sounds. You may have to perform steps similar to the following:

1 Insert an audio disc in the CD-ROM player.

2 Run the CD-ROM audio player application that came with your CD-ROM drive. In Windows, double-click on its icon. In DOS, type the command used to run the application, and press [↵Enter]. The CD control panel appears.

CHAPTER 17

An audio CD
control panel

3 Click on the buttons as desired to pick a song, rewind, fast forward, or scan.

4 To stop the CD, click on the stop button.

MORE YOU CAN DO WITH SOUND AND CDS

- **Talk to your computer.** With a sound board, a microphone, and the right software, you can bark commands at your computer, such as "Save this file!" instead
of opening a menu or typing a command. The technology isn't perfect yet, but it
does a fair job.

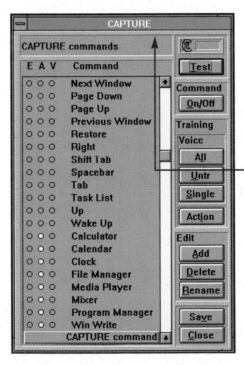

*SoundBlaster Pro comes
with VoiceAssist, an application that lets you control
your other software using
spoken commands.*

- **Photo albums on discs.** With a Kodak Photo CD compatible CD-ROM drive, you can have your photos placed on a CD when you have your film developed. Each CD can hold about 100 color photos. You can then view the photos on-screen, as shown here, or insert the files in your documents (for example, into a family newsletter).

You can keep your photos on a disc.

Greg Kopchak–It's All Relative Software

EXERCISE

If you have a sound board, a microphone, and Windows 3.1, you can record and play sound files. Here's how you do it:

1 Double-click on the [Accessories] icon.

2 Double-click on the [Sound Recorder] icon.

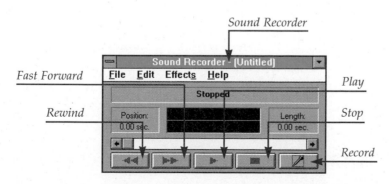

CHAPTER 17

3 Click on the Record button and start talking or making some other sound into the microphone.

4 Click on the Stop button when you're done.

5 Open the File menu and select Save.

6 Type a name for the file (no extension) in the File Name text box.

7 Click on the OK button.

8 Click on the Play button. Sound Recorder plays the sound.

If you don't have a microphone, Windows comes with a couple of sound files in the \WINDOWS directory that you can open and play. You can also use the options on the Effects menu to increase or decrease the volume and modify the sound in other ways.

CHAPTER DIGEST

CD-ROM Drive Minimum Requirements

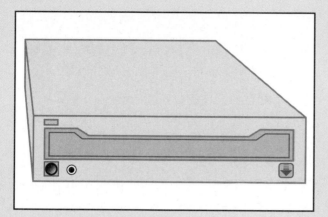

Transfer rate: 150Kbs/300Kbs

Double-speed or faster

Access time: 200ms

64Kb on-drive cache

MPC 2 compatible

CD-Audio

*Kodak Photo CD or
XA Mode 2 compatible*

*High Sierra and ISO-9660
compatible*

Sound Board Minimum Requirements

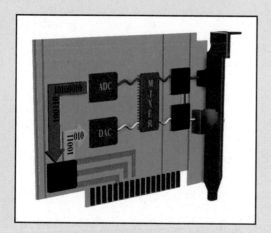

MPC 2 compatible

16-bit sound

Microphone input

MIDI stereo input

SoundBlaster or AdLib compatible

Volume control

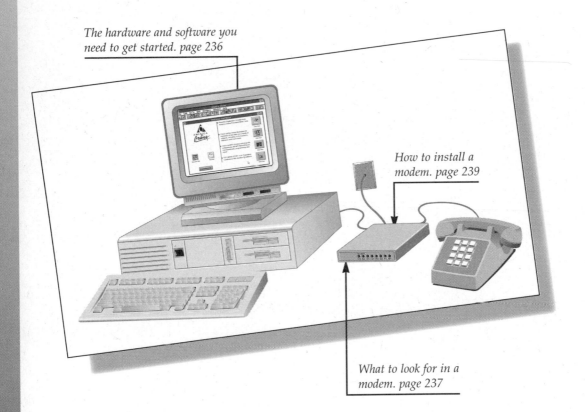

The hardware and software you need to get started. page 236

How to install a modem. page 239

What to look for in a modem. page 237

BUYING AND INSTALLING A MODEM

I n the last year or so, modems have become essential computing tools, enabling people to connect their computers to other computers using their phone lines. With a modem and the right software, you can connect to online information services, send and receive mail electronically, send and receive faxes, research topics, make flight reservations, shop, and even invest your money—all without leaving your desk. In this chapter, you'll learn how to choose a modem and install it. In the next chapter, you'll learn how to use a modem to do all these nifty activities.

WHAT IS A MODEM?

The term *modem* stands for MOdulator/DEModulator. To send information, the modem *modulates* (translates) the data into a form that can be sent through the phone lines. To receive information, the modem *demodulates* the incoming information, translating it into a form that your computer can understand. Modems even make it possible for two different types of computers to communicate. A person in Atlanta can use an IBM-compatible computer to call a Macintosh computer in Los Angeles, as long as each computer is connected to a modem.

WHAT YOU NEED TO GET STARTED

Before you can use your computer to connect to other computers, you need two items: the modem itself and software that enables the modem to perform a specific task. The software you need depends on what you want to do with the modem:

- **To connect to an online service**   To connect to an online service (such as PRODIGY, CompuServe, or America OnLine), you need to subscribe to the service. The service usually provides the software you need to get online. To try PRODIGY for free, call 1-800-PRODIGY (using your phone, not your modem). To try America OnLine for free, call 1-800-827-6364.

- **To send and receive faxes**   Not all modems are capable of sending and receiving faxes. You need a special fax modem, as explained later in this chapter. You also need special software, such as WinFax PRO, that helps you put together the cover sheet and files you want to fax.

- **To transfer files between two computers**   Telecommunications software enables you to connect to another computer and transfer files. Windows comes with a basic telecommunications application called Terminal. You can purchase better telecommunications applications, such as ProComm Plus or WinCOM.

- **To connect your home and office computers**   You can purchase a remote computing application that allows you to control your office computer from home and vice versa. However, make sure you have a speedy modem (9600bps or faster). Remote computing applications include pcANYWHERE and Carbon Copy.

- **To connect to the Internet**   The Internet is a huge network of networks. You can connect to the Internet by using an online information service, by subscribing to a special Internet service, or by connecting to a network that is part of the Internet. For details, see Chapter 19.

- **To set up your own voice mail system**   With a modem that can handle voice calls, and with special software, you can turn your computer into an answering machine.

- **To transfer files between a laptop and a desktop**   No modem required. To transfer files between two computers, you can connect the computers with a cable (serial or parallel) and use a file transfer application, such as LapLink or WINLYNX.

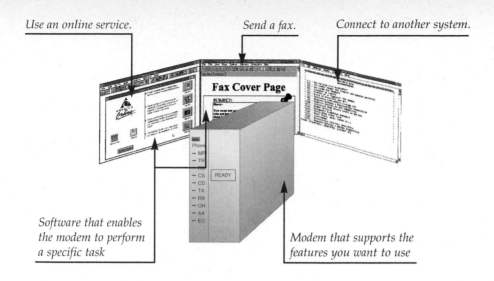

Use an online service. | *Send a fax.* | *Connect to another system.*

Fax Cover Page

Software that enables the modem to perform a specific task

Modem that supports the features you want to use

SHOPPING FOR A MODEM

Before you go shopping for a modem, you should understand the language of modem ads and some of the features available. Otherwise, you might end up purchasing an obsolete modem or paying for features you'll never use. To get some idea of how confusing modem shopping can be, read the following ad I lifted from my favorite computer catalog:

V.32bis External

The SupraFaxModem V.32bis features 14,400bps communications with up to 57,600bps throughput with another modem that supports both V.32bis and V.42bis data compression. And of course, it also maintains downward compatibility with millions of V.32, 2400, and 1200bps modems already in use. With any fax software that supports Class 1 or Class 2 fax commands, you'll be able to send and receive high-quality faxes without ever leaving your desk. Includes a status display with 25 different messages and DOS and Windows software.

If this ad makes your head spin, read the following list to learn how to translate it:

- **9600 or 14,400bps.** Bps stands for *bits per second*, a unit for measuring the speed at which the modem sends and receives data. Most online services offer 9600bps service, and you'll need a 9600bps modem (or faster) to take advantage of it. Don't buy a 2400bps modem. No matter how inexpensive the modem is, you will lose time and money in the long run.

- **Automatic fallback (downward compatibility).** In order to communicate effectively, both the calling and answering modems must work at the same speed. Most modems offer an automatic fallback feature that enables the faster modem to communicate at slower than maximum speeds.

- **Internal or external.** Internal modems are less expensive, take up less desk space (they plug into the inside of the system unit), and require only one connection (the phone line). External modems require a serial or COM port connection, and you have to plug them into a wall outlet, too. If you have an open expansion slot inside your computer, buy an internal modem.

- **Hayes-compatible.** Most modems are Hayes-compatible, meaning they understand Hayes commands. This is important because most modem applications use Hayes commands.

- **V.32 bis.** A modem standard that allows the modem to send and receive data at the same time.

- **V.42 bis.** An error correction, data compression standard used in modem communications. V.42 bis data compression allows more data to be transmitted at one time. For example, a modem with V.42 bis can send four times as much data per second as a modem without V.42 bis. However, both modems involved in the conversation must follow the same compression standard.

- **Throughput.** A measure of how much data a modem can transfer given its speed and data compression capability. For example, a throughput of 57,600bps means that when the modem is operating at maximum speed (say 14,400bps) using data compression (V.32 bis), the modem can transfer data at 57,600bps.

- **Fax send/receive.** Most modems offer fax send/receive features at no extra cost. However, make sure the fax modem is capable of both sending and receiving faxes. Also, make sure the fax modem supports Class 1 and Class 2 Group 3 fax machines. Nearly 90 percent of faxes in use today are the Group 3 variety.

Tip: If you have a laptop or notebook computer that has a PCMCIA expansion slot, you can purchase a fax modem that is about the size of a credit card that slides easily into the expansion slot.

- **Voice support.** If you plan to turn your computer into an answering machine, you need a modem that can handle incoming voice calls.

Do You Need Another Phone Jack for the Modem?

If you already have a phone jack near the computer, but your phone is plugged into it, you don't need to install an additional jack. Most modems come with two phone jacks: one that connects the modem to the incoming phone line and another one into which you can plug your phone. When you are not using the modem, you use the phone as you nor-

Tip: Keep in mind that most residential phone lines can handle only one call at a time. If you plan to use your modem and phone at the same time on a regular basis, you may want to call the phone company and have a second phone line installed.

mally would. If your modem doesn't have two phone jacks, you can purchase a split phone connector from an electronics store. The split phone connector allows you to plug both your phone and your modem into the same jack.

Installing a Modem

Modem installation varies depending on whether you are installing an internal or external modem. With an internal modem, you must take the cover off the system unit, plug the modem card into an open expansion slot, and then connect the phone cable to the card, as shown here. If you are a new user, seek help from a more experienced person, or follow the precautions and instructions that came with the modem.

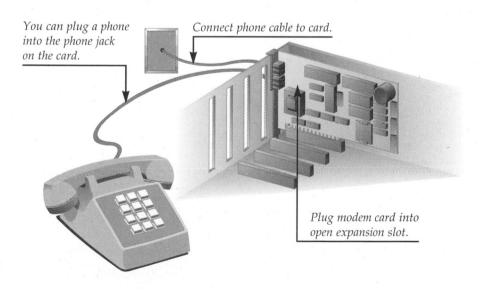

You can plug a phone into the phone jack on the card.

Connect phone cable to card.

Plug modem card into open expansion slot.

Just about anyone can install an external modem; you only make three connections. Before connecting anything, turn the computer off. First, use a serial cable to connect the modem to a serial port on the system unit. Second, plug the modem's power cord into an electrical outlet or your power strip. Finally, connect the modem to a phone jack; this is just like plugging in a phone.

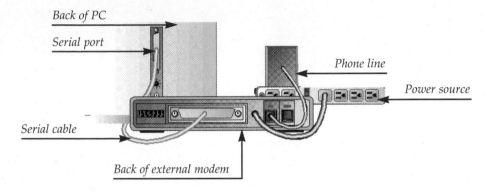

INSTALLING YOUR MODEM SOFTWARE

Most modems come with basic software that allows you to use the modem to perform specific tasks. For example, if you purchased a fax modem, it probably came with software for sending and receiving faxes. Before you can use your modem, you must install this or comparable software. If you have an external modem, make sure the modem is turned on before you install any modem software. The installation or setup program may need to use the modem to complete the process or test for a successful installation.

You install a modem application in much the same way that you install any other application: start the install or setup program, and then follow the instructions that appear on-screen. In most cases, the program will ask you to specify the brand name and type of modem and its location and speed. If you are installing the software for an online service, the installation process will be slightly more complicated (refer to Chapter 19 for details).

Select a fax/modem for WinFax PRO 4.0 to use. If your fax/modem does not appear on the fax/modem Model list, choose the Generic entry at the top of the list.

Fax/Modem

Port : COM2   Test...

Type : Class1

Model : Practical Peripherals, Inc. - PM 14400 FXSA

Init : AT&F1&K3S7=55\

Reset : ATZ\

Continue   Exit Setup   Help

The installation program normally asks you to specify the COM port and modem type.

COM PORT PROBLEMS

Although most modem installations are fairly simple, you may have trouble if you have two devices (for example, your mouse and modem) set up to use the same communications (COM) port. You may find that the modem cannot dial a number, or the application may display a message that no modem is installed. In either case, you will have to change the COM port setting for one of the devices. Changing the setting for the modem is usually easiest. You simply flip DIP (dual in-line package) switches to the desired COM port setting. Usually, the mouse is on COM1, so changing the modem COM port setting to COM2 fixes the problem.

After you change the COM port setting for the modem, you usually must specify that setting in the modem software, as well. Look on the menus for a Communications Settings option, and select the COM port setting that matches that of the modem.

OTHER MODEM SETTINGS YOU MAY NEED TO CHECK

If you are installing software for an online service, a fax application, or some other specific purpose, you don't have to worry about any other settings. The installation program will enter the required settings for you. However, if you are planning to connect your computer to your computer at work or to a friend or colleague's computer, make sure the following communications settings match those of the other computer:

- **Baud rate** The speed at which the two modems transfer data. The transfer can only be as fast as the slower of the two modems allows. Baud rate is commonly measured in bits per second (bps). You can often leave the baud rate setting high, and the modem will automatically choose a lower setting if it is necessary.

- **Parity** Tests the integrity of the data sent and received. Common setting is None or No Parity.

- **Data bits** Indicates the number of bits in each transmitted character. Common setting is Eight.

- **Stop bits** Indicates the number of bits used to signal the end of a character. Common setting is One bit.

- **Duplex** Tells the computer whether to send and receive data at the same time (Full), or send data or receive data but not both at the same time (Half). Common setting is Full.

To check these settings, search the application's menu system for an option called Communications, Settings, or Preferences. Selecting that command usually displays a dialog box like the one shown here.

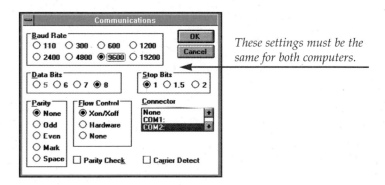

These settings must be the same for both computers.

DIALING OUT WITH A MODEM

Once your modem and software are set up, try to dial a phone number with your modem. Enter the command for dialing out or signing on, and then type the number as you would normally dial it. If you need to dial a number to get an outside line, make sure you type that number first, followed by a comma (to allow a pause before dialing the rest of the number). For example, you might call a local number by typing 9,555-5678.

The modem dials the number, connects with the other computer, and performs the required task or displays a screen that enables you to enter commands. The screen shown here is the one that appears when I use the Windows Terminal application to connect to the computer at the Indianapolis-Marion County Public Library.

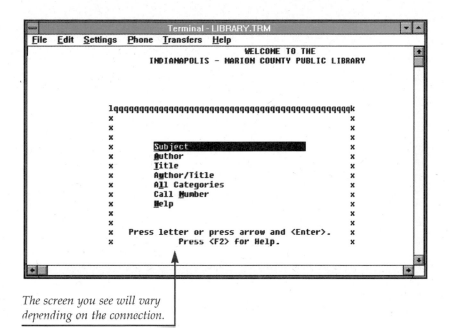

The screen you see will vary depending on the connection.

EXERCISE

The most difficult part of modem communications is buying the right modem. Try to decipher the following computer ad for yourself and answer the questions that follow it:

> **2400/9600 Super Fax/Modem $39.95**
> This internal 2400/9600 baud data/fax modem is Hayes compatible, offers V.42 bis data compression, and supports Class 1 and 2 fax commands with Group 3 fax machines.

Questions:

1 What is the maximum data transfer rate of the modem?

2 Can the modem both send and receive faxes?

3 Can the modem handle Hayes commands?

4 Can the modem communicate with most types of fax machines?

5 Can this modem be used for voice mail?

6 Is the price reasonable?

Answers:

1 2400bps. The 9600 in the ad refers only to the fax send and receive rate. If you connect to another computer or online service, this modem communicates at 2400bps maximum.

2 Yes. The modem can send and receive faxes.

3 Yes. The ad says that the modem is Hayes compatible.

4 Yes. Most fax machines are of the Group 3 variety.

5 Probably not. The ad does not specify whether the modem supports voice calls. You would have to ask to make sure.

6 No. At any price, a 2400bps modem is a bad buy.

CHAPTER DIGEST

Minimum Modem Requirements

9600bps

Automatic fallback or
downward compatibility

Hayes compatible

V.32 bis support

V.42 bis support

Fax send/receive Group
3 fax support

14,400 fax send/receive
speed

Installing an Internal Modem

Connect phone
cable to card.

You can plug a phone
into the phone jack on
the card.

Plug modem card into
open expansion slot.

Installing an External Modem

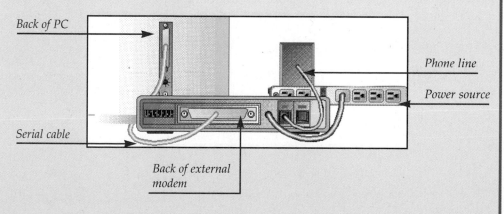

Back of PC

Serial cable

Back of external
modem

Phone line

Power source

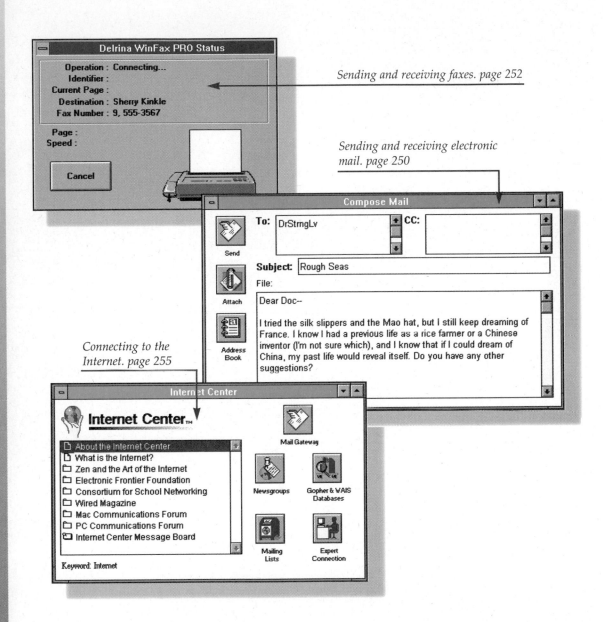

Sending and receiving faxes. page 252

Sending and receiving electronic mail. page 250

Connecting to the Internet. page 255

Delrina WinFax PRO Status

Operation : Connecting...
Identifier :
Current Page :
Destination : Sherry Kinkle
Fax Number : 9, 555-3567

Page :
Speed :

Cancel

Compose Mail

Send

To: DrStrngLv   CC:

Attach

Subject: Rough Seas

File:

Dear Doc--

I tried the silk slippers and the Mao hat, but I still keep dreaming of France. I know I had a previous life as a rice farmer or a Chinese inventor (I'm not sure which), and I know that if I could dream of China, my past life would reveal itself. Do you have any other suggestions?

Address Book

Internet Center

Internet Center™

About the Internet Center
What is the Internet?
Zen and the Art of the Internet
Electronic Frontier Foundation
Consortium for School Networking
Wired Magazine
Mac Communications Forum
PC Communications Forum
Internet Center Message Board

Mail Gateway

Newsgroups

Gopher & WAIS Databases

Mailing Lists

Expert Connection

Keyword: Internet

USING YOUR MODEM TO GET CONNECTED

O nce you have your modem installed, you can start using it to connect to other computers, information sources, and people. You can check the daily news, weather, and sports; send and receive mail; check job listings in your field; chat with other people all over the country; shop for clothes and other items; and do much more. In this chapter, you'll learn the basics of how to use your computer and modem to perform these common activities.

USING AN ONLINE SERVICE

If this is your first experience with modems, the best way to learn about them is to subscribe to an online service, such as PRODIGY, CompuServe, or America Online. When you subscribe to the service (usually for about 10 to 15 dollars a month), you get a program that enables you to connect locally to the service (assuming you live near a major city), and you get access to what the service offers.

*Connecting to
PRODIGY or
America Online*

*Sending and Receiving
E-mail*

Using the Internet

*Controlling Your Work
Computer from Home*

*Sending and Receiving
Faxes*

*Transferring Files
Between Computers*

Three Popular Services Compared

Most services charge a monthly fee that provides various degrees of access to the service, but they waive the first month's charge so you can try before you buy. The following list gives you a general idea of how the services compare.

- **PRODIGY** charges a flat monthly rate (about $15) that allows you to use the service as much as you want during the month and send up to 30 e-mail messages per month. Additional messages cost $.25 each. Special services (such as travel and financial services) also cost extra. PRODIGY is a family-oriented online service. Call 1-800-PRODIGY for a membership startup kit.

- **America Online** charges a flat rate (about $10) for five hours a month, and $3.50 for each additional hour at any time of the day or night. You can send as many e-mail messages as you like. America Online is an online information service for the Me generation. Call 1-800-827-6364 for a membership startup kit.

- **CompuServe** charges $8.95 for unlimited connect time to many basic services, including news, weather, and business information. Many services cost extra, and you are usually charged by the minute. E-mail charges vary depending on the length of the message and the speed of your modem. CompuServe also has a CB Simulator feature that enables you to chat with other people connected to the service. CompuServe has traditionally been considered more technical and business-oriented. To get started with CompuServe, get a startup kit at your local computer store. The kit costs about $25, but you get a $25 usage credit from CompuServe.

Starting Your Online Account

When you subscribe to an online service, you get a startup kit that includes the software you need to connect to the service, an account number and password, and documentation that teaches you how to get started. You install the software just as you install any new software—by running the installation or setup program on the first disk. (Refer to Chapters 6 to 8 for installation details.)

The installation program copies the necessary files to your hard disk and then asks you to specify which COM port and type of modem you are using. Some installations test the COM port and modem settings for you, and simply ask for your confirmation.

The installation program then uses the modem to dial a toll-free number that gives you access to local connections in many cities. By selecting a local number, you avoid any extra long-distance charges. Once you select a local number (and usually an alternate number, in case the first number is busy), the installation program disconnects from the toll-free connection.

CONNECTING AND DISCONNECTING

Once you have a local number to dial, you can sign on to the service and start using it. To sign on to PRODIGY or America Online, you simply click on an on-screen button. The service dials the local access number and then asks for your screen name (online nickname) and your password. With CompuServe, you must select a feature (for example, News or Mail) before you sign on; CompuServe then dials the local access number, connects to the service, and takes you immediately to that feature.

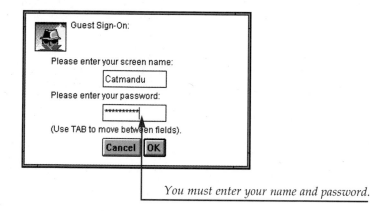

You must enter your name and password.

When you are done with the service, you hang up. You usually do this by opening the File menu and selecting Disconnect or Exit.

NAVIGATING THE SERVICE

Although each online service offers different tools for moving around in the service, the tools are very similar. Most services display buttons and menus that allow you to access commonly used features, such as mail, news, and games. In addition, you can use keywords to quickly access a feature. For example, on America Online, you can press Ctrl+G, type the name of the feature you want to use (News, Mail, Help), and press ↵Enter. On CompuServe, you can use keywords by pressing Ctrl+G (and on PRODIGY, you press F6).

Menu bar provides additional options   Button bar provides quick access to features

Click on a
feature to
go to it.

SENDING AND RECEIVING MAIL

All services allow you to exchange electronic mail (e-mail) with other users of the same service. To send an e-mail message, you enter the Create Mail command, type the name and address of the user to whom you want to send the message, and then click on ▣OK▣ or click the Send button. Your message is then sent to the storage area of the online service, where it is kept until your friend or colleague reads it.

> *Tip: On America OnLine, press* Ctrl+K, *type Help, and press* ↵Enter *to go to a free Help area. On CompuServe, press* Ctrl+G, *type Practice, and press* ↵Enter *to go to a practice area where you can get additional help.*

When someone sends you mail, the mail waits in your personal mailbox until you get around to reading it. When you sign on, a message or other indicator appears on-screen showing that you have mail. You can then select the Get Mail command or click on the Mail button to view a list of the waiting messages. Double-click on a message to read it.

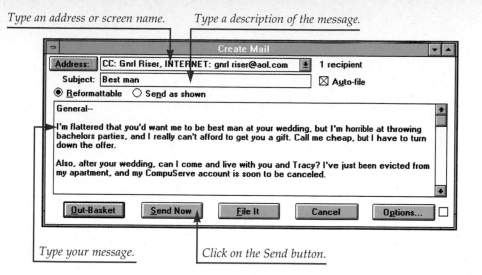

Type an address or screen name.   *Type a description of the message.*

Type your message.   *Click on the Send button.*

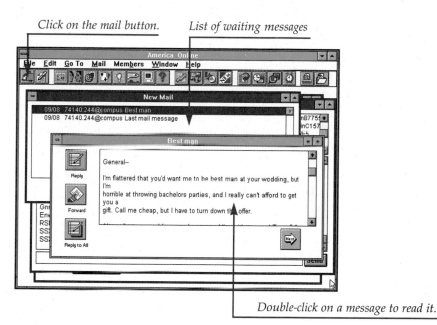

Click on the mail button.   *List of waiting messages*

Double-click on a message to read it.

CHATTING WITH OTHER MEMBERS

If you don't like waiting for mail, you can converse with your friends and colleagues on the service. You pick a room in which 20 or so people are hanging out and start typing. Your messages appear on the screens of the other people in the room, and their messages appear on your screen. If you prefer to talk in private with one or more other users, you can create your own private room and invite other users to join you.

CHAPTER 19

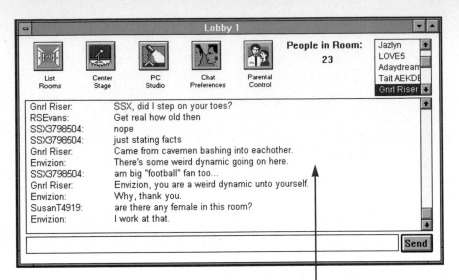

In chat rooms, you can converse with other members.

Sharing Common Interests

Online services started as computerized community centers where people could share their ideas, problems, and solutions. This tradition is still alive in online *forums* and *boards*. You can find a forum or board for almost any special interest category—from gardening and parenting to computers and automobiles. If you have a question, you simply post a message on the board. In a day or so, other members will post answers in an attempt to help you out. You can get free legal advice, find information on how to grow prize roses, and even get help finding long-lost relatives.

> *Tip: If you have children who might be using the service, you must be careful with mail and chat rooms. Although most service members attempt to be civil, some members may be a bit unruly.*

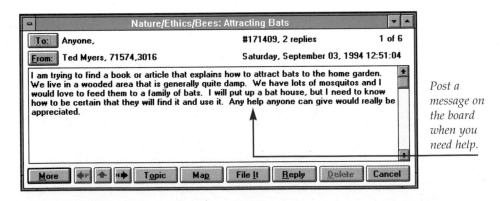

Post a message on the board when you need help.

DOWNLOADING AND UPLOADING FILES

Online services provide a convenient method for exchanging computer files, freeware (free programs), and shareware (programs you can try for free and then pay for later). You can copy files from the service (download files) or copy files to the service (upload files). In either case, the procedure is fairly easy. You specify the file you want to download or upload, then enter the required command. The modem then transfers the file as specified.

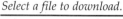
Select a file to download.

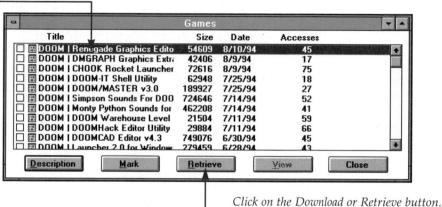

Click on the Download or Retrieve button.

Many files you download (especially program files) are in a format that you cannot immediately use. The files are compressed (usually using a program called PKZip or StuffIt), for the sake of faster file transfer. To use the file(s) (whose names usually end in .ZIP), you must decompress them. You can download the program you need to decompress files from any online service.

CHANGING YOUR PASSWORD

It's a good idea to change your membership password every month or so, to prevent other users from using your account and any account information, such as a credit card number. Changing the password is easy. You sign on as you normally would, enter the Change Password command (you can use the keyword Password), type your current password, and then type the new password. Use a password that is easy for you to remember but difficult for anyone else to guess.

CHECKING YOUR BILL

If you subscribe to a service that charges extra for e-mail or connect time, you should check your bill regularly. On CompuServe and America Online, you can use the keyword Billing to check your current charges.

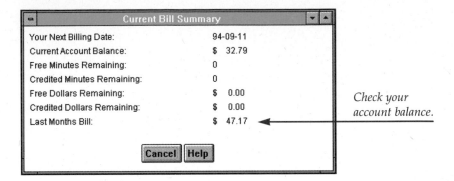

Check your account balance.

SENDING AND RECEIVING FAXES

A fax modem and the required fax software can transform your computer into a fax machine. With the right application (for example, WinFax PRO), sending a fax is as simple as printing a document. You use your favorite Windows word processing application to create the document you want to fax, then you enter the Print command. Select WinFax PRO as your printer. WinFax PRO then displays a dialog box asking you to specify the name and fax number of the person to whom you are sending the fax. Enter this information and an optional fax cover page message, then click on OK. WinFax dials the number, connects with the remote fax machine, and transmits your document.

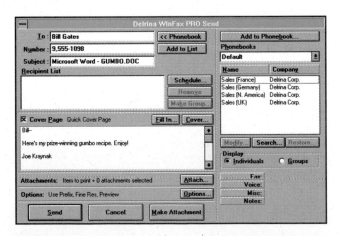

To receive faxes, you run WinFax PRO and turn Automatic Receive mode on. When the remote fax machine calls, WinFax PRO answers the call, connects to the remote fax machine, and receives the incoming fax. You can set up WinFax PRO to automatically print all incoming faxes, making it act like a true fax machine. In addition, WinFax PRO saves the received fax, so you can mark it up, add comments, and send it back to the sender or pass it on to another person.

CONNECTING TO THE INTERNET

With the aid of Vice President Al Gore, the Internet has become well-known. The idea behind this vast network is that everyone in the country (and the world) will be connected via computers, allowing people to exchange information, develop and market products, and communicate more freely. If you're wondering why the Internet gets so much press, and why so many people spend so much time playing with it, here are two good reasons:

- **The Internet is a great research tool.** Because the Internet connects your computer to university and government computers, it gives you access to unclassified government documents, electronic books and magazines, research materials (such as the *Reader's Guide to Periodical Literature*), and other information that may be stored on various networks.

- **The Internet provides connections with other users.** Because the Internet connects the various online services in addition to government, business, and educational networks, it provides a vast resource of people you can talk with. You can post messages in special interest areas, read messages, and even send electronic mail to anyone on the Internet (assuming you know the person's e-mail address).

FINDING A WAY ONTO THE INTERNET

Before you can navigate the Internet, you have to find an entrance ramp, a way onto the Internet. You have several options:

E-mail gateway   Most online services (America Online, PRODIGY, and so on) provide an Internet connection called a mail gateway, which allows you to send and receive electronic mail. When you send mail, you type your letter and then enter the person's online mail address. Here's what an Internet address might look like:

joekraynak@aol.com

Online service connection   Most online services are currently developing ways to connect their subscribers directly to the Internet to offer more than just e-mail. The Delphi service already offers access to the Internet and provides the best way for a beginning user to connect and get started. America Online and other services offer basic tools for searching the Internet for specific information.

Permanent connection   If your company or university has a network that is part of the Internet, and your computer is connected to the network, you have access to the Internet through the network. This is the least expensive way to go. Your network administrator can tell you if you're connected.

Special Internet service   One of the most practical ways to connect to the Internet is through a special service. You use your modem to connect to the service's computer, which is part of the Internet. Ask your local computer store or computer user group for a list of service providers in your area.

WHAT TO EXPECT

To sign on to the Internet, you generally use your modem to dial the phone number of your Internet connection. The process for navigating the Internet depends on the connection you have. If you use a typical online service, it probably offers several Internet tools for sending mail and doing research. For example, if you go to the Internet area using America Online, you'll get the screen shown here.

If you sign on using the Delphi service, you don't get the fancy welcome screens that you get with most online services. At best, you get a menu of options that can help you get started. To select a menu option, you type the first few letters of the option's name and press ⏎Enter.

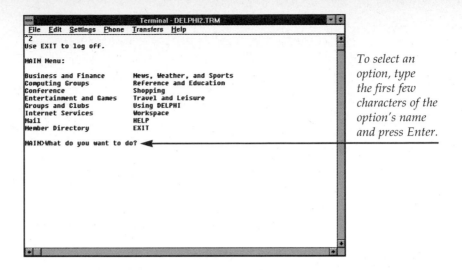

To select an option, type the first few characters of the option's name and press Enter.

In addition to the crude menu systems that you can use to stumble around the Internet, there are some other tools you can purchase separately (or download) to help you search for information across the Internet. A couple of the more popular tools include:

- **Gopher** A play off the phrase "go for," Gopher is a menu system that helps you access data from an Internet server (a network computer to which you connect). When you connect to an Internet server, the Gopher accesses the server's index and uses it to create a menu.

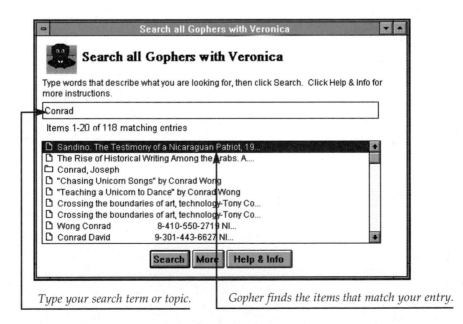

Type your search term or topic.   *Gopher finds the items that match your entry.*

- **Telnet**   A program that lets you connect to other computers anywhere in the world (assuming that computer system lets you in).

- **Archie**   A tool you use to find a file when you know the file's name. Archies (there are more than one) are file indexes that contain lists of files along with their locations (on the Internet network) where you can get those files.

- **WAIS (wide area information server)**   A computerized bloodhound that can sniff out information in hundreds of databases on the Internet. Because the Internet is packed with information about everything from weather reports to pharmaceuticals, you need some way to quickly search for specific information. WAIS does the searching for you.

Tip: To make World-Wide Web easier to use, obtain an Internet program called Mosaic. This program provides a push-button interface for gaining access to popular Internet features.

- **World-Wide Web (W3 or WWW)**   An Internet tool that lets you skip around from article to article till you find what you need. Each article contains one or more key terms that cross reference other articles. Key terms may be underlined or followed by a bracketed number, such as [1] or [2]. When you select a key term, its article is displayed on-screen.

LEARNING MORE ABOUT THE INTERNET

The Internet is too large and complex to cover in such a brief section. However, if you want to learn more about connecting to the Internet and navigating it, try the following books:

10 Minute Guide to the Internet provides instructions on connecting to the Internet; reading, writing, and sending e-mail; joining Internet news groups; downloading files; and using the various information hunting tools.

The Complete Idiot's Guide to the Internet explains in plain English how to connect to and navigate the Internet. This book includes a disk that contains Internet tools and information.

CONNECTING TO BULLETIN BOARD SYSTEMS

If you don't want to pay a subscription price to an online service, and you really don't want to venture onto the Internet, you may be able to connect to a local bulletin board system (BBS) at no charge or for a fraction of the cost of the other options. Don't expect to get the fancy features of a costly online service, but the local bulletin board may let you share files with other computer users, make valuable local contacts, and get help for your computer woes. To find out about local bulletin boards, call around to various computer dealers. If they don't know of any local bulletin boards, they may know of some computer clubs you can ask. You may even want to set up your own bulletin board.

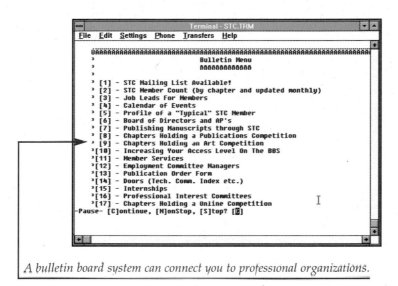

A bulletin board system can connect you to professional organizations.

CONTROLLING YOUR WORK COMPUTER FROM HOME

With a remote computing program and a modem, you can connect your home and office computers and use one to control the other. For example, you can use your home computer to run a program installed on your office computer and edit a document stored on its hard disk. Or, if you forgot to bring a file home to work on, you can use your modem to call your office computer and download (copy) the file from its hard disk to your home computer.

To take advantage of remote computing, the same remote computing program must be running on both computers. These programs include Carbon Copy, pcAnywhere, and Commute. The computer you want to call must be turned on and set up to wait for your call. You can then call the remote computer, establish the connection, and start using it.

More You Can Do with a Modem

In this chapter, you learned about some of the obvious things you can do with a modem. The following list reveals some not-so-obvious activities:

- **Shop from your home.** With a modem, an online service, and a credit card, you can do all your Christmas shopping without leaving your keyboard.

- **Make travel plans.** You can connect to an online travel agency and book your own flights.

- **Take college courses.** Take a correspondence course using your computer.

Exercise

If you're hesitant about modem communications or online services, take the plunge:

1 Borrow a 2400 bps external modem. You can usually find someone who has an obsolete 2400 bps modem junked in a desk drawer.

2 Connect the modem as explained in Chapter 18.

3 Pick up the telephone, call PRODIGY (1-800-PRODIGY), and ask them to send you a free membership kit. Get the Windows version if you have Microsoft Windows on your computer—it's easier.

4 When you get your kit, turn on your computer and modem.

5 Follow the directions that come with PRODIGY to install the program, set up your modem, and sign on to the service.

6 Play around until you figure out how it works. You'll catch on fast.

7 If you don't like the service, be sure to call PRODIGY and cancel your membership before your one-month free trial period runs out.

CHAPTER DIGEST

Signing On to an Online Service

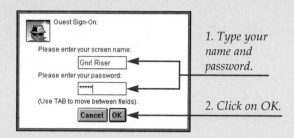

1. *Type your name and password.*

2. *Click on OK.*

Sending E-mail

1. *Select Send Mail button.*

2. *Type person's address or screen name.*

3. *Type message description.*

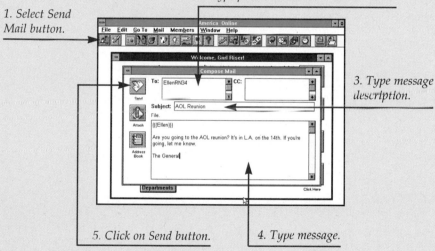

5. *Click on Send button.*

4. *Type message.*

Reading E-mail

Click on Get Mail button.

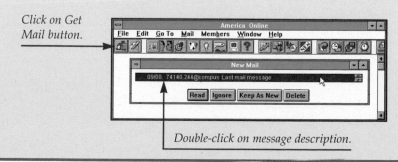

Double-click on message description.

Selecting a good monitor. *page 267*

Shopping for a multimedia PC. *page 269*

Telling the difference between microprocessors. *page 264*

Picking the right printer. *page 270*

What to look for in a hard disk drive. *page 265*

Getting enough memory. *page 265*

BUYING A NEW COMPUTER

T he ultimate goal of computer shopping is to find the most computer for the least amount of money. The concept is easy enough, but as you flip through the Sunday newspaper's sales inserts and wander around a few computer stores, reality hits: finding the perfect computer is sort of like searching for the Holy Grail.

However unachievable the goal might seem, if you understand the sales language, the options, and the standards, you can make a fairly well-educated choice. In this chapter, you'll learn all you need to know before setting out on your quest.

MAC OR PC? DESKTOP OR PORTABLE?

Before you start trying to decipher computer ads, you should make some general decisions about the type of computer you want. Do you want a PC or a Macintosh? Do you want the computer to sit on a desk, or do you want to be able to tote it along on trips?

The biggest question is whether you want a PC or a Mac. And the most obvious answer is to get the computer with which you have the most experience. If you have a Mac at work or you have kids who

Differences Between a Macintosh and a PC

Making Sure You Get Enough RAM

How to Avoid Obsolete Equipment

Picking the Right Monitor

What to Look for in a Laptop or Notebook Computer

Making Sure You Can Expand Your System

use Macs at school, a Macintosh computer is probably the best choice. It is easy to use, and is excellent for education, graphics, sound, and music. If you have more experience with PCs, get a PC. PCs typically offer more power for the same price, and enable you to use a wide variety of relatively inexpensive software.

The answer to the second question (whether you should get a desktop or portable computer) may have more to do with what you can afford. Portable computers offer less memory, are slower, and offer less disk space than comparably priced desktop models. In addition, portable computers require batteries, and usually do not offer CD players, sound boards, speakers, and other equipment you may find essential. In other words, if you don't need to lug your computer around with you, a desktop model is the wisest choice.

Shopping for a Modern Microprocessor

The microprocessor is the computer's brain. It sets up and controls the communication network that is your computer. Processor names are usually numbers, such as 80386 or 80486, and are often abbreviated as 386 or 486. The chip label, which is printed on the chip and usually on the front of the system unit, tells you three things:

- **Chip number** The chip number (for example, 486) tells you how relatively advanced the chip is. A 286 is prehistoric; 386 is on its way out; 486 is a good bargain; and the Pentium is the hot new chip. For a Macintosh, 68030s are on their way out; 68040s are a good bargain; and the PowerPC is cutting edge.

Tip: To get the best bargain in a chip, find out what the newest chip is and then shop for its next younger sibling. For example, now that Pentium chips are cutting edge in PCs, 486 chips are selling cheap. PowerPCs for Macs are the newest technology, so you can get a powerful 68040 chip at a reasonable price.

- **Chip speed** Chip speed is measured in megahertz (pronounced "MEG-a-hurts"). The higher the number, the faster the chip processes data. But be careful: a 25MHz 486 processes data faster than a 33MHz 386, because the 486 is more advanced. In general, compare speeds only between chips that have the same number.

- **Chip type** The chip number may be followed by an abbreviation, such as SX or DX. DX is a step up from the SX chip. Usually, the SX chip is a scaled-down version of the DX; for example, the 486SX is a 486DX without a math coprocessor. The DX2 operates at twice the speed of a DX; for example, a 33MHz DX2 has an effective speed of 66MHz. For portable computers, SL is commonly added to the chip type, indicating that the chip is specially designed for portable computing.

Recommended chip type:
486 or Pentium for PCs
68040 or PowerPC for Macs

MEMORY: HOW MUCH IS ENOUGH?

Today's operating systems and applications can barely function without at least 4 megabytes of RAM. Many applications, especially multimedia programs, need 8 megabytes. If you do a great deal of work with graphics, video, or sound, get at least 16 megabytes. Whatever amount you decide on, make sure you can add memory up to 32 megabytes.

Minimum memory: 4 megabytes
Recommended memory: 8 megabytes

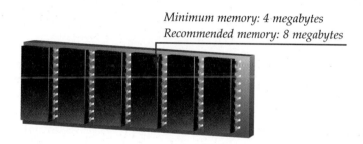

Some computers come with a RAM *cache* (pronounced "cash"). This is a set of fast memory chips that stand between the normal (slower) RAM and the microprocessor. The RAM cache stores frequently used instructions and data, so the microprocessor can get the instructions and data more quickly. One reason a 486 chip is faster than a 386 is that a 486 has a built-in cache.

A HARD DISK: HOW BIG? HOW FAST?

The size of a hard disk is measured in megabytes (about a million bytes or a million characters). A small hard disk is about 100 megabytes. Large hard disks can be over 500 megabytes. The size you need depends on the number of programs you want to run, the size of each program, and how much space your data files take up. Make sure you get a hard disk that can store at least 200 megabytes.

When shopping for a hard disk, don't focus just on size. Compare speeds as well. Speed is measured in two ways: access time and transfer rate. *Access times* are measured in milliseconds (the lower the number, the faster the drive). Good access times are between 15 ms and 20 ms. The *transfer rate* is a measure of how much information the drive can transfer from the disk to your computer's memory in a second. A good rate is between 500 and 600 kilobytes per second. (Here, the higher the number, the faster the drive.)

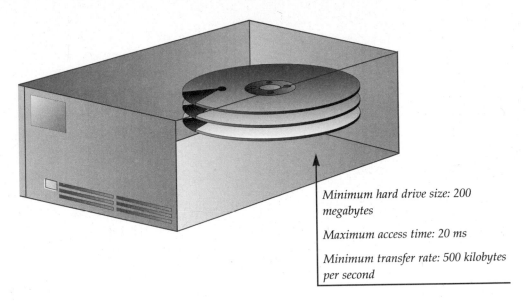

Minimum hard drive size: 200 megabytes

Maximum access time: 20 ms

Minimum transfer rate: 500 kilobytes per second

FLOPPY DISK DRIVE SIZE AND CAPACITY

A computer should have at least one floppy disk drive so you can transfer programs and data files from floppy disks to your hard disk. When considering floppy drives, look at size and capacity:

Disk size   Most new computers come with a single 3.5" floppy disk drive. This should be sufficient unless you use 5.25" disks to share files with friends or colleagues or if you have some programs on 5.25" disks. 5.25" drives are becoming obsolete, so don't get a computer that has only a 5.25" drive.

Capacity   New computers come with high-capacity drives. Because they can use both high- and low-capacity disks, there's no reason to get a low-capacity drive.

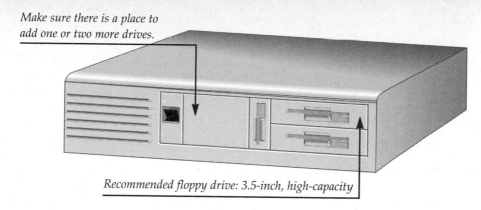

Make sure there is a place to add one or two more drives.

Recommended floppy drive: 3.5-inch, high-capacity

MONITOR AND DISPLAY ADAPTER

When you shop for a monitor, pretend you are shopping for a TV. You want the picture to be big and the image to be clear. In addition to those obvious points, look for the following:

Color   Most monitors for desktop computers come in color.

Size   Most monitors measure 14" or 15" diagonally. Try to get a 15" monitor, even if you have to pay an extra $100 or so. A 17" is an even better choice, if you can afford it.

SVGA or VGA?   VGA monitors are quickly becoming obsolete, because they display photos and other detailed graphics poorly. Insist on an SVGA monitor.

Dot pitch   Dot pitch is the space between the dots that make up the display: .28mm is good, .39mm is fair, .52mm is bad.

Non-interlaced   Look for a non-interlaced monitor. Interlaced monitors have an imperceptible flash that can be hard on your eyes. Non-interlaced monitors don't flash.

Tilt/swivel base   You'll want to adjust your monitor for comfort, so be sure the base can be adjusted easily.

Flat screen   Most monitor tubes are curved, making them more susceptible to glare. Look for a flat screen.

Anti-glare   Some monitors are built to prevent glare. With other monitors, you have to purchase a special anti-glare screen that fits over the monitor, but these can be cumbersome.

Swedish MPR II low-emissions standard   If you're worried that the low-level emissions coming out of your PC might cause health problems, make sure the monitor meets the Swedish MPR II low-emissions standards.

> *Tip: Many computer stores advertise low prices by not including the monitor in the price of the computer. Make sure you figure in this cost when comparing prices.*

Once you have the monitor problem solved, you need to focus your attention on the display adapter into which you plug the monitor. The adapter type (SVGA or VGA) should match the monitor type. In addition, the adapter should come with sufficient *video memory* (at least 1 megabyte) to help the adapter update the screen image more quickly.

GETTING ONLINE WITH A FAX MODEM

A year ago, a fax modem was an optional device. Now it is essential. Make sure the modem can transmit data and faxes at 9600 bps or faster. Many systems now offer a 2400/9600 data/fax modem, or a 9600/2400 fax/data modem. Both of these devices are obsolete, transferring data at only 2400 bps. Insist on a 9600/9600 fax/modem or more commonly a 9600/14400 data/fax modem.

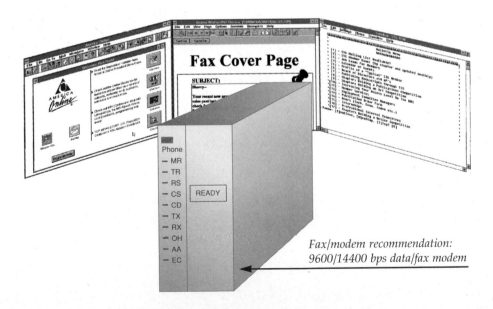

Fax/modem recommendation:
9600/14400 bps data/fax modem

CD-ROM Drive and Sound Board

If you think you may be able to do without the CD-ROM for now, think again. Last Christmas, computer stores were packed with CD-ROM hungry people. They were all buying multimedia upgrade kits (for $600–$800) to add a CD-ROM drive and sound board to their computers, and they were all worried about how to do it and whether they could even use the kits with their computers. If you buy a multimedia PC, you pay less for the CD-ROM capability, and you don't have to worry about installing it yourself. Here's what you should look for:

- **Double-speed CD-ROM drive or faster.** Slower CD-ROM drives cannot access the vast amounts of data stored on a CD fast enough. Refer to Chapter 17 for more details about what to look for in a CD-ROM drive.

- **16-bit stereo sound card with speakers.** Many computers come with a CD-ROM drive but with no sound board. To hear the CD sounds, you have to plug some dinky headphones into the CD-ROM drive. Get the sound card and speakers.

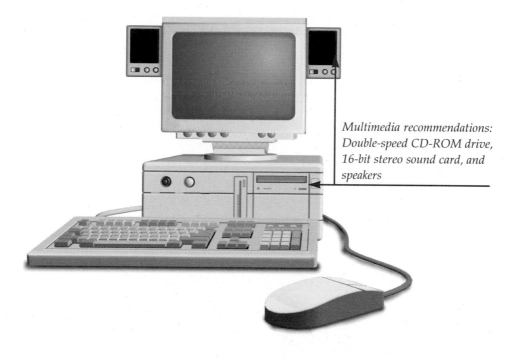

Multimedia recommendations: Double-speed CD-ROM drive, 16-bit stereo sound card, and speakers

Keyboards and Mice

Keyboards look different when they have different arrangements and numbers of keys, but there's not much difference between them; they all perform the same tasks. The important thing is how the keys feel to you. Some keys click when you press them, some offer little resistance, and some just feel funny. Buy a keyboard that feels comfortable.

In addition to a keyboard, make sure the computer comes with a mouse. With today's applications, you can't get around without one. Also make sure the mouse feels right to you. I recently worked with a mouse that was more like an exercise machine for my index finger. Make sure you can click without too much effort.

Printer Included?

The price of a computer rarely includes the price of a printer, so you usually purchase that separately. For low-cost printing, look for a dot-matrix printer. For affordable quality, check out inkjet printers. For high quality and speed, laser printers are the best choice. When comparing printer prices, consider the price of the printer and its consumables. Consumables are office supplies (ink ribbons, toner cartridges, paper) that you use up during printing.

Printer Type	Price Range	Consumables	Output Quality	Speed	Paper Handling
Dot-matrix	$150–$500	1/2–2 cents per page	180–360 dpi	1 4 ppm 80–450 cps	Tractor continuous form
Inkjet or Bubblejet	$250–$600	3–10 cents per page	300–360 dpi	2–4 ppm	Sheet feeder tray
Laser	$650–$3000	3–7 cents per page	300–1000 dpi	4–10 ppm	Sheet feeder tray

* dpi stands for dots per inch
cps stands for characters per second
ppm stands for pages per minute

Software Included?

Some dealers include the cost of the operating system in the price they quote you; others don't. (Most PCs come with DOS and Microsoft Windows, and most Macs come with System 7.1.) If the computer does not come with an operating system, you won't be able to use it.

> **Tip:** Don't purchase a computer solely because it comes with a lot of freebies. Often, dealers will bundle a bunch of software with a computer to sucker the buyer into purchasing an obsolete computer.

Many dealers also offer free applications with a computer, including a word processor, spreadsheet, and graphics application. If you purchase a computer with a CD-ROM drive, the dealer usually throws in a CD-ROM encyclopedia, a game, and a few other tidbits. Consider these extras when comparing the prices of two comparable computers.

Energy Smart Green Computers

As you shop for a computer, you may encounter dealers offering "green PCs," and you may wonder why they don't look green. The "green" label marks the PC as meeting the U.S. Environmental Protection Agency's criteria for its Energy Star program. To meet these criteria, the computer must consume no more than 90 watts (30 for the system unit, 30 for the monitor, and 30 for the printer) when not in sleep mode (not in use). Some computer manufacturers go even further, making their computers out of recycled plastic, and being careful about the waste materials produced during manufacturing.

Planning for Expansion

After you pay $2,000 for a computer, the last thing you want to think about is spending more money to make it better. Therefore, when you purchase a computer, you should think ahead. The following sections list some of the things you should consider.

Adding Internally with Expansion Boards

Every part of a computer plugs into a big circuit board called the *motherboard*. The motherboard contains several *expansion slots* that enable you to increase the capabilities of your system by plugging in expansion boards (or cards). For example, you can plug a sound board into the slot so you can connect speakers and a microphone, or add an internal modem to your computer by plugging it into one of the slots. Make sure you get a computer that has at least four open expansion slots.

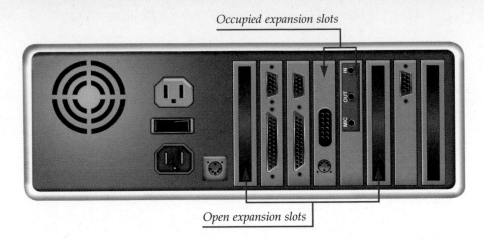

Occupied expansion slots

Open expansion slots

DRIVE BAYS: FOR FLOPPY DRIVES OR CD-ROM

Some computers come with only one floppy drive, but they contain additional *drive bays* so you can add drives later (for example, a CD-ROM drive, another floppy drive, or a tape backup unit). Look for a computer with at least three bays: one for a 3 1/2" drive, one for a CD-ROM drive, and one for an optional drive.

ADDING MEMORY TO YOUR SYSTEM

Knowing that you can add memory to your computer later is not enough; find out what it takes to add the memory. You should be able to add memory in 1-megabyte units by plugging chips (or *simms*, single in-line memory modules) into the mother-board (this costs about 70 bucks per megabyte). If you have to buy a memory board and then add chips, you may end up paying over $100 per megabyte, and the memory usually won't be as fast.

ON THE ROAD WITH LAPTOPS

More and more users are opting for the portability of laptops (small), notebooks (small-er), and subnotebooks (smallest). Laptop computers enable you to work anywhere and keep your information with you at all times. But what makes one laptop better than another? Here is a list of things to look for:

- **Weight**   Keep in mind that you'll be carrying this laptop around with you. Get the lightest laptop you can afford (4–8 pounds). In the laptop arena, the light-weights win.

- **Display**   Laptops generally offer three types of displays: gas plasma, liquid crystal (LCD), and active matrix. Gas plasma screens can crack if they freeze. Liquid crystal screens are the most popular and affordable (make sure you get a backlit screen). Active matrix screens produce the clearest picture, but they are more expensive.

- **CPU**   Most laptop computers come with 386SL or 486SL chips. The SL means they consume less energy than do comparable chips in desktop computers. With these energy savers, you can use the computer for longer intervals between charges.

- **Hard drive**   Hard drives on laptop computers are usually smaller than those on desktops. A 210 megabyte hard drive is considered large.

- **Battery**   Look for a laptop with a nickel metal-hydride battery or nickel cadmium battery. Find out how long it takes to charge the battery, how many hours you can operate the laptop between charges, and how many times you can charge the battery. Also, make sure you get the AC adapter you need to recharge.

- **Keyboard**   The last thing you'll think about when shopping for a laptop is the keyboard. However, the keyboard and display are the two things you'll use most, so give them a good test. Make sure the keys aren't too close together for your hands, and that they feel "right" when you type.

- **Trackball**   If you want to run Windows applications on your laptop, make sure it comes with a trackball for pointing and clicking. Also make sure you like the location of the trackball, or get an adjustable trackball.

- **Floppy drive**   If you have to swap files between your laptop and desktop, or exchange files with a colleague, make sure the laptop has one floppy drive.

- **PCMCIA expansion slot**   The newest feature in portable computing is the PCMCIA expansion slot. This slot enables you to insert credit-card sized expansion boards into the system to add devices such as a fax/modem, CD-ROM drive connection, tape backup system, network card, or even a hard disk drive. You simply pop one card out and another one in, depending on what you want to do.

> *Tip: If you can't decide between a desktop and portable computer, consider purchasing a portable computer with a docking station. To use the portable as a desktop computer, you slide it into the docking station, with which you can connect the portable computer to an SVGA monitor, CD-ROM drive, and other desktop equipment.*

CHAPTER 20

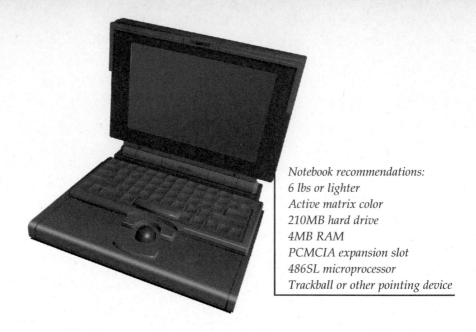

Notebook recommendations:
6 lbs or lighter
Active matrix color
210MB hard drive
4MB RAM
PCMCIA expansion slot
486SL microprocessor
Trackball or other pointing device

EXERCISE

Get the Sunday newspaper and find a computer ad. Use the following checklist to see if the computer offers the following essential features:

____ 200 megabyte hard drive or larger

____ 8MB or more of RAM (memory)

____ 14″ SVGA color monitor

____ 1MB or more video memory

____ Double-speed CD-ROM drive

____ 16-bit stereo sound card with speakers

____ 9600/14400 data/fax modem

CHAPTER DIGEST

The Least You Should Get

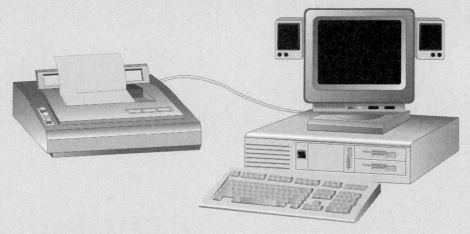

80486 microprocessor (for a PC)
68040 microprocessor (for a Mac)

8 megabytes RAM expandable to
32 megabytes

200 megabyte hard drive

Double-speed CD-ROM drive

3.5" high-capacity floppy drive

9600/14400 data/fax modem

SVGA monitor and display adapter
with 1MB video memory

16-bit stereo sound card with
speakers4 open expansion slots

Inkjet printer

3 drive bays

Mouse

Protecting your disks and files. page 281

Cleaning a monitor. page 280

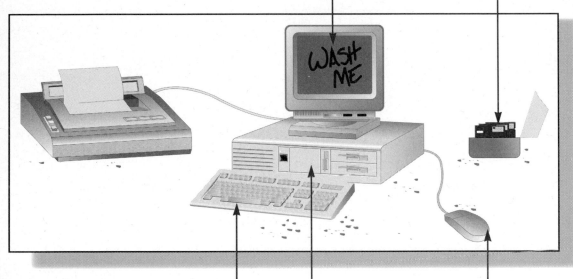

Vacuuming a keyboard. page 280

Cleaning a mouse. page 280

Maintaining a hard disk. page 281

KEEPING YOUR COMPUTER IN TIP-TOP SHAPE

Y our computer, the applications it contains, and the files you create are all a big investment of your time and money. To protect this investment, you need to perform some basic maintenance on both your equipment and data. In this chapter, you'll learn how to clean your computer, protect against data loss, and prevent your files from being infected by computer viruses.

FINDING A PLACE FOR YOUR COMPUTER

One of the first actions you can take to ensure that your computer lives a long and healthy life is to house it in a good location. Select a place that meets the following requirements:

- **Cool, dry, and out of direct sunlight.** If it gets too hot around your computer, it may overheat, which burns out some of its circuits and costs you money.

- **Clean and dust free**. Don't set your computer next to the clothes dryer, where lint can pour through every opening.

- **Near a stable outlet.** Choose an outlet that is on a separate circuit from appliances that draw a lot of current, such as clothes dryers and toasters. These appliances cause fluctuations in the power that can damage your files and computer.

- **Near a phone jack.** If you plan to use a modem, you will need to plug the modem into a phone jack.

PROTECTING THE MONITOR

If you leave your computer monitor on for extended periods, the image on the screen can physically etch itself into the screen, leaving a permanent *ghost*. To protect your monitor from ghost images, turn down the brightness of your monitor when you're not using it. You can also get a screen saver program that automatically blanks your screen or displays moving images after a set amount of idle time. Microsoft Windows comes with a screen saver. To turn it on, here's what you do:

Tip: If you just set up a new computer, turn it on and leave it on (except the monitor) for a couple of days to make sure the computer will outlast its warranty. This test is called a burn-in. You can use your computer during this time—just don't turn it off when you're done. If the computer fails, return it before the warranty runs out.

1 Double-click on the ▦ Main group icon to open the Main window.

2 Double-click on the Control Panel icon.

3 Double-click on the Desktop icon.

Screen saver options →

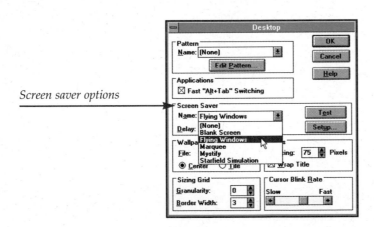

4 Open the Screen Saver Name drop-down list.

5 Click on the name of the screen saver you want to use.

6 To see what the screen saver will look like, click on the Test button. When you're done previewing, move the mouse or press a key to stop it.

7 Click on OK. You are returned to Windows, and your screen saver kicks in when you leave your computer inactive for the specified amount of time.

PROTECTING AGAINST POWER DROPS AND SURGES

Computers depend on a steady source of electricity. Unfortunately, household electricity sometimes fluctuates. Sudden surges or drops in power can damage your computer or destroy the files you worked so hard to create.

To solve these problems, many people buy a *surge suppressor* and *uninterruptible power supply* (UPS) to ensure a consistent power supply. Surge suppressors can protect the computer against sudden increases in current. However, they have little or no effect on power drops. An uninterruptible power supply uses a battery to keep a constant supply of current going to the computer. This gives you at least enough time to save your work to disk if there is a power outage. Most users get by with a surge suppressor. UPSs are used mainly in businesses to keep a network up and running during power outages.

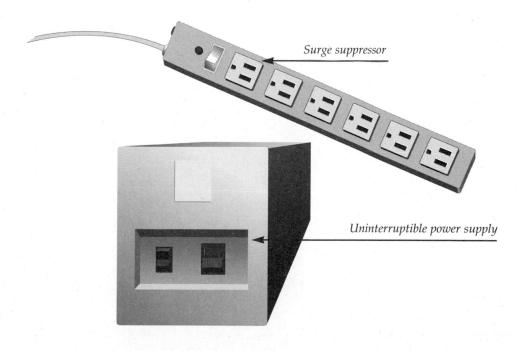

Surge suppressor

Uninterruptible power supply

KEEPING YOUR COMPUTER CLEAN

The least you can do for your computer is to keep it clean. The following list provides some DOs and DON'Ts for computer cleanliness:

- Do not smoke, eat, or drink around your computer. Food, smoke, and liquids can damage your computer.

- Dust your computer once in a while with a clean, dry cloth—don't spray anything on the computer. To keep your keyboard dust-free, buy a can of compressed air from a photography shop or computer store and spray the dust out from between your keys.

- To remove dust from the monitor, wipe it with a clean, dry cloth or a towelette designed especially for cleaning monitors. Anything wet can seep into the monitor and damage the circuits. A used dryer sheet is perfect for cleaning monitors.

- Clean your computer's disk drives once or twice a year. You can get a special kit for cleaning the floppy disk drives.

- Clean your CDs once a month. Use a soft cloth, and wipe from the center of the CD out to the edges. Do not wipe in a circular motion.

- Clean your mouse. If the mouse gets too dirty, it may cause the mouse pointer to skip erratically across the screen. Flip the mouse over on its back, remove the ball cover, and remove the ball. Wipe the ball with a paper towel dipped in window cleaner. Inside the mouse are some rollers. Gently pick any dust balls out of the rollers. Make sure the mouse ball is dry before you reassemble the mouse.

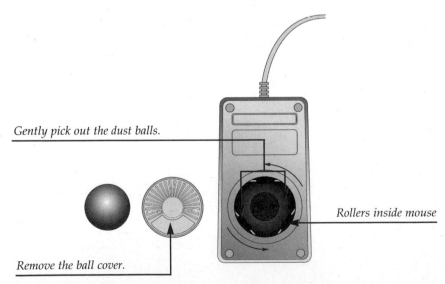

Gently pick out the dust balls.

Rollers inside mouse

Remove the ball cover.

A First-Aid Kit for Your Computer: A Utility Program

No matter how careful you are, you and your computer will eventually have an accident. It may be human error or machine malfunction, but sometime (usually the worst possible time), something will go wrong. To recover from the occasional mishap, you should purchase a utility program and learn how to use it.

A utility program is actually a set of programs designed to help you manage your files, get information about your computer, diagnose and repair common problems, recover lost or damaged files, and keep your system operating efficiently. Most utility programs offer the following features:

- **File undelete** The undelete feature can help you restore files you accidentally deleted.

- **File backups** Some utility programs come with a backup program that copies the files from your hard disk to floppy disks or to a separate backup drive. If anything happens to your original files, you can use the backups to restore them.

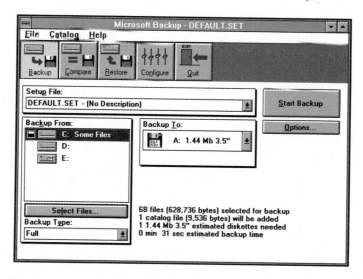

- **File passwords** Most utility programs provide a way for you to prevent unauthorized people from viewing your files.

- **Disk fixing** If a disk is unreadable or if a file on disk gets damaged or lost, the utility program will try to help you find and correct the problem.

- **Disk performance**   As you store files on your hard disk, some may be broken up and stored in different locations. These files are more difficult for the disk drive to read. Utility programs reorganize files so each one is stored in a single location.

- **Emergency disk**   Many utility programs lead you through the process of creating an emergency disk that you can use to boot your computer if you can't boot from the hard disk drive. In addition, the emergency disk usually contains the programs you need to get your hard drive up and running.

- **Virus protection**   This feature checks your computer and your diskettes for viruses or for the effects of viruses.

> *Tip: Store your backups away from your computer. Burglars rarely practice the courtesy of leaving backups, and fires are even less considerate. If you use a computer at work, take the backup disks home with you at the end of the day. If you work at home, store the disks in a separate room as far as possible from your computer.*

- **System information**   Provides information about your computer, including how much memory it has, how the memory is being used, how fast the hard disk is, the type of monitor connected to the computer, the speed of the central processing unit, and more.

Two good utility programs are The Norton Utilities and PC Tools. If you have a PC that runs DOS 6.2 or later, you have most of the utilities you need, including ScanDisk (for fixing disks), AntiVirus (for virus protection), Defragmenter (for disk performance), Microsoft Backup (for backing up the files on your hard disk), Undelete (for restoring accidentally deleted files), and Microsoft Diagnostics (for getting information about your system). To use these valuable tools, type **help** at the DOS prompt and press ⏎Enter.

DEFENDING YOUR COMPUTER AGAINST VIRUSES

A computer *virus* is a program that can get into your system, delete files, command your computer to do strange things, and destroy the information that your computer needs to function properly. Left untreated, a computer virus can bring your computer to a grinding halt. Now the good news: viruses are rare.

Computer viruses are not airborne diseases that your computer can mysteriously contract. To get a virus, your computer must be turned on, and the virus must be introduced to your system through one of its ports or drives. Your computer may be at risk for catching a virus if:

- **You are connected to other computers via modem.** If you run programs that you obtain from BBS (Bulletin Board System) services or online information services, your computer is more at risk.

- **You are connected to other computers on a network.** You can't do much to protect your individual computer in this case. Protection is up to the Network Administrator.

- **You obtain program or data disks from outside sources.** If you use only commercial programs, and you work only with the files you create, your system is as safe as you can make it.

- **Somebody else uses your computer.** Somebody else may use an infected floppy disk on your system without your knowledge.

KEEPING VIRUSES AT BAY

The best way to stop viruses from destroying files is to prevent them from infecting your system. Take a few precautions:

- **Isolate your system.** Don't let anyone insert a floppy disk into your computer without your knowledge. Any disk could contain a virus. However, if you're hooked up to a modem or if your computer is networked, this type of prevention is not very practical or effective.

- **Write-protect program disks.** Before you install a commercial program, write-protect the disks you purchased. If your hard disk is infected with an undetected virus, the write-protection will at least protect the program disks. You can then use the disks to reinstall the program after you destroy the virus.

- **Back up your data files separately.** Although viruses can wipe out data files, they rarely hide in them.

- **Install an anti-virus program.** Anti-virus programs protect your system by warning you of incoming viruses. Some popular anti-virus programs for the IBM include FluShot+, Norton AntiVirus, and Central Point's Anti-Virus. (Use the anti-virus program to check any floppy disks you get from outside sources.)

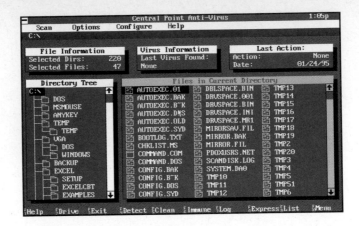

MORE MAINTENANCE TIPS

What more can you do to protect your computer and data? The following list provides additional tips:

- If you must house your computer in a dusty area, you can purchase a special cover for the keyboard similar to the covers used on fast food cash registers.

- If you spill a drink on your keyboard, flip the keyboard over, and turn off your computer. Let the keyboard dry, or use a blow dryer if you're in a hurry.

- Keep your floppy disks and CDs in a special storage case. Dust and dirt can make these disks unreadable.

EXERCISE

Use the following checklist to make sure your computer is properly set up and maintained:

____	Running screen saver program	____	Cleaned mouse (monthly)
____	Installed surge suppressor	____	Backed up data files (weekly)
____	Made emergency disk	____	Backed up all files (monthly)
____	Vacuumed around system unit (monthly)	____	Defragmented files on hard disk (monthly)
____	Vacuumed keyboard (monthly)	____	Used check disk program for lost file pieces (monthly)

PART 4

CHAPTER DIGEST

Making an Emergency Disk (PC)

1. Format disk using the FORMAT /S command.

2. Copy AUTOEXEC.BAT and CONFIG.SYS from C:\.

Note: An emergency disk should also contain a virus scanning program and an undelete utility.

Backing Up Files

1. Run your backup program.

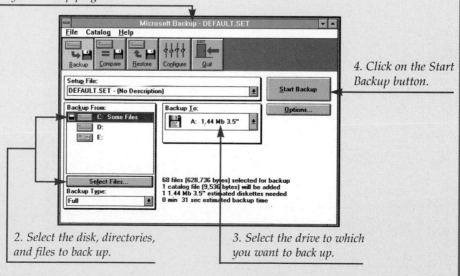

4. Click on the Start Backup button.

2. Select the disk, directories, and files to back up.

3. Select the drive to which you want to back up.

INDEX

graphics
    clip art, 163
    desktop publishing docu-
      ments, 184
    file formats, 184
    importing, 185
    morphing, 174
    sizing, 185
    stacking, 186
    word-processing documents,
      131
    wrapping text around
      graphics, 186
graphics applications, 7, 163-176
    drawing programs, 171-173
    paint programs, 168-173
    text, 173
graphs (spreadsheets), 146-147
grayed-out commands (menus),
  82, 94
green PCs, 271
group windows, 76
    closing, 78
    creating, 86
    opening, 78
GUIs (graphical user interfaces),
  75

H

Happy Mac icon (Macintoshes),
  28
hard disk drives, 15, 45-46, 50
    buying, 265-266
    cleaning, 280
    defragmenting, 282
    logical drives, 47
    organizing, 53
    partitioning, 47
    physical drives, 47
    portable computers, 273
      retrieving, 8
      storing, 8
hardware, 13
Harvard Graphics, running from
  DOS, 69
Hayes-compatible modems, 238
Help
    applications, 116
    DOS, 70-71
    hypertext links, 116
    Macintoshes, 100
    searching, 117-118
    Windows, 77-78

high-density floppy disks, 48,
  61-62
hypertext links (Help), 116

I

icons (Macintoshes), 76, 90-91
illustrations, *see* art
importing
    graphics to desktop publish-
      ing documents, 185
    text to desktop publishing
      documents, 181
income tax estimators, 197
initializing floppy disks, 96-97
    see also formatting, floppy
      disks
inkjet printers, 270
input ports, 14
inserting
    clip art into documents, 164
    floppy disks into drives, 49
installation
    applications, 111
    CDs, 226
    CD-ROM drives, 224
    DOS, 112
    drivers (CD-ROM drives),
      226, 228-229
    Macintoshes, 112
    modems, 239-240
    sound cards, 225
    Windows, 112
Internet
    Archie, 258
    connecting, 236, 255-256
    Gopher, 257
    telnet, 258
    WAIS, 258
    World Wide Web, 258
investment managers, 197

J-K

joysticks, 19, 216

kerning text, 183
keyboards, 6, 16, 35
kilobytes (K), 47
Kodak Photo CD, 223, 231

L

labels
    columns (spreadsheets), 141
    floppy disks, 48, 53, 61-62
    mailing labels, 157
    rows (spreadsheets), 141
landscape orientation (printing),
  146
laptops, 272-273
laser printers, 270
LCD (liquid crystal display)
  monitors, 273
ledgers (accounting), 199
letters (form letters), 156
lock ups (Macintoshes), 29
logical drives (hard disk drives),
  47
Lotus 1-2-3, running from DOS,
  69

M

Macintoshes, 89
    applications
      installation, 112
      running, 91
    booting, 27
      emergency disks, 282
      power keys, 27
      rebooting, 29
      troubleshooting, 28-29
    buying, 264-271
    clocks, 100
    Desktop, 89-90
    dialog boxes, 95-96
    files
      copying, 99
      deleting, 99
      finding, 100
      folders, 53
      moving, 99
      selecting, 99
      undeleting, 99
    floppy disk drives, 46, 97
      floppy disks
      copying, 111
      ejecting, 29, 97
      initializing, 96-97
      naming, 97
    folders
      creating, 98
      finding, 100